PENGUIN BOOKS

THE NEW ITALIANS

Charles Richards was born in 1955 and after Oxford University spent ten years as a correspondent for British newspapers around the Mediterranean. He was based in Cairo for the *Financial Times* and the BBC, and in Jerusalem and Rome for the *Independent*. He now works for the BBC in London.

CHARLES RICHARDS

THE NEW ITALIANS

PENGUIN BOOKS

PENGUIN BOOKS

Published by the Penguin Group
Penguin Books Ltd, 27 Wrights Lane, London W8 5TZ, England
Penguin Putnam Inc., 375 Hudson Street, New York, New York 10014, USA
Penguin Books Australia Ltd, Ringwood, Victoria, Australia
Penguin Books Canada Ltd, 10 Alcorn Avenue, Toronto, Ontario, Canada M4V 3B2
Penguin Books (NZ) Ltd, Private Bag 102902, NSMC, Auckland, New Zealand

Penguin Books Ltd, Registered Offices: Harmondsworth, Middlesex, England

First published by Michael Joseph, 1994
Published with a preface and epilogue in Penguin Books 1995
10 9 8 7

Printed in England by Clays Ltd, St Ives plc

NOTE

Throughout the text I have used a rough conversion of £1 sterling equals between
2,100 and 2,400 lire. I make no apology for any inconsistency. As anyone who has
converted one currency to another knows, banks, hotels and foreign exchange bureaux
all give different rates and none tallies with the posted price. During the time of
writing both Italy and the United Kingdom withdrew from the European Exchange
Rate Mechanism and allowed their currencies to float. Both sank by over 20 per cent
against the main European currencies, the Deutschmark and the French franc. The
dollar behaved in its own imperious way, improving by over a third. At the time of
going to press (March 1994) the approximate exchange rates were:

1,000 lire	sterling	0.40
	US dollars	0.60
	Deutschmarks	1
	French francs	3.5

To Tina

CONTENTS

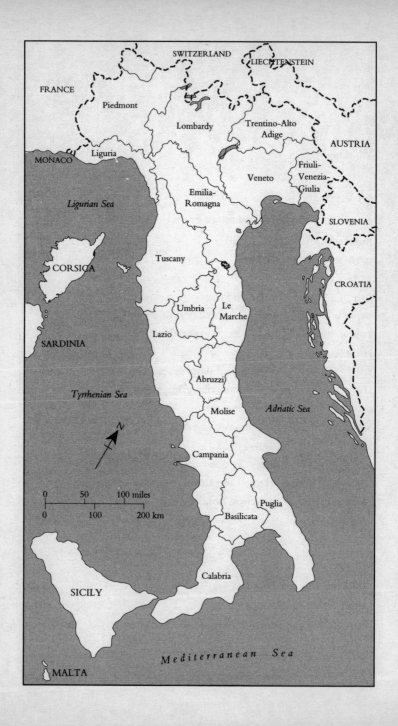

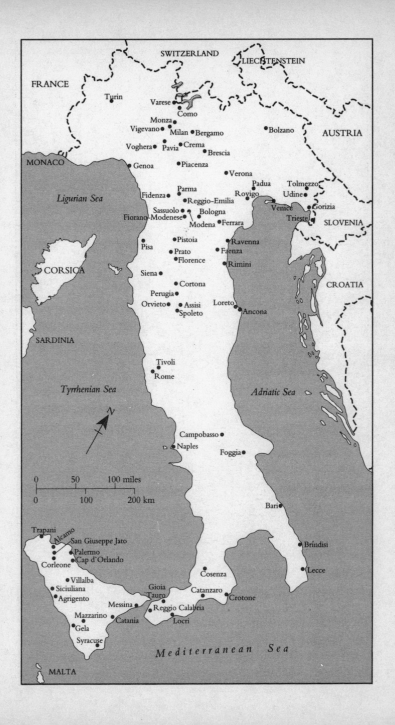

The Penguin edition has an epilogue to take account of some of the great political changes since original publication. Some minor errors kindly pointed out by readers have also been corrected. Otherwise the text remains the same.

London 1994

ACKNOWLEDGEMENTS

Very many people have helped with the creation of this book, many of them before the seed was first planted by the publishers Michael Joseph. I should thank my parents, who first took me to Italy, and Nick Ashford, may he rest in peace, foreign editor of *The Independent*, who overruled my reservations and sent me off to what became the most enjoyable assignment a journalist can hope to have.

In Italy my greatest debt is to the staff of the Rome daily newspaper, *La Repubblica*, particularly the wonderful, warm, helpful journalists on the foreign desk and especially Pietro Veronesi, Magdi Allam and Vincenzo Nigro, who made me so welcome, who always had time for a chat, and pointed me in the right direction. Italian journalists are the best of colleagues. Never was a door closed, never an enquiry, however mundane, too much trouble to answer. From Palermo to Milan, Bari to Verona, Bologna to Rome, journalists on small local papers and stars of the national press and television were unstinting in their generosity. I thank them all.

A book such as this is the fruit of hundreds of conversations and discussions, in smart hotels and seedy dives, with government ministers and street bums, with academics and grocers. I should like to mention a few, mostly in the inky trade, who have shared their thoughts with me, especially James Ruscoe, Neliana Tersigni, Enrico Palandri, Beppe Severgnini, William Ward, Matt Frei, John Ashton, Alison Jamieson, Robert Graham, David Willey, Robert Fox, Melanie Knights, Bruce Johnston, Tana De Zulueta, Ed Vulliamy and Wolfgang Achtner.

My editor Louise Haines first asked me to write what she called an idiosyncratic portrait of Italy and the Italians. She subsequently endeavoured to ensure that I kept to the subject. John Wyles encouraged me to write it, and gave of his great wisdom. And Tina my wife was with me from the beginning, making many sacrifices to help see it through and offering the most constructive and helpful criticisms of early drafts.

It goes without saying that all tendentious judgements or errors of fact are my responsibility.

Everyone knows something of Italy. Our collective cultural baggage is festooned with labels from Rome and Florence. Italy is Roman law and Renaissance rules of perspective, it is the universal Church and the roots of western civilization. Italy is a summer's lease of a Tuscan villa. It is swifts – visitors from the South – screaming and wheeling over terracotta roofs in Trastevere. It is sunshine and blue skies, extra-virgin oil and olive-skinned lovelies entangled on a Vespa. It is the world's best-dressed people, and cappuccino in the Mecca of Mocha. Italians can also have execrable taste. As a sign of their new wealth, they are the biggest importers of Persian carpets in Europe, but they prefer garish, floral patterns to more muted tribal designs. Once upon a time Italy was a place where rich Northern Europeans found their money went a long way. But fifteen years of high inflation have made Italy today one of the more expensive countries in Europe.

Italy as a modern state, a country with the same-sized population as the United Kingdom or France, is much less well understood. Luigi Barzini, whose *The Italians* published in 1964 remains a timeless portrayal of the feats and foibles of his countrymen, warned about the difficulties in seeking to decipher the Italian puzzle. 'Italy,' he wrote,

> is universally considered a particularly unpredictable and deceptive country. Some people even believe that this is the only absolutely certain thing about it. They are, of course, right some of the time, but also wrong as often. There are no sure guides to what Italy is and what it might do next. Italians themselves are almost always baffled by their own behaviour. The only people who have no doubts and hold very definite and clear ideas

about the country and its inhabitants are foreigners who streak through it in a few days.

And he quoted a foreign correspondent who said, 'In Moscow one knows nothing but understands everything, in Rome one knows everything and understands nothing.'

When I was asked to transfer to Italy as a correspondent, I was reluctant to go. It might be a wonderful place for a vacation, I said, but to report on? Nothing ever happened. Tranquillity had descended since the political turbulence of the 1970s and early 1980s, when the Red Brigades and other groups engaged in murderous urban terrorism. My friends thought I was insane. I now recognize that this was the only explanation for my strange reaction. At the time I saw it differently. In terms of political importance, Italy always seemed secondary to the mainstream. All the significant decisions on the future of Europe were taken in Paris or Bonn, Brussels or London. Italy was not a key player (or so I thought). Don't worry, I was told. Just go and enjoy yourself.

Rome is seen as a plum posting for foreign correspondents, a place to enjoy life rather than to earn an honest living. American TV networks once used it as a semi-retirement home, where old warhorses who had covered the conflicts of the Middle East were put out to grass and told to enjoy the pasta and the wine and not to bother the editors too much. I too came to Rome from the Near East and I saw it initially from a more Eastern perspective. The frustration of waiting in line at the post office to pay a telephone bill with great wads of used high-denomination banknotes was all too familiar. So was performing an everyday transaction like cashing a cheque, which could entail many different visits to various counters, and was inevitably held up when the only clerk with the necessary authority in these overmanned temples of waste was off sick, or having the ritual coffee break. The Italians may have invented banking, but their practices at the end of the twentieth century are way behind the European norm. More importantly, it was easier to come to terms with the fact that the shortest route is not always the quickest. To get my shipment out of customs, there was absolutely no point at all in trying to be Anglo-Saxon and expecting a set procedure that any private citizen could follow. There was only one way: to do in Rome as the Romans do and pay someone else to deal with all the paperwork. It was not a question of time. Italian bureaucracy is oriental in its opaqueness. When I wanted to get hooked up on a computer link through a subsidiary of the national telephone company, I found that this was not such a simple task. Elsewhere it may be possible to make a single phone call to a telephone company keen to sell its services. A colleague said he had managed to get his personal user code within twenty-four hours – in the Ivory Coast. Not so in Italy. Dealing with the telephone company was a nightmare. In the end I did what I should have done at the beginning: used the services of a fixer. The newspaper *La Repubblica*, where I had an office, had a highly efficient administrative manager whose job was to smooth the way through the national bureaucratic obstacle course. One of the employees there was a telephone engineer. He worked from 8 a.m. until 2 p.m. for the telephone company, and then like most public-sector employees took a second, better-paid job in the afternoon, in his case at the newspaper. With his help, and his contacts, I managed to get my computer link in a record six weeks.

In Italy, supplicants must still hang around ministries seeking to obtain permits or renew passports (for all the country's commitment to the European ideal of free movement of people across borders, Italian citizens need to renew their passports once a year).

Coming as I had from elsewhere in the Mediterranean, what had always endeared me most to the region was the warmth and openness of the people. Every British visitor through the centuries has noted how much more agreeable the Italians are than the sour French. They may rob you, steal your handbag or break into your car, but they will always do so with a smile. Personal contact works both ways. It may be well-nigh impossible to get something done or fixed without what the Italians call a 'saint in paradise' or a patron, but once personal contact is established, doors will be thrown open. I found the lack of punctuality, and the frequency with which appointments were not kept, could be infuriating. But by the same token, I could turn up without any warning at a senior judge's chambers in Florence or Milan and be admitted after only the briefest of pauses and some speech about how busy he was, how little time he had to speak, before he would launch into some lengthy exposition of the penetration of organized crime into local businesses. It was a sign of the Italians' quick thinking and rapid reactions, as well as their sense of hospitality, that I was able to secure an invitation to the President of the Republic's official residence, the old papal palace at the Quirinale, for a National Day reception twenty-four hours before the event. Imagine the response a foreign journalist would get if he or she sought an invitation to the White House for Fourth of July celebrations, or the Elysée on Bastille Day, or Buckingham Palace for a garden party a day or two before the event?

I was seldom able to plan a schedule in advance. When I tried, most of the arrangements would fall through. Italians like to make their arrangements at the last minute. So too with their work. How often they would seem to leave jobs so late they had no apparent hope of finishing on time. Yet they would manage, with their genius for improvisation, to install all the telephones for a conference centre, or lay the turf of a football stadium or finish the car park, just as the opening ceremony began.

Not that these Mediterranean attitudes, of expressiveness and warmth and openness, apparently rubbed off on me. Shortly after the birth of my son, a Roman friend asked me what he was like. I said he was fine, but looked at that early stage like any other baby. It was definitely not the right response. She treated me to a tirade, a torrent of invective the like of which I never want to hear again. 'You bloody English bastard! How can you say such a thing? All those years living in the Mediterranean. Have you learnt nothing? You should be ashamed of yourself. Why are you so repressed? Why can't you bring yourself to say that he is perfect, unique, the most gorgeous, wonderful, marvellous, beautiful, intelligent baby in the world and he is *your* son?!'

She was right, of course, even if when she was ranting she was conforming to two of the stock images of the Italian: child adoring and highly emotional. They talk as we know with their hands. When a social psychologist went round orthopaedic wards he found those patients with arm injuries were tongue-tied: they could not talk if they could not move their hands.

My brief was to write a personal attempt to come to understand Italy and its people. What struck me, as it has struck others, was how the Italians manage to appear both rich and happy, to have money and know how to spend it with such, well, with what else but such *brio* and *gusto*. This was the question to which above all others I sought an answer. Now I know that, underneath, the Italians are not so happy. How else does one account for the high incidence of suicides, and the rising numbers seeking psychiatric help? The huge drugs problem was a further sign of escapism, mainly of young people seeking ways of not facing up to reality. But on the surface the Italians seemed to have the best way of life in the world. Was the reason for this lifestyle the Italian model of an apparently anarchic system of government? Could this be replicated elsewhere, or was the Italian way of life confined to the peninsula?

Many others have made the same investigation at different times. Hans Magnus Enzensberger, that most perspicacious observer of the differences within the great European family, was dismissive of Italy as the laboratory of the post-modern.

The Germans, the English, or the Finns could not act like the Italians even if they wanted to. They're not astute enough, not cynical enough, not talented enough; they're too stubborn, too set in their ways, too amateurish, too inhibited. They've invested too much energy in their well-ordered systems, delegated too many resources, responsibilities, and hopes to the state. They're out of practice when it comes to relying on their own initiative and can't say, 'Me and my clan, my family, my shop, we'll manage – and all the rest can go to hell.'

We'll never go so far as the Italians. Only when we're left with no other choice will we, somehow or another, borrow this or that number from the Italian repertoire. However, we will continue to regard Model Italy, which is not a model at all but an unpredictable, productive, fantastic tumult, with mixed feelings of fear and admiration, dismay and envy.

By the 1990s the Italians had one of the highest disposable incomes in the world. Italy had the fourth or fifth highest gross domestic product. In individual terms, this made the average

Italian considerably richer than his British counterpart. An Italian with a salary of £20,000 a year had far more spending power than a Briton earning the same amount. The Italian would more successfully find ways to avoid paying tax, he would have a second or third income from making wine or running a shop part time on the side, he would seldom be burdened by crippling mortgage repayments, and he would seldom have to consider paying school fees.

The statistics may show that more rain falls on Rome than on London. Not that you would ever have anyone say so in quite such concise language. Italy's weather forecasters are as prolix as their uniforms are splendid. The main television channel Rai 1 uses an air-force colonel who expounds at length on the 'intensification of nubilosity'. He means it will be cloudy. Rain is never merely rain. It is always precipitation. Milan's airports are closed more often by winter fog than is Heathrow. But statistics deceive. Italy, North and South, has some of the finest weather in the world. And it is essentially an outdoor society. People are always out parading themselves, on their evening passeggiata or lunch-time stroll in one great daily show (although in part because many are forced to be outside, their flats are so small). Even in Milan, hectic, fervid Milan, people rush around at a furious pace, but outside. Beppe Severgnini, an Italian journalist who has dissected the habits of the English, has tried to explain some of the reasons why the Italians are so different. First, he says, you must 'learn the Terrazza Law. Italians always seem to be on the point of blowing their tops, but · never do. We like our country (the weather, the towns, the food, the wine, the charming people) as much as foreigners do. We may have had a lousy day. We may have been told that we are going to have to pay more taxes because someone in government has made off with another few billion lire. But in the evening we can have a meal al fresco with our friends, maybe on a terrazza under a clear sky; and our bitterness evaporates. This is the Terrazza Law. If we had British weather in Italy, our politicians would have come to a sticky end long ago.'

Severgnini is an Anglophile. Al fresco is an English expression. But then, Italians have none of the open disdain that the French have for foreigners who massacre their language. In Italy if he were eating outside in the open he would dine *all'aperto*. Only politicians now sup *al fresco*, a slang expression meaning 'in the cooler'. For while I was living there, Italy's chickens came home to roost, as all the stored-up problems of a generation suddenly exploded at the same time.

Of course, many of the old commonplaces about Italy held true well into the 1990s. Governments still had an average life similar to the human gestation period. Southern farmers continued to blast away with shotguns in an annual slaughter of songbirds. Scandals erupted with depressing regularity. There was massive defrauding of EC tobacco and milk support funds, the adulteration of lakes of wines with banned chemicals, and tales of venal politicians and Mafia killings. Public transport was perennially disrupted by unofficial strikes by the train drivers, the air-traffic controllers or the bus companies. Sardinian and Calabrian gangs were kidnapping the children of rich northern industrialists. Forest fires in areas of natural beauty in Sardinia were started by organized crime syndicates: this would destroy land earmarked for conservation areas, and make it available for lucrative development. Neapolitans still had to boil their water to avoid the risk of diseases eradicated elsewhere in Western Europe in the last century. Abuse of social benefits was rife. Thousands of men and women with pensions for the blind had driving licences, star footballers in local teams lived off disability pensions. These old habits were unchanging. What did change was the unravelling of the entire political system, and all the accepted rules as to how the country should be governed and administered.

For some time there had been Cassandras warning that the bubble would burst, that Italy was living beyond its means, that it only managed to achieve such spectacular growth because it faced no competition in its highly protected home market from international industry or services such as banks. With the advent of the single European market after 1992, they declared, Italy would find itself up against the best of the world, and be found wanting. And by 1994 their doom-saying appeared vindicated.

This book was not intended as a travel guide nor as a textbook.

Nor was it meant as a political study. The byzantine intrigues of the politicians in Rome are an arcane interest. There is an excellent analysis of the Italian political system in English in *Italy: A Difficult Democracy* by Frederic Spotts and Theodor Wieser. My book draws shamelessly on the issues raised and conclusions reached in it. Nor is it a modern history of Italy. Here I can recommend the magisterial work by Paul Ginsborg, *A History of Contemporary Italy*.

Rather, I have tried to give a picture of the Italians themselves, at the end of the twentieth century, of the creators of Italy rather than of the creation. However, it is not possible to write about the Italians without dealing with the country they have made, and the systems they have devised for ordering their lives, from daily social contact to the reasons for the success of their industry. I have touched on how inefficient is its system of justice (and forgiving too: the ministry in charge of handling the prosecution of justice is called the Ministry of Grace and Justice, thus incorporating in its very name the concept of absolution as much as retribution).

The challenge of writing at this time is that the country is in such a state of flux. When I started working on this book in 1991, many of the old stereotypes about Italy seemed set in stone. Two years later, the future was far more uncertain. *The New Italians* might therefore be seen as an X-ray of a patient, revealing the bone structure but also an ominous dark patch. It is not clear how malignant the tumour is. No diagnostician would be prepared to say whether or not the growth would respond to drastic surgery or require a course of treatment sustained over a long period. He or she could only point to the causes of the malignancy and provide a cautious prognosis for recovery and restoration to health.

The Italians could change the system. But would the Italians themselves change so readily? In Giuseppe Tomasi di Lampedusa's classic novel *The Leopard*, first published in 1958, which is set during the unification of Italy, the hero Tancredi expresses the need for intervention, for taking action: 'Unless we ourselves take a hand now, they'll foist a republic on us. If we want things to stay as they are, things will have to change.'

Can Italy change? Can the Italians? For years a combination of a forgiving Mother Church and the understanding Italian *mamma* helped engender a society with little sense of personal accountability and responsibility. But when the Italians found their politicians partaking of the rape of the state like potentates from some Third World banana republic, they cried 'Basta!' 'Enough!' A tremendous social and moral pressure grew for reform. Yet would this head of steam create a real momentum for change, or would it evaporate as so often in the past? I remain fundamentally doubtful of how much the Italians will change. It is hard to imagine that Sicilian householders will suddenly start applying for planning permission to develop their homes. It is equally difficult to believe businessmen will stop paying small bribes to the telephone technicians to get a line installed more quickly. Or that the sun will stop shining, and end the Terrazza Law.

It is not merely the romanticism of north Europeans who do not have to live in Italy which hopes that the Italians do not change too much. Romano Prodi – distinguished economist, former industry minister in the Christian Democrat administration, a man with a reputation for personal probity, privatizing head of the behemoth state holding company IRI (Institute for Industrial Reconstruction, founded in 1933) until he was sacked, later rehired to head IRI again – with great faith in the richness of the Italian entrepreneurial spirit, made an appeal for a different Italy, but one recognizably Italian. 'I want Italy to be a normal country,' he told me. 'I don't say an honest one.'

ONE

Sic transit gloria mundi

It was the end of the regime. The triumvirate who had dominated Italian political life for a dozen years were out, tainted by assocation with corruption scandals or by alleged links with the Mafia. The last political system in Europe to owe its existence to the continent's division into Western and Eastern blocs at Yalta fifty years before was being dismantled as surely as the Berlin Wall.

Even one year before, it had seemed that the regime would survive, if not another half century, then at least a few more years. The general elections of April 1992 had appeared to be a formality. All the pundits agreed that Bettino Craxi, the leader of the Socialist Party, would become prime minister, even though his party would only get the third largest number of votes. Giulio Andreotti, the outgoing Christian Democrat prime minister, would be 'elected' president – that is, preselected by the cabal of party leaders, then confirmed by vote of parliament. The third member of the triad, Arnaldo Forlani, would continue to pull the levers of power from his post as secretary-general of the Christian Democrat Party. Craxi, Andreotti, Forlani – CAF as they were collectively known – would remain in place. It really did not matter how the voting went. This was Italy. The deal had been stitched up beforehand.

As the initial results came in, it became evident that the elections were a watershed in the history of the country. The party bosses of the ruling Christian Democrats and Socialist Party watched with growing dismay as the computer projections showed that, for the first time since the Second World War, the Christian Democrats and their allies would lose their overall majority in both houses of parliament. Italy, unlike the United States or Britain, but like most countries in continental Europe, had an electoral system that produced no single winning party, so governments were formed by cobbling together coalitions. Bettino Craxi spoke with studied understatement of an erosion of support. Arnaldo Forlani proffered his resignation. They were only partly relieved as counting progressed and it emerged that, by a margin of one-tenth of a percentage point, they would garner enough votes to secure a slender majority of seats in parliament.

When the elections were called, as they must be every five years, Italy was into its fiftieth government since the foundation of the republic after the end of the Second World War. It was one of those features of Italian life which observers and commentators have, in the absence of other explanations, dubbed 'paradoxes' that the apparent fragility of government coalitions had disguised a concrete stability in the Italian political system and its denizens. The same grey men had been in office, in one guise or another, for two generations. The same faces had appeared nightly on television (introduced albeit at first only in the North of the country in 1954) with the only occasional titillation provided by the disporting of porn stars such as La Cicciolina or Moana Pozzi.

Unique among Western European democracies, Italy had a political class whose stultifying hold on power over fifty years was comparable only to that of the one-party states of the Eastern bloc. The same party, the Christian Democrats, dominated the government and its institutions, although sometimes it had to concede the prime ministership to one of its coalition partners. And the opposition Communist Party was always in opposition, except for a brief period when it was co-opted to be in the area of the government if not actually of it. Yet it never really behaved like an opposition. A look at the voting record over the last fifty years shows that very often those outside government voted with it.

The frequent change of governments did not help the projection of Italy's image abroad. Alan Clark, Britain's former overseas trade minister, described in his diaries a summit in 1988 with his counterpart Renato Ruggiero.

What a nice, thoughtful, civilized man he is. It is always a pleasure, I always learn something. But the Italians are useless, the country is a mess – corrupt and unreliable – what earthly point is there in having a 'summit'? Even if we did a deal the Italians wouldn't stick to it. Or the government would change before they had time to deliver.

Now, at last, the system was being challenged, and overthrown. The private vices of the individuals at the top were being exposed to a public whose own cynicism of the foibles of the political class was not prepared for the scale of the excesses. That cynicism I heard in the case of a doctor whose position in a local health unit (Unità Sanitaria Locale or USL), one of the most politicized and corrupt institutions in the country, was owed to a national politician. When asked how he would cast his vote in the forthcoming referendum on electoral reform, he shrugged and responded with the pessimism of those who had long since despaired of changing things, that he would ring up his political master, and then ring up the thirty people he had promised to bring with him to vote according to whatever they were instructed.

Within a year of the crucial 1992 elections, Craxi and Forlani were being investigated for corruption over public-works contracts for the illegal financing of the parties. And the great survivor, Giulio Andreotti himself, had been notified that he too was under investigation for association with the most deadly criminal organization, the Sicilian Mafia known as Cosa Nostra. Mafia turncoats have come forward with some shattering accusations. They have accused Giulo Andreotti, a man who has been seven times prime minister, of arranging for Mafia killers, eleven years before in 1982, to gun down the former carabinieri commandant Carlo Alberto Della Chiesa, whom he himself had sent to fight the Mafia in Sicily, because the general had found out too much about government collusion with terrorism in the 1970s. (The carabinieri are the paramilitary police under the defence ministry.) Andreotti also astonishingly has been accused of giving the nod to the killing of journalist Mino Pecorelli, well-known conduit of officially inspired leaks, who may have discovered too much about the kidnapping and murder by the Red Brigades back in 1978 of Aldo Moro, the Christian Democrat leader. The charge of association with the Mafia was far more serious than pillaging the treasury. It was the first time that a genuine effort was being made to investigate the widely held contention that organized crime in Sicily and the South had only been able to flourish because the political establishment had provided a protective umbrella. It was in areas controlled by the different Mafias – the hard men of Sicily, the more *arriviste*, consumerist Camorra of Naples, and the brutal 'ndrangheta of Calabria – that the Christian Democrats traditionally had been able to rely on having most electoral support.

No one personified the history of modern Italy more than Giulio Andreotti. The careers of few statesmen in the world have been so closely entwined with the fortunes of a single country. Andreotti's political career spanned nearly the entire second half of the twentieth century, from 1946 until after he was made senator for life in 1992. Andreotti was the most experienced statesman of his generation. He was born in Rome on 14 January 1919, and took his degree in law from the University of Rome, where he became active in Catholic student organizations. While engaged during the war in obscure research into the naval power of the old papal states, he had a meeting in the Vatican Library that was to change his life. He came across a Vatican employee, Alcide De Gasperi, who took him under his wing. De Gasperi was to become one of the most revered of Italian statesmen in the new Italy, heading all the governments for eight years from December 1945 until 1953. Andreotti was brought in almost from the outset. After a time on the drafting committee for the new constitution after the proclamation of the republic in June 1946, Andreotti was given the key post of under-secretary to the presidency of the council of ministers (the prime minister's office). It was one of the most powerful jobs in government. Not only did Andreotti in effect control De Gasperi's agenda, he also obtained first-hand experience of how the delicate balancing was achieved of the different parties and opposing factions within government coalitions. Although not a full minister, Andreotti uniquely was allowed by his post to sit in on cabinet meetings. There he learnt too about the importance of arranging deals to avoid issues, rather than confronting them head on. It was the politics of the bazaar. Everyone had their price, every issue could be bargained for. Principled stands were foolish when the best course was to seek harmony between opposing forces.

This was a specifically Catholic view of the world, a view that in the grand scheme individuals could achieve little. After his schoolmaster father died when he was only three, Andreotti was brought up by his mother and a religious aunt whose philosophy left a lasting impression. 'She brought me up in the Catholic wisdom of the Roman populace: never overdramatize things, everything sorts itself out in time, keep a certain distance from things in life, not many things are really important.'

He struck an ecclesiastical figure, sitting with his legs together and rubbing his hands unctuously like one of those brilliantly clad cardinals with whom he was so familiar. Few politicians have so deserved the epithet Machiavellian for their expertise in the exercise of power, and their skill at manipulating a situation to gain advantage. Explaining how he had not tired of power, he quipped in one of those one-liners which were his trademark, 'Power only tires those who do not have it.'

During his political career, he was to hold every major office: minister of foreign affairs, defence, interior, and presidency of the council of ministers seven times. He impressed his supporters with his formidable intellect, acerbic wit and unflappability, but exasperated his opponents with his cynical indifference. Andreotti could claim to have presided over a period of unprecedented prosperity, although he never claimed to have a detailed grasp of economics. Only once did he hold an economic portfolio. The system he represented made much of the boom possible, because of a very loose administration. The country achieved a growth rate that was second highest in the developed world, especially during the boom years of 1958–63. And in contrast to the preceding era of world wars, fascism, and foreign adventure, ignominy and defeat, Italy enjoyed a time of political stability. The murderous assaults of the Red Brigades and right-wing terrorists shook but did not overturn the political system.

But Andreotti's approach, his deferral of hard decisions, his lack of a coherent vision or detailed programme for the future, his habit of minimizing problems, reached their nadir in his last government. It was a government that was all about pretending to change, while changing nothing. It saddled Italy with the highest public debt in Europe and a political class whose rapaciousness had no equal outside the Third World. Because of government in-action or ineptitude, by the 1990s organized crime was rampant. The budget deficit hit 11 per cent of gross domestic product, and the total public debt was 110 per cent of GDP. Public services, particularly health care, were a scandal. Overmanning in the huge, bloated state industries, dictated by the parties' need to ensure jobs for life in exchange for votes and favours, was crippling the treasury.

In the end Andreotti paid for subordinating political and moral principle to the overriding one of survival. For he had always shown too few scruples in the selection of his friends and support-ers. Many were of dubious reputation. He was on more than a nodding acquaintance with many of the shadier figures of Italian life, people like the Mafia financiers with Vatican connections, Michele Sindona and Roberto Calvi, boss of the 'priests' bank', the Banco Ambrosiano. Both died in mysterious circumstances. Sindona was to die in prison after drinking a cup of coffee laced with strychnine. Calvi's body was found hanging under London's Blackfriars Bridge. Many Italians refused to accept police findings that it was suicide. When the bank, Italy's most important private bank, collapsed, some $1,300 million was found to be owed to a number of Panamanian and Liechtenstein shell companies owned by the Vatican's Istituto per le Opere di Religione (IOR).

Other suspect acquaintances included Prince Valerio Borghese who launched the farcical coup in 1970, although there was never a suggestion that Andreotti had any part in it. More sinister was Licio Gelli, Venerable Master of the P2 Masonic Lodge which subverted the security services, who had his men in key positions of Italian political and establishment life. In 1981, a raid on Gelli's Tuscan home uncovered the long list of nearly a thousand prominent Italians who were members of P2. And most dubious of all was Andreotti's openly declared friend-ship with Salvo Lima, his pro-consul in Palermo, kingmaker for the Andreotti faction of the Christian Democrats in Sicily, who was the Mafia's middle-man with Rome.

The allegations made by the Mafia *pentiti* or turncoats had been the stuff of rumour and innuendo for years. Conspiracy theories thrive in a country such as Italy, where government processes are so opaque, and the public has so little faith in the honesty of its politicians. Italy's leading cartoonists had portrayed Andreotti either with the devil's horns and tail, or with the mask of the grim reaper. He had been investigated twenty-six times previously for various scandals but proceedings were always dropped. Like all parliamentarians he enjoyed immunity from prosecution, a privilege extended by Article 68 of the constitution. The measure was introduced to protect elected representatives from the experience under Mussolini when his opponents were often prosecuted on trumped-up charges. But parliamentary immunity was corrupted into impunity, as members systematically flouted the law, knowing they were safe from prosecution.

Andreotti rejected as absurd the suggestion that he or any of his governments had favoured the Mafia. His governments had introduced much of the tough legislation intended to combat organized crime, he said. It is no small irony that those who made the accusation against him were Mafia *pentiti* who had profited from laws passed under Andreotti's presidency of the council designed to protect informants. He also observed that many of the accusations could only have been confirmed by people who were now dead.

Yet Andreotti's long tenure of office reinforced the view of many Italians who saw the turning point as one of generational change. Like Chinese leaders, most of those at the top in Italy had clung to power longer than anywhere else in the world. Not only in politics, but in nearly every sphere of business, a gerontocracy was being challenged with no heirs apparent. When top construction-company officials were locked up during investigations over paying bribes, construction virtually came to a standstill, less because of fear of the consequences of continuing than because a new generation of experts had not been nurtured. A whole generation had had their youthful energies and talents stifled by the old guard.

The fall of the regime was the culmination of a process, rather than a single, mould-breaking event. Most called it a revolution, although some would still argue it was not a true revolution, but merely a restoration of those democratic principles enshrined in the constitution but traduced over half a century by the most corrupt political class in Europe, comparable to the worst excesses of the French Fourth Republic. The agents of change were several, representing very disparate trends. They all conspired – not in the legal sense, though many of the victims used to seeing hidden hands sensed there must have been a plot – to bring about the most radical change in fifty years.

First, there was Mikhail Gorbachev. The changes he wrought to end the Cold War and the fall of the Berlin Wall undermined the main basis on which the Christian Democrats and their political allies had claimed their right to govern since the war: the need to spare Italy from being taken over by a Communist Party that was once the largest in Europe. The electoral fortunes of the Italian Communist Party, already in steady decline, dropped sharply after the decision in 1990 to reform the party as the Democratic Party of the Left (PDS), a move which provoked a schism by hardline members who formed the breakaway – they would claim they were the original rump – Communist Refoundation.

Within Italy two other movements had begun. One was an opposition movement that challenged directly the rule of Rome. This was the Northern League, once called the Lombard League, headed by Umberto Bossi, a gruff, crude, ex-medical student and former salesman. Bossi's straight-talking diatribe against the politicians in Rome who squandered billions in taxes paid by hard-working Northerners to pay off the Mafia and to fund their extensive networks of patronage in the south of the country had won considerable support in the rich, modern industrialized North. In two years, the movement jumped from nowhere to make impressive gains in the national elections. In many of the towns of Northern Italy, frustration with the corruption of the government and party political system in Rome had carried the League to become the largest party.

The other political movement, more modest in scope but no less iconoclastic in its repercussions, was a reform one. The Referendum Movement, later to become the Democratic Alliance, was fronted by a highly respectable figure from the heart of the Christian Democrat establishment, Mario Segni. The son of a former president – a not very good one – this stubborn Sardinian sought evolutionary change in the electoral law to reduce the opportunities for ballot fraud. He was always in favour of a first-past-the-post system, known in Italian as 'uninominale maggioritaria'. His referendum was always intended to be a step towards this goal. He sought to change the system from within, to purge his own party of its rotten elements. Many said it was impossible, that the only way was to leave the party. Finally he did, but only after agonizing for months.

Segni's referendum in June 1991 was the first clear internal sign that the desire for change extended beyond the large but still minority parties to the left of centre. The referendum merely fine-tuned the highly arcane system of voting in Italy. The objective was to reduce the number of preferences a voter could express on his ballot slip. Previously this system had been subject to consider-able manipulation. The result of the referendum was devastating. It demonstrated that the mass of electors was fed up with the status quo. Bossi had urged his supporters not to vote, Craxi told his to go to the beach. Both had underestimated the desire for change. Some 63 per cent of the electorate, or 27 million people, ignored the admonitions of these political leaders and did indeed turn up (referendums need a 50 per cent turnout to be valid; a referendum to restrict the shooting of game was invalidated by too low a turnout). Of these, 96 per cent voted for change.

A second referendum on 18 April 1993 had even greater success. Over 83 per cent of voters (and more than 80 per cent turned out – for it is one of the paradoxes of Italian life that, however improbable the politics, voters regularly come out in droves to cast their ballots) voted to reform the electoral procedures for two-thirds of the senate to a British-style first-past-the-post system. It was a significant date. For in the Italian political calendar, 18 April was celebrated as the great victory of the Christian Democrats in the first general elections of the new republic in 1948, when they almost secured an absolute majority of votes. That the referendum on the old style of elections should have taken place on that date was in a sense a cancelling of that historic achievement, and reinforcement of the factor of change.

Francesco Cossiga, president until 1992, played his part too. For all but the last two years of his presidency he kept mum, hardly making any provocative or controversial remarks. Then he

underwent a metamorphosis. He started making increasingly out-
rageous comments, apparently off the cuff, but more precisely
calculated barbs aimed more often than not at his Christian
Democrat rival Andreotti. By nature authoritarian and irascible,
with a history of mental instability (he had a breakdown after
Moro's murder, when he had been interior minister), Cossiga
could also at times be charming and long-winded, at others direct
and blunt. He had always lived in other worlds, the worlds of
academic scholarship and the low cunning of Italian politics. Yet
he got it into his head that he was voicing the concerns of the
common man. By challenging the existing order with his *picconate*,
his blows of the pickaxe, he also set the terms of debate about the
future cast of government in Italy. He recognized earlier than most
that the fall of the Berlin Wall had a direct impact on the self-
justification of the Italian ruling class.

The other agents for change were ordinary servants of a state
who for so long had suffered from lack of support. It was to
Judge Antonio Di Pietro that the task of investigating the bribery
for contracts in a Milan old people's home fell. His investigations
snowballed into the biggest political corruption scandal in Europe,
known as *tangentopoli* – 'bribesville'. Some jealous colleagues,
anxious that Di Pietro should not claim too much credit personally,
have suggested that he just happened to be handling the case when
the political circumstances changed to permit him to pursue it. Yet
his dogged persistence, and his knowledge of computers, put him
in a stronger position than most to uncover the wider picture. He
symbolized the new moral climate, the search for justice, a
twentieth-century Savonarola who yet did not cast all the best
aspects of Italian life on a huge bonfire of the vanities.

More than any other event to provoke a widespread mood for
change, for justice, was the murder in Palermo in May 1992 of the
leading anti-Mafia campaigner Judge Giovanni Falcone. Nothing
illustrated more the degeneracy and ineffectiveness of a state that
was unable to protect its loyal servants. When Rosaria Costa, the
young widow of one of the bodyguards killed with Falcone, spoke
out at the televised funeral service against the Mafia killers who
had taken these lives, she struck a chord across the country. It was
an electrifying speech. With all the dignity of a woman brought

up in the Catholic tradition, she declared that she had been taught by the scriptures to forgive. But, she said, she knew members of the Mafia were there, inside the church, and if they wanted forgiveness they would have to come on their knees. The seething congregation heard her anguished wails, and jostled the police chiefs and political leaders who represented a state that had for so long abandoned the people of the island to their fate. The Mafia was a formidable adversary, but never was there a clearer demonstration that many of the people of Palermo passionately wanted a change from the old order.

The events of the early 1990s signalled the beginning of a process to change the relationship between people and government. This was when the first real signs appeared that the Italian people had determined that politics was too serious an affair to be left to the politicians. The left, the traditional repository for opposition to the regime, had long decried the system. What altered were the views of those masses who for so long had supported it. Most establishment politicians could only see the shift as politically motivated. Yet there was also a current seeking moral change. People simply said, 'Enough!' How deep was that current? How deep was the conviction of those who heckled the disgraced Bettino Craxi with cries of 'Send him to jail!' when for so long these same people had sought his favour, voting in ever-increasing numbers for his party? How fickle public opinion was. As *The Times* of London noted in a famous leader fifty years before, one day forty million Italians were Fascists. Overnight, forty million Italians discovered they were anti-Fascist.

The change also had economic causes. The fiscal pressure on the government was forcing reforms, which began to hurt more and more people. The majority of working people, whose main income is taxed at source, found they were being asked to bear a larger burden in increased taxation. The government came up with ever more ingenious schemes to make people pay taxes. A tax meter was devised to gauge a person's worth according to their assets. People would then be taxed on their visible wealth, rather than their declared income.

Prime ministers came and went with the regularity of the past. During his ten-month term from 1992–93 the former university professor known as Doctor Subtle, Giuliano Amato, was able to talk frankly about his being a transitional government. The occasion was a lecture at the London School of Economics in 1993. On the Ides of March, he took as his theme 'The Rules of Chaos'. He cited in a self-mocking manner the bibliography of Chaos Theory, of the dripping tap as a modern chaotic system. And he defined chaos as the absence of rules. He said that often there were rules which we did not see. There were causes and effects. If you do not understand what is going on, you might be tempted to say there are rules of chaos. When a butterfly flaps its wings in Japan, there is a hurricane in New York. What was needed, therefore, was flexibility. What was dragging Italy down were two main factors: the gigantic public debt, and excessive expenditure. The Italian state was spending more than it was earning. There was an excess of political appointees, in economic and social spheres, even in the public health service (although this was changing). Amato had been credited with initiating an economic restructuring by starting the process of privatizing the huge state-owned holding companies, but tripping up on political reform. This, he showed, demonstrated a fundamental lack of understanding of how Italy worked. He was not selling off the state sector to raise money to reduce the country's deficit (although that was a consequence). His aim was political: to break the connection between this economic sector and the political parties. For Italy was a place where governments did not pursue national interests, but were engaged in the protection and promotion of partisan interests, whether of a party, a faction within a party, of commercial and industrial groups. Decisions were taken behind closed doors, by men who were not accountable to an electorate or shareholders, in secret cabals that served common interests but rarely the common good. This entanglement had been most clearly seen in the *tangentopoli* scandal that had erupted in Milan.

Perfectly aware that by these charges he was introducing factors of instability into the system, Amato hoped that the next elections would bring a stable majority.

I represent a transitional government with the job of breaking old rules for a new stable period, possibly with a new electoral system. That is why I flapped my wings. What is needed in Italy is a totally new political class, not necessarily a system. This was something nobody could foresee until a few months ago. Writers have said of Italy it is a blocked democracy. It is now in need of a change, of profound change. Italians now want a different political class . . . the new electoral system must not be a new atmosphere for the old party and the old men. The new electoral system must be a new atmosphere for the new party and the new men. The old people will not be accepted any more.

Professor Amato was not to survive. His was, as he had said, a transitional government, but to what was unclear. It was appropriate that, in a country which had produced such distinguished scientists as the Nobel Laureate Enrico Fermi, the metaphors used should have come from physics: the fragmentation of the vote as more and more smaller parties, from the Greens to the Pensioners, emerged; the centrifugal force of the Leagues; but above all the fear of political vacuum.

He said that business and politics in Italy work on corruption. Why else was the administrative secretary of any party always bound to have parliamentary immunity from prosecution? Why else than because he was breaking the law? But they went too far. 'Italy went beyond the usual level of corruption. That is why it was discovered.'

What surprised most Italians was not the fact of political corruption. Everyone knew that the parties disposed of sums far in excess of what was voted by parliament. But the devices set up to raise revenue for the parties and spirit it out of the country were so perfected, Professor Amato said, that it was almost a matter of national pride that the parties could be so efficient in raising money in this illegal way, demonstrating that the shortcomings of the Italian revenue service were not necessarily the national norm.

Very few people were aware of the kinds of devices being employed. Most accepted the system of political financing. It was accepted by politicians, by the courts. So what changed? Why were the judges acting now? Why had they not acted before? Professor Amato asked the same question. 'I asked a friend who was a judge. He said that in the past when he started making investigations he would only get so far. Then he would encounter obstacles. These were difficult to explain. If Italians accepted these devices as a system in the past, and do not accept them any more, that is good for the country. The politicians have to change and we have to find new politicians.'

TWO

Il Belpaese and *la bella figura*

It all seemed such a short time since Italy and Italian goods, style and tastes were the flavour of the decade. The Mediterranean diet was in. Italian suits clad young males across the world. Italian designers became household names. In the 1980s, Italians were everywhere, a generation of big spenders. Italians were buying up property in the South of France and antiques in London. Italian businessmen like Luciano Benetton were profiled in every business magazine. Fiat's Gianni Agnelli was hailed as Renaissance man. Silvio Berlusconi was buying up half Europe's TV stations (and half its footballers for the best club team in Europe, AC Milan).

Berlusconi was doing what Italians are best at: communicating and having fun. For football is not just life and death in Italy. It is more important than that. When a friend of mine was trying to secure a deal with one of Berlusconi's communications companies, he found there was no one available to handle the contract: all the company lawyers were in South America signing up footballers.

For the industrial barons of Italy, the acquisition of a football team is an equivalent social cachet to owning a newspaper (Fiat, of course, did both, owning the newspaper of its company town *La Stampa* as well as *Corriere della Sera*, and backing local team Juventus). But Silvio Berlusconi (who had also owned a newspaper, *Il Giornale*) made his club the most glittering star in the firmament of Italian club sides that dominate European competition in the 1990s. And he did it by spending lots of money, and managing it well.

Berlusconi's genius was to exploit the passion of his countrymen (and countrywomen) for football in the most commercial ways. AC Milan was run less like a sporting club and more like a modern corporation. After he bought AC Milan in 1986, he made his wishes clear. He took all his top managers to a castle near the

Italian lakes and told them they had a mission to become the best football club in the world. He first ensured he had the best product range, acquiring the three top Dutch players: Marco van Basten, Ruud Gullit and Frank Rijkaard. He then marketed them. The players themselves are some of the best paid in the world. They are also very well looked after. Most will be given a car and a flat, and a club functionary will help pay household and other bills. Both players and club benefit from lucrative sponsorship contracts. The players' physical health is assured by a team of top-rank doctors and physiotherapists.

For Berlusconi, AC Milan was not just a rich man's bauble. In a way that other owners cannot, he could exploit his team on the television companies controlled by his Fininvest holding company. He thus owned the entertainers and the stage on which they performed to millions of Italians throughout the season. And he had a captive audience. Italians are football crazy. They have the most magnificent stadiums in the world. Many were rebuilt specially for the 1990 World Cup finals held in Italy. Magistrates may now be investigating the allocation of contracts for the building works, of the millions paid in bribes, and the massive overspend on quotations, but the legacy is one for future generations.

Every Sunday afternoon during the season you see couples sitting at café tables, a small transistor between them, or a father out with his family for a stroll, a radio pressed to his ear listening to live coverage of the local game. Even those who profess not to follow the game too closely are well informed about the sport. Not just Berlusconi's channels, but all the television stations in Italy – it has more than fifty – give total coverage to the game. The only other sport which commands such a following is Formula One motor racing. It is possible on a Sunday, zapping the remote control to switch from channel to channel, to watch ten hours of uninterrupted football, from match previews to the game itself, to replays and discussion. The most popular chat-show-cum-analysis of the game is presented by a Junoesque female professional player. The show provides a combination of sexual allure and passion for sport which conforms to the national stereotype.

In Italy, as elsewhere in continental Europe, sports papers are

among the most popular newspapers. *La Gazzetta dello Sport* – one
of three newspapers in Italy devoted to sport – is one of the
publishing success stories of the continent. It has the largest circula-
tion of any daily sports newspaper in Italy. Its print run of 700,000
(which goes up to a million on Mondays after the weekend sports
programme) is nearly as high as the major national newspapers
such as *La Repubblica* and *Corriere della Sera*. Its distinctive pink
pages – it went pink as a gimmick in 1899 – are visible up and
down the country and wherever Italians and Italian sports-lovers
(usually one and the same) are found abroad. Unusually the
newspaper has been helped by the advent of television. As more
and more television was devoted to coverage of sport, so the
demand rose for complementary coverage in the press, with more
in-depth interviews and analyses. Football was a real subject of
intellectual debate. The great football writer Gianni Brera made
reporting on the game an art form, inventing words and expres-
sions for his lucid commentaries, which had the impact that the
New York Times theatre critic has on Broadway shows.

I was given a good idea of the primacy of football in the life of
Italians during the World Cup finals held in Italy in 1990. It was a
turbulent time in Western Europe. The Berlin Wall had fallen.
The old Eastern bloc was rapidly disintegrating. In Germany a
great debate was raging over the proposed unification of the
currency. At what price would former East Germans be able to
exchange their ostmarks for deutschmarks? What were the strategies of Chancellor Kohl and foreign minister Genscher? The word
'mark' cropped up again and again in conversation. But even in
the foreign newsroom of *La Repubblica* where I worked, the
references were to how the defence would mark out the talents of
Germany's strikers Jurgen Klinsmann and Rudi Völler.

The conversations followed the pattern. For discourse in Italy
can often have a numbing superficiality. Did not Luigi Barzini
himself deride his countrymen for their 'eternal search for shallow
pleasures and distractions'? They certainly seemed more interested
in the pursuit of physical gratification than in the world about
them. Indeed, Italians more than most other Europeans seemed
blissfully unaware of and uninterested in the great developments all
around. Little serious in-depth public debate was ever held about

the advantages and disadvantages of the treaty on European monetary and political union signed at Maastricht.

Despite the huge numbers of Italians who emigrated to Australia and the Americas, those who remained behind had a curiously introverted, peninsular view of the world. The growth of mass global tourism permitted many Italians to travel abroad on holiday. However, such was the variety of vacation resorts within Italy that most would spend at least one holiday within the *Belpaese*, the 'beautiful country'. Yet, like the Japanese, Italians would almost invariably travel abroad in groups. One problem, of course, was language. An older generation of the educated class spoke French. Today younger Italians are becoming more at ease in English. But the habit of dubbing foreign films into Italian, rather than keeping them in the original language with subtitles (a hangover from Mussolini's pursuit of Italian nationalism) has retarded a more generalized fluency in foreign languages.

You can get some idea of what Italian businessmen get up to abroad by appreciating that in Moscow the second language of most prostitutes is Italian not English. In hotels throughout the eastern bloc, Italian businessmen would traditionally spend a couple of hours each evening trying to get through on antiquated telephone systems to their wives, and, having salved their consciences, set about getting off with the switchboard operator.

Within Italy it has become chic to use English words in Italian, although not always in a sense recognizable to native speakers. Furthermore, many are simply synonyms of perfectly acceptable extant Italian words but are used to convey a sense of modernity and efficiency. Words like *manager*, *executive*, or *VIP*. There is a magazine called *Class*. *Top* is used as a prefix as in *top models*, or *top managers*. When there are perfectly good Italian equivalents, the only explanation for their use is to create an impression. Less explicable is the use of imported words in a context which one would have thought provided an entire lexicon of precise meanings, namely that of organized crime: words like *racket* or *boss*. Many of these words are tortured in the process. Hence *baby killer* does not mean a Herodian slaughterer of innocents, but a pre-pubescent professional hitman (a *killer* being specifically a hired gun, not an everyday murderer). Other words like *babysitter* are used because there is no equivalent in a culture where an aunt or grandmother or sister would perform this function.

The image Italians have of themselves, the image they project to outsiders, is a classic stereotype of the sensual, funloving, genial, exuberant, extravagant, vainglorious, bombastic and essentially superficial. Image or *bella figura*, which roughly translated means cutting a dash, is closer to the Arab and oriental concept of face, of not revealing to the outside world what is behind the mask, especially when once the mask slips there is nothing, nothing of substance, no backbone, moral or otherwise, to be found underneath. *Bella figura* meant that Mussolini lined the road into Rome with painted cardboard façades of elegant villas to deceive the visiting Hitler into thinking that Italy was richer than it was. *Bella figura* means always looking one's best to conceal indigence, or unhappiness. The Terrazza Law both encourages *bella figura* and makes it easier to indulge. To parade around in one smart jacket and one well-pressed pair of trousers does not mean one is well-heeled. But no one is to know that they are a young blade's only decent clothes.

Bella figura explains Italians' obsession with appearance. How often does one see a round-shouldered young person? It is not just their breezy self-confidence. More, it is that desire to project an illusion of self-assurance. *Bella figura* explains Italy's posturing on Third World issues, yet Italy has seldom played an international role. It is true Italians are proud that the founding treaty of the European Community was signed by the six original members in Rome. True, too, that Italy is the world's fifth largest industrialized power (some would say fourth), with manufacturing output by value larger than Britain's. Yet despite the energetic enthusiasms of Gianni De Michelis, the Falstaffian chemistry professor from Venice who wrote a guide to the country's best discotheques and was foreign minister until 1993, Italy has never played a global role commensurate with its economic vitality. Indeed, at both government and popular levels, Italy has appeared to take a lighthearted view of world affairs.

One explanation is that Italians have found that the daily political drama in their lives has overshadowed all outside developments.

Another is that they feel unsure of what it means to be Italian. While I was in Italy the media was afflicted with a surprising lack of self-confidence. Every time the *Financial Times* reported that Fiat's results showed improvement, or *The Economist* urged Italian voters to cast their ballots for the Republicans or the Northern League, these opinions were reported prominently with fawning reverence for these august journals, as though somehow the opinions of distant foreigners had more gravitas.

In a country as diverse as Italy, there are many different answers to the question of what constitutes being Italian. Leo Longanesi founded his periodical *L'Italiano* in the 1920s to express the sense, the taste and the smell of a national character based on the concept of *strapaese*, of the crucial importance of local values.

> The people of Northern Europe have the fog [you would have thought he had never been to the Po Valley, which is swathed in dank mist for much of the winter], which goes step by step with democracy, with spectacles, with Protestantism, with utopia, with universal suffrage, with five meals a day, and with Marxist theory. Italy has the sun, and with the sun one cannot help but conceive the Church, classicism, Dante, enthusiasm, harmony, philosophical health, Fascism.

Italians will tell you that Italianness is an elusive concept. Older ones will tend to emphasize regional origins or local differences. Many is the time one is reminded of the old slogan of the Piedmontese Massimo D'Azeglio after the unification of the . country: 'We have created Italy, now we must make the Italians.'

A survey of students at a *liceo classico*, a top high school, in Milan confirmed that the concept of the nation among young people was dying. The word *patria* was no longer taboo because of its association with the Fascist past. Yet of the 406 students questioned in the survey, 41 per cent said they were in complete agreement with the declaration of the veteran political philosopher Norberto Bobbio that 'Italy is no longer a nation in the sense that in the new generation there no longer exists a national sentiment. Italy has become little more than a geographical expression and the Italians are becoming once more a common mass with no name.'

So the mid-nineteenth-century jibe of Metternich that Italy was a mere geographical expression was once more finding currency. Only a quarter of the students believed that the feeling of national pride still existed. Over half – 58 per cent – felt it in some sporting occasion: the World Cup finals, or the successes of skiing champion Alberto Tomba, as previous generations had derived patriotic pride when Ferrari's bright red racers were winning Formula One. A very small proportion obtained some national pride from the judicial struggle against the Mafia. Many preferred to express their identity as Europeans or citizens of the world, although the majority did not think these concepts made national sentiment obsolete. Over half said they would not hesitate to take up a well-paid job abroad, and 37 per cent said they would do so even if they were never to return to Italy.

Whether a European identity can really replace a national one is a dubious proposition. Yet the vision of a Europe of the regions is enormously appealing to Italians. For years they have turned to the European Commission in Brussels to impose the fiscal and monetary discipline that successive governments have been unwilling to take. The Italians have quite the opposite feeling to the British towards Brussels. Whereas for years Britons have felt animosity towards those they regard as meddling Eurocrats, the Italians turn to Brussels for the kind of decisive and wise (since controlled by the French and Germans) leadership they themselves have lacked. Italy's aspirations towards Europe are also an agent for change. Europe's function is to provide some modernizing influence, particularly in terms of legislation. Now Italy's respect for European laws and regulations may be more in their breach than in their observance, but Italians of all classes are intent, for reasons of self-image as well as pragmatism, that Italy should keep up with the pack and maintain some status in European politics. Advantages accrue. Europe can be cited as a means of justifying otherwise difficult policies. It is fundamental to keep in touch with developments in Europe. For if Europe was not there, and Italy was not part of the European venture, then the naturally parochial Italians would be even more turned in on themselves.

The lack of a sense of national identity has many causes. Besides the relative newness of the Italian state, a questioning of the role of the nation was inevitable in all the countries defeated in the Second

World War. The weakness of the state may not be reason enough for the decline in a sense of national identity, but it is a contributory cause. Some historians have also attributed a diminished sense of the state to the overriding power and influence of the political parties, which demanded loyalty and ties over and above any elsewhere accorded to the state. The weakness of the institutions also undermined any respect for the state. Furthermore, the two prevailing political orientations were supra-national: the universal Catholic Church and international Marxism.

But, taking the historical view, dismissing Italy's lack of apparent national sense of self-esteem as an inevitable product of its recent formation as a unitary state does not fully account for the underdeveloped feeling of nationhood. After all, Italians have fought as Italians, not as Piedmontese or Sicilians or levies for some foreign power, but as Italians, in two world wars this century. That said, the defence of national territory has been a low priority. Or rather, Italy has been prepared to seek the protection of Nato, basking under the security umbrella provided by the United States so long as the Americans paid for it. There has never been any real debate about national defence. Even when, in 1986, Libyan missiles landed off the sparsely inhabited island of Lampedusa, which showed that Italian territory was vulnerable to external threats, there was little serious public discussion about defence needs.

The lack of its own investment in defence expenditure – the Italians may not have spent more on uniforms than on tanks, but the priority was the parade ground rather than the field of battle – meant that during the Gulf War Italy could send only a token force of Tornados to help the US-led coalition. Its army has been better equipped for such humanitarian missions as distributing food to Kurds and Albanians, and peacekeeping in the former Italian colony of Somalia and in Mozambique. In April 1992, when Italian air-force jets were scrambled to intercept a Libyan airliner entering Italian air space in breach of an UN security council embargo, the warplanes were thirty-four-year-old F104s built before the pilots who were flying them were born.

Italian defence policy has been a gamble that paid off. Most countries in Western Europe have been prepared to pay higher defence costs as insurance. Successive Italian governments cut corners. Italy spent 1.9 per cent of GDP on defence, including the carabinieri, half that of Britain. But they won the bet. Italy has not been invaded, or forced to yield to the threat of a greater external power. Indeed, for much of the postwar period, Italy's treasury has been the grateful recipient of monies dispensed as into a war chest by a United States concerned at the size of the Italian Communist Party, the largest in Western Europe.

Now it is customary to laugh at the Italians' lack of martial spirit, at their readiness to throw down their weapons. The cruel schoolboy joke – What is the title of the world's shortest book? Italian War Heroes – misses the point. It is true that generally Italians seek to avoid confrontation, preferring to find a way round a potential dispute to arrive at the required destination. It is not true, however, that Italians are cowards. Many daily run risks on matters of principle or conscience which few elsewhere in the western world could contemplate. I have a friend, a Sicilian journalist, who many years ago transferred to Rome where he worked his way up one of the Roman newspapers. But all the time he was thinking of Sicily, of how he could help to make his birthplace a better place to live. Then one day he was given the opportunity he had longed for: to become a senior editor on a newspaper in the Sicilian capital, Palermo, where he was born. It was a terrific post on a paper with a fearless reputation for a campaigning style of journalism against the greatest ill on the island, the Mafia. Once upon a time he would have leapt at the job. But now he had a young daughter. He needed to think about her. He knew that, in such a job, the chances were that sooner rather than later he too would become one of those bare statistics computed each year under the heading Mafia Killings. It was an unenviable choice: to serve his people by seeking to confront the Mafia, or to take care of his daughter by staying out of trouble. Was to refuse the opportunity cowardice? It is not fair for those who do not have to put themselves in his position to pass judgement.

My friend, who had to face a real personal moral choice, one that required great courage, was the antithesis of Raul Gardini. Gardini's life (and death) was the single most telling allegory for the rise and fall of the new Italian. When the lean, tanned, silver-haired, chain-smoking, raffish former head of one of the four largest private companies in the land shot his brains out because he was implicated in the unfolding corruption scandal, it sparked a wave of national self-examination. Was it really right that the judges had hounded him to take his life in this way, it was asked?

Raul Gardini saw himself as an outsider to the *salotto buono* of the Italian industrial and commercial establishment dominated by the likes of Fiat's Gianni Agnelli. He encouraged his nickname 'Il Contadino' ('the peasant') even though he came from a family of moderately well-to-do landowners near Ravenna. (The top big businessmen in Italy are known by their nicknames: Gianni Agnelli is 'L'Avvocato' ('the advocate'); Carlo De Benedetti is 'L'Ingegnere' ('the engineer'); and Silvio Berlusconi, in parody of His Eminence, Cardinal . . . , is known as 'Sua Emittenza' ('his emittence').) Yet Gardini was an outsider only in that he took on the establishment. He was a corporate raider, yet he conformed totally to type: he advanced through family connections, allied to undoubted talent and ruthlessness, and ripped off the state for personal gain. He married Idina Ferruzzi, the daughter of Serafino Ferruzzi, founder of the cereal and commodities trading group of the same name. In 1985 Gardini switched his attention to chemicals, and started buying up stock in the chemicals giant Montedison. It was an audacious move, and one which was to put him into conflict with the business community. Having turned Ferruzzi-Montedison into the country's second largest industrial group, he then embarked on his most controversial move: the formation of a joint venture with the state-owned chemicals company, Enichem. The commercial marriage, blessed as Enimont, quickly came to grief. The two companies divorced, citing incompatibility. But the settlement was hugely beneficial to Gardini. He managed to unload much of Ferruzzi's debt on to the combined company, which was picked up by the state holding company ENI when it regained control of Enichem.

Shortly afterwards Gardini said he was leaving Italy for good, because he could not work in the Italian business climate. It was a barely hidden critique of a system that survived only on the payment of huge bribes. Yet in the days before his death, it emerged from the confessions of the former chairman of

Montedison that not only had Gardini not been immune to the affliction of Italian enterprise, he had been a prime exponent of the system. Gardini was accused of creating a slush fund to pay off politicians. And he was also blamed for some $202 million extra losses on Montedison's balance sheet.

The revelations were too much for Gardini. After a full life, his lawyer explained, the prospect of spending the next twelve years in prison next to HIV-positive drug addicts was intolerable. At the age of sixty, a year after making his spectacular but ultimately unsuccessful bid to capture the America's Cup, he killed himself.

But why? Why had he not tried to fight the allegations? If he was merely playing the system, a system which had driven the motor of national growth and wealth for so many Italians, why did he not stand up and fight? What lack of fibre, of backbone, was it that led a man in the prime of life to end it without a struggle? What was it that led Gardini, and five days before him the former head of the state holding company ENI, to kill themselves? What kind of immaturity, in a sixty-year-old, made him unable to face up to his responsibilities? It was not guilt, the acknowledgement of some personal failure, or some breach of conscience or inner morality. It was shame, the realization that his image of success was for ever to be tarnished within society, and inability to face the family he had been married into, whose trust he had repaid with chicanery.

For if Raul Gardini was one of the beautiful people, he also personified other sides of the Italian character. He was the shining example of the dynamism of Italian enterprise, which contrasts so strongly with the inertia of the institutions. Italians work hard, are creative, and when confronted by an obstacle seek a way round it. The positive side of this is the flexibility of the Italian way of doing business and their energy. But often those energies are spent being *furbo*, that portmanteau Italian word which usually expresses admiration and which means being cunning and sly to try and outwit the next guy, to get round the state or the law.

Italy is a country where in 1987 the government officially recognized that the black economy, of people working in family shops, of plumbers and artisans not declaring their income to the tax authorities, was worth 20 per cent of GDP. And this was regarded as a conservative estimate! There are few in Italy who can assert that they too have not bent the rules, paid off a local official to obtain a building permit or a driving licence. The practice among the self-employed of underdeclaring income to the taxman is widespread. Landladies write one contract for the tenant, another for the tax authorities. Favours are exchanged. If you want something done, you seek a friend, a contact, a politician who can fix things for you. And in return some favour will be demanded, not necessarily immediately, possibly not for years.

Italy is a country where laws are turned upside down. Elsewhere, power tends to corrupt, and absolute power corrupts absolutely. In Italy the absence of absolute power has not prevented its absolute corruption. Italian political life is about co-operation and consensus. As Gore Vidal observed, the genius of America was to separate State from Religion. The genius of Italy was to separate the State from the People.

The lack of strong government or definite policies has allowed Italians to mould a society without any real ideological boundaries. It has also fostered two nations, one of private enterprise and initiative, the other dependent on state hand-outs. The state sector is the largest in Europe. The huge loss-making state-owned industrial holding companies, IRI and ENI (EFIM, which ran into major financial difficulties, was much smaller), accounted for 10 per cent of GDP, but suffered from overmanning and inefficient manage- ment. Nearly 40 per cent of the workforce was employed by the government, either in the civil service or in one of the state enterprises. One million people lived off politics, which had become the principal channel for social advancement, occupying the position the Church once held.

The interaction of the two sides of Italy, of private and public, is paraded each year in a regular event. The last day of May is an annual fixture in the social and business calendar of every industrial baron and major financier in Italy. From early in the morning, traffic in Rome's Via Nazionale is clogged. Outside the baroque entrance to the Bank of Italy, chauffeurs manoeuvre on to the pavement the regulation navy blue limousines beloved of oh-so- conformist Italian businessmen and politicians.

The annual meeting of the shareholders of the Bank of Italy

may not sound as exciting an event as a weekend's skiing in Cortina or a first night at La Scala. But as surely as all roads lead to Rome, it draws silkmakers from Como, sleek brokers from Milan, and prosperous manufacturers from Turin. The occasion is an enormous cocktail party, without the cocktails.

Inside the great conference room the governor of the bank delivers his yearly diatribe against government. The bank is unique in Europe for being a central bank owned by private shareholders. The governor rails against the government's failure to tackle the country's serious economic problems and its lack of preparation for the great single European market. No politician to whom the message is addressed is in sight. In the marbled halls outside, paying scant attention to these proceedings – they have heard it all before, and can pick it up in the next day's papers – friends meet, dealers rub shoulders, businessmen shake hands, entrepreneurs clinch deals, brokers exchange gossip. For in Italy business and advancement, from the obtaining of the smallest of favours, still largely depends on who you know, rather than what you do or are. Introductions are crucial. Promotion in most private companies hinges more on family connections than on merit. The business environment is essentially clannish and Masonic.

The occasion at the Bank of Italy sheds light on one of Italy's many paradoxes. How can the private sector be so successful when government is so poor and public services so diabolical? How is it that the country can prosper when telephones (until recently) and railways and government and the postal service work at the standard of a Third World nation (or in many cases worse: the quality of international telephone lines from Ethiopia is far higher than that of its former colonial power)? How can Italians live so long when some of their hospitals are such deathtraps?

Some argue that Italians thrive on the absence of strong central government, rather than despite it (local and regional government in the North is often quite good). Alternatively, they prosper despite their politicians, rather than because of them. It is a question that ceased to be academic. For as Italy started the difficult and painful process of reform, the question had to be asked again: What had led them to their current pass? Was it the system, or the Italians themselves?

THREE

Così fan tutti or Everyone's on the take

It all began with a woman scorned. And as first Mario Chiesa learnt to his cost, and subsequently the whole political establishment in Italy, the failure to pay a few million lire maintenance payments to an estranged wife turned out to be an expensive mistake. It was as if the removal of one single brick from the financial foundations underpinning the political system had brought the Italian party structure crashing down.

It was bad enough for Lara Sala that her husband (like many Italian women, she kept her maiden name after she married Chiesa) had taken up with another woman twenty years younger. What broke her was her husband's stinginess. She complained to the authorities that he had not been making the payments she considered appropriate for a man of his standing. His salary as head of the Pio Albergo Trivulzio old people's home in Milan known as La Baggina was modest. But she knew sufficient about his activities to realize that he was making a great deal more than that. She should have done. After all, the luxury apartment in Via Monte Rosa where he lived in central Milan had cost rather more than a civil servant and party functionary could ordinarily have afforded.

At the same time, the judicial authorities were trying to match together other pieces of gossip they had heard about this official. Then came their second break. A businessman, Luca Magni, had gone to the authorities to complain that he was being asked to pay Mario Chiesa in order to win a cleaning contract for the old people's home. There was more than a hint of irony that a cleaning contractor helped spark the big purge. Chiesa was asking him for 10 per cent, he said, which would have halved his profits. He was asked to co-operate with the authorities, and to pass by

Chiesa's office to make the pay-off. A tiny microphone was hidden in a ballpoint pen he carried in his jacket. He was also given what he described as a hideous black attaché case. Inside was hidden a television camera. As important as these high-tech accoutrements were the ten marked notes he was given to entrap his man. This was a technique the investigating magistrate Antonio Di Pietro had learnt during his days as a police officer. When Magni handed Chiesa the money, 7 million lire (about £3,200) in hundred-thousand-lire notes – the largest denomination at the time – the carabinieri burst in. Chiesa made an effort to protest his innocence. It was his money, he claimed. But the marked notes demonstrated their true provenance.

Under interrogation, Chiesa at first declared that he had been taking money to fund his party, the Socialists, who dominated Milan's municipal politics. But it was clear from his lifestyle that he had also been cheating on his party, and raking off money for himself. In a short time other businessmen began to come forward. Then, when Chiesa saw that he had been disowned by his own party, he began to talk too. It emerged that every contract associated with the old people's home, from the undertaker's contract for interment of the deceased to the provision of food, was won on payment of a flat, set commission. After his arrest, some 12 billion lire (nearly £5 million) was found in his personal bank accounts. More importantly for the investigators was another find: not a black book, but a floppy disk with the names of 7,000 contacts. Chiesa was the first person convicted in the scandal. He was sentenced to six years in prison and fined 6 billion lire – leaving him with at least 6 billion, some believe twice that amount, waiting for him on his release.

The tangle of spaghetti that Chiesa's arrest uncovered revealed itself to be never-ending. As the investigators tugged at one strand, a whole new knot appeared. Within weeks, a complete network of pay-offs came to light. A network so institutionalized, so systematic, so extensive that it was a wonder to all that it had remained undiscovered for so long.

Hardly a single public-works contract in Milan was signed without a commission being paid, whether for roads, the metropolitan underground line, the rebuilding of the San Siro stadium whose costs soared as the World Cup finals approached, or the airports authority. Each area of activity attracted a different rate. Public-works contracts could carry 3 or 4 per cent, while property development might carry twice that. If a contract had to be extended for any reason, then a further commission was payable, pro rata.

The investigations fascinated the public and had immediate popular support. Within days the graffiti artists of Milan had daubed the entrance to the city with signs saying *Benvenuti a Tangentopoli* (Welcome to Bribesville). It was all the more galling for a city which prided itself on being the most hardworking of the Italian peninsula, and the country's moral capital. For such a scandal to happen in the South would have been considered the norm. But Milan was meant to be different. Critics of the Milanese jibed that this demonstrated that Milan was as flawed as the cities of the South. Apologists for the city countered that only in Milan could a judge, Antonio Di Pietro, have pursued his investigations with such vigour without them being derailed or sabotaged by political interests.

On a political level, Chiesa's revelations spelt the end of the aspirations of the Socialist Party leader Bettino Craxi. Milan was the Socialists' flagship of a modern administration. The mayor had long been a Socialist, and the local party was run as the personal fief of Bobo Craxi, the then twenty-eight-year-old son of the party leader. It was not long before the party headquarters was closed by judicial order. Banners appeared reflecting the new popular desire for moral rectitude: 'Get out of Milan, Ali Bobo and the forty thieves.'

This number proved somewhat conservative. Within a few weeks, the whole sleazy picture was exposed of how Italian mainstream political parties were financed by robbing from the public purse. When Chiesa declared in a statement released to the press that he had assisted in the re-election of Bobo Craxi to the city council, this was strenuously rebutted. Craxi *padre* tried to shrug off the scandal. Every party, he said, had a few bad apples. What emerged was that the entire barrel was rotten to the core.

Bettino Craxi did not go without a fight. He was the first

former prime minister to have been tainted in the scandal. He was one of Italy's very few statesmen of world stature. At home, he had transformed the Socialist Party from a small faction of the left into a major political force. It was he who understood the Socialists' role as the fulcrum between two main political power blocs. He would cajole concessions out of the Christian Democrats by threatening to join forces and form a government with the Communists. It was an empty threat, since the Socialists were bent on sharing power within Christian Democrat-led coalitions and gaining with it first-class seats on the gravy train. As prime minister in the 1980s, Craxi was responsible for grasping the nettle and introducing austerity measures to correct an economic downturn. But the reverse side of his decisiveness was his reputation for authoritarianism. Italy's best political cartoonist, Forattini, caricatured him in Gestapo boots.

Craxi could not, however, stem the inexorable tide of scandal. One of the early arrests was of a man directly connected to his leadership. Paolo Pilliteri was an ex-mayor of Milan. He was also Bettino Craxi's brother-in-law. When he was arrested, Craxi shouted that there was a plot against the Socialist Party, and his leadership of it. He refused to surrender. But he was doomed. First he failed to be called to form the next government. And eventually he was forced to give up his post as the leader of the party. It was inevitable that Bettino Craxi should have devised all sorts of fanciful conspiracy theories as to why Judge Di Pietro was acting. He claimed that the Milan magistrates were investigating him specifically as part of a plot to kill off the Socialist Party. He even suggested that Di Pietro was acting on behalf of a Catholic reform group.

The net grew wider. In the following year the spreading scandal hit most of the Italian political establishment. All the other main political parties lost their leaders. Several politicians or businessmen took their own lives and hundreds were arrested.

A less obvious candidate for a fall was Giorgio La Malfa. He had become leader of the small but influential Republican Party after the death of his distinguished father Ugo. He had taken his party out of the government coalition because he sought institutional reform. And he had personally hunted out of the party the man most associated with corruption and the Sicilian Mafia, Aristide Gunnella. Gunnella was said to have brought with him 20 per cent of the Republican vote in Sicily. An inquiry showed that many of the votes cast for him in Catania for the regional elections were, in fact, those of the dead.

The Republicans, the small party of the private-sector business community, had often admonished the big parties for their excessive corruption. Giorgio La Malfa had campaigned openly for a 'party of honest people'. But inevitably the Republicans too were tainted, even if far less than the other parties. Giorgio La Malfa failed to ensure his own house was in order. Whether through an oversight or because he simply did not think it mattered, he allowed someone to pay 50 million lire for printing party-political propaganda which he failed to declare. It was enough, in the new moral climate he had himself played a part in achieving, to force him out.

It was not only the politicians who were accused for demanding commissions to finance the parties. Businessmen who paid the bribes were also implicated. The scandal spread beyond Milan to the other cities of the Po Valley and the North. And it grew to encompass senior executives of many of the blue-chip companies in the country.

One of the first men to be investigated in the commercial world was Salvatore Ligresti, a Sicilian-born financier who was one of the richest men in Italy. Don Salvatore had interests from construction to insurance to banking. He had come penniless to Milan from his native Catania at the end of the 1950s. By 1976 he was in a position to buy the SAI insurance group from Fiat. His greatest successes were in construction. Many of the appalling, cheap, high-rise blocks around the suburbs of Milan were built by him. He also contrived to sell off some ghastly offices for use by the Catastro, the housing register. At the time of his arrest his companies were said to be worth some 5 trillion lire (£2.2 billion). His meteoric rise had been helped by the excellent relations he maintained with local politicians, including Bettino Craxi. Throughout the 1980s, he was to receive a plethora of charges for breaches of planning regulations. But no charge ever stuck. One of the more opaque links was Don Salvatore's connection with Mediobanca, the near-legendary privately-owned merchant bank. It was known for what was not known, for the secrecy surrounding its founder, Enrico Cuccia, another Sicilian, as much as for its fruitful role in most of the main commercial and financial deals in corporate Italy.

Other companies, private and public, were swept along by the dragnet, as the magistrates trawled the murky waters of the financing of Italian political parties. The state railways and roads organizations were tarred with charges of paying commissions to win contracts. Even Fiat was hit. Two of its top executives were arrested for paying commissions on the contract for the extension to the Milan metro, built in part by Fiat's construction subsidiary Cogefar. Subsequently Fiat was to deny with vigour that it had operated a slush fund through companies in offshore tax havens.

But why Fiat? Why would Fiat need to pay bribes to politicians to secure business? Not for nothing was it seen as a state within the state. Fiat had enjoyed an unrivalled dominance in the economic and political life of the country for most of the century. Through an elaborate network of alliances, by the early 1990s it directly employed a quarter of a million, and an estimated two million workers in feeder industries depended on Fiat. Its turnover was equivalent to some 5 per cent of gross domestic product. Fiat was not just a maker of cars. It made tractors and trucks, owned banks and insurance companies. It had construction arms and was heavily engaged in defence and the aerospace industry. It wielded extraordinary influence, owning two newspapers and placing a seventh of all advertising in Italian media, so that journalists were reluctant to criticize the company lest they lose advertising income.

Because of Fiat, the road lobby had time and again diverted resources to motorway construction away from rail. From the 1950s onwards, Fiat had a captive market, desperate for new consumer goods and the cheap Fiat 500. Furthermore, Italy was to have one of the most protected markets in Europe, with high tariffs on imported cars, particularly the bigger ones which Fiat did not make, favouring the smaller models which it did build. By the early 1990s, however, Fiat's share of the domestic market (the total number of registered cars was 28 million, more than in comparably sized Britain) had fallen below 50 per cent, because of aggressive marketing by Volkswagen, Peugeot, Renault and Ford.

Fiat had always acted on the principle that politics depended on business and business depended on politics in a chain of *intrecci* or conspiratorial links. Some hint that the management of Fiat was being asked to pay too much to the politicians came in an unusual outburst in 1987 by Cesare Romiti, Fiat's long-standing managing director and the bruiser of Italian industry. Like so many messages it was issued in the mysterious language of Italian public speaking, the key to whose decipherment is possessed only by a small number of people.

Somewhat belatedly, Fiat unveiled its own code of business ethics to govern future relations between the company and government, public-sector companies and civil servants. The new rules were clear. In no circumstances should employees provide 'money or goods of any kind to promote or favour the interests of one or more groups or companies following illegitimate pressure.' It may seem extraordinary to people outside Italy that employees of the largest company in the country had to be given a specific code of ethics instructing them not to break the law. Yet the evidence of past misdemeanours was clear. Fiat, for example, was alleged to have paid 2.4 billion lire (£1 million) for a luxury Rome apartment for a senator. And it was clear that bribes had been paid on many major contracts.

Fiat was not alone. The corruption scandal took another turn with the confessions of Carlo De Benedetti of the Olivetti computer and office-equipment maker. De Benedetti was to the business world what La Malfa was to politics. For years he had beaten his chest with righteous indignation about the climate of bribe-paying. At a meeting of shareholders in 1993, he was giving assurances that their company had never paid bribes. Then, three weeks later, De Benedetti seized the initiative. He presented himself voluntarily to the magistrates in Milan. And he told them about instances when his companies paid bribes to secure contracts. In an eleven-page document he listed illicit financing of parties – mainly the Christian Democrats and Socialists – to the tune of nearly 20 billion lire (£8.5 million). He said that he had had no option if he was to stay in business in the highly competitive office-equipment sector. In his account, the ministry of posts had threatened to stop buying from Olivetti unless the group paid bribes. When in 1988 he agreed to pay 2 per cent commission to the ministry on its purchases from Olivetti, the group's revenue from the postal ministry soared, from a little over 2 billion lire (£850,000) in 1987 to more than 200 billion lire (£85 million) in 1988. Olivetti was obliged to prime the home market because it relied for two-thirds of its sales on exports. The German and Swiss postal authorities were reluctant to buy Olivetti products if they saw that Olivetti was not successful in its domestic market.

Yet De Benedetti did not concede any wrongdoing, or admit guilt. He was, he said, a prey of the system. 'The pressure from the parties and their representatives in the state entities reached an impressive crescendo of menaces and extortion to become in the last few years nothing short of racketeering . . . The demands from the representatives of the parties were systematic and unavoidable on everything they controlled without exception.'

Thus did he cast the Italian business community as the victim, and the politicians as the true corruptors. In Italian law there is a distinction between *corruzione*, where two parties conspire to steal money, and *concussione*, or extortion. De Benedetti sought to portray Olivetti as an innocent and unwilling victim of extortion, not itself an originator of paying bribes.

In that first year nearly a thousand people, including a hundred members of the Italian parliament, had been formally notified they were under investigation. The means used was an *avviso di garanzia*. These formal notifications, *avvisi di garanzia*, rained down like tickertape. Although the *avviso* was meant to guarantee a citizen's rights, it became in itself an instrument of accusation and was seen as a public declaration of a suspect's guilt.

Magistrates have considerable powers of preventive detention in Italy. Even before charges are preferred, they can order a suspect to be locked away for up to three months while investigations are pursued. The period can be extended. During that first heady summer after the investigations began, Milan's San Vittore prison became, in the words of one former inmate, 'like La Scala on a first night', such were the prominent figures who passed through its portals. Indeed, a VIP was redefined as *visto in prigione* – 'seen in jail'. San Vittore was built in 1889 to take 800 prisoners. During the height of the investigations it was holding over 2,000. One of the Fiat executives inside complained about having to share a mattress with other inmates including HIV-positive drug addicts and the local population of rats. Small wonder that after a spell inside suspects were more willing to talk.

There have been many scandals in the history of the republic but never one such as this. What was different this time was the sheer scale of collusion uncovered between corporate business and party treasurers. Another difference was both the determination of the investigators to pursue their inquiries, and the extent of malfeasance that these investigations revealed. For the first time there were no limits imposed on the scope of the inquiries, either by the press, the magistrates, or the political establishment.

Why then? Why had it not happened before, if the corruption of the political parties had been an open secret for years? Indeed, one of the protagonists, seeking to downplay the extent of the practice, had declared that the division of spoils, carving up the cake between the parties, in this way had only been going on since the late 1970s. Fifteen years! It was a staggering confession.

The usual explanation given is that the whole mess began to unravel with the fall of the Berlin Wall in 1989. Until that time the parties which since the end of the Second World War had joined in coalitions to all governments had argued that the main danger came from the Communist Party, which received funds from Moscow. They argued that they therefore needed to take exceptional measures to ensure the Communists did not take over the country. It was justification for the abuses of power during those years. Subsequently the collapse of Communism, and the visible demonstration of the ideological bankruptcy of the left, deprived the traditional political forces of their unifying factor.

Romano Prodi summed it up in one word: Yalta. Because of the postwar division in Europe, and the need to keep the Communists from power, 'there was no punishment in democracy. The political market was not working.' Hence Italy had a 'blocked democracy', where there was never an alternative. The opposition was always understudy, patiently waiting in the wings for the opportunity to come on stage, but knowing that however sick were the ruling parties, however incapable of proper government, they would always be given a *bis*, an encore, by the audience, many of whom had their tickets paid for them, so that the show would go on.

Professor Prodi contrasted Italy to Japan. There the parties financed themselves illegally, but an efficient state machine acted as a counterweight. In Italy, the difference was that the bureaucracy had not been resistant to the corruption of the political parties.

Some magistrates conceded that they had operated under a self-denying ordinance. They too had not pursued their inquiries in the past with such vigour because of concern that to prosecute the ruling parties might have undermined the bulwark against the Communists. In time, the Italian Communist Party and its officials had also been cut into the commission-sharing scheme with the other parties in some areas, though it received a smaller share than they did.

Very early on in the unfolding events in Milan, I asked the state prosecutor why it had taken so long. Why was it that, if the system of pay-offs and commissions had been so institutionalized, it had not been uncovered before? Judge Francesco Saverio Borrelli was in overall charge of investigations in the metropolis. His office was the largest and grandest of all the offices on the fourth floor of the Fascist-era tribunal in Milan. Beneath a huge oil painting he stated what prime minister Amato was to say in his lecture at the London School of Economics, that Operation Clean Hands (Mani Pulite) was different in scope and extent from previous investigations into political bribery. These were isolated episodes. 'This time it is spreading like an oil stain. The problem has probably existed for some time. But it never came to light before.'

He said that in the past one could not bring prosecutions on the evidence merely of gossip at drinks parties. 'The trouble was we needed real evidence of the people, their collaboration. In its nature, this kind of practice is conducted without written records or documentary proof. What is indispensable is the wish to speak.'

And that will to speak had emerged, slowly at first, then quickly gaining momentum. As Judge Borrelli's deputy Gerardo D'Ambrosio was to declare, in one of those phrases which expressed the magnitude of the problem even as it was only just coming out, the evidence was being shovelled in 'by the pallet load. Everywhere you look there is corruption.' In the end, people were queuing up – in so far as Italians were able to overcome their national aversion to standing in line to be dealt with on the basis of first come first served – to tell the magistrates their stories.

These top magistrates and prosecutors were to admit that everyone knew about incidents of collusion between the business community and the political parties. In every bar and every workplace one could hear gossip about kickbacks and backhanders. Everyone had their story of petty corruption. Ten years previously the contractor Adriano Zampini had explained how he had paid off not one, but several different parties in order to win contracts in Turin. What no magistrate had until then begun to comprehend was the way that the commissions paid to the parties had become as institutionalized as the tribute levied on subject tribes in the outreaches of the Roman Empire.

Nor did it emerge at first what were the destinations of the bribes demanded: how much went for personal enrichment, and how much for the party the corrupt official was working for. In one estimate, one-third of the bribes went to the party or a particular faction within it, one-third to the individual, and one-third to all those who needed paying off to ensure the smooth running of the system. The total sums estimated to have been paid in this distortion of economic activity were over 17,000 billion lire a year, or £7 billion.

The reason for the eruption of the financial scandal was quite simply that the parties became too greedy. They had more and more expenses as they grew in size. And as more and more companies were facing economic difficulties, they were less willing to pay the ever greater sums demanded by the parties for their collaboration.

The man who harnessed the public mood for change was Judge Antonio Di Pietro. Although many political figures find this hard to accept, Judge Di Pietro was thus the judicial corollary of the Northern (formerly the Lombard) League, the political protest movement against the corruption of Rome.

Di Pietro was an unlikely hero. He would not win prizes for his looks, his dress sense, or his delphic pronouncements. But no one else better evoked the changing spirit of the age. He was born in 1950 of humble peasant stock in the village of Montenero di Basaccia, near Campobasso, in the southern central province of Molise. Even after he had risen to national prominence, he maintained a touching relationship with his elderly mother. He would phone her each day before dawn as they each left to work, she to her fields, he to the fertile pastures of the Mani Pulite investigation (Operation Clean Hands).

There were few prospects for a young man growing up in the poor rural area. As for so many of his peers, there were three possibilities: he could go abroad, he could join the priesthood, or he could join one of the branches of the armed forces or police. There was a fourth option: to turn to crime. If he had done that Italy would have been the poorer. He chose two of the former possibilities. First he migrated, going to West Germany for the better part of a year. He earned some ready cash as a factory worker, which he was able to send back to his mother. He also earned enough to pay for his studies. On his return to Italy he passed an exam to join the defence ministry as an electronics technician. It was neither a glamorous nor a typical training for a future investigating magistrate. But it gave him the technical expertise for some of his later coups. His work was always described as methodical, rather than inspired. While working for a defence contractor, testing computer-guidance systems for warplanes, he started studying law. He passed another exam for entry into the police, and after studies in Rome went off to Milan to work in a small police station. There he specialized in investigations into drug trafficking and fraud.

In Italy, to become a judge, as for so many jobs, you need to pass a *concorso* or competitive exam. The competition is tough. In 1992, there were over 10,000 applicants for 300 posts. Although institutionally there is a separation of functions between the police and investigating magistrates, many of the tasks they undertake are similar. The transition from policeman to investigating magistrate is not unusual. The system in Italy, as in France, is that the magistrate is responsible for preparing a case for prosecution. He or she lays down the areas of inquiry, and instructs the branches of law and order – the police, the carabinieri, the guardia di finanza – to assist where required. The system changed in 1989 to take on some of the methods of the approach in Britain and America, yet the office of the examining magistrate remained.

The investigating magistrates in Italy have traditionally enjoyed a reputation as a corps of highly intelligent and dedicated men and women. At times their self-governing body, the Consiglio Superiore della Magistratura, has been beset by factional strife. Yet often the judges took on cases alone which revealed shadowy links between a corrupt political class and some form of organized criminal activity. Those in the areas of risk, in Sicily and the south of Italy, frequently paid the price.

No one would attribute to Di Pietro the brilliance of the anti-Mafia judge Giovanni Falcone, with whom he was collaborating shortly before Falcone's death. But he had dogged qualities. His rise is proof that it is still possible to achieve great things in Italy without having a political patron or compromising oneself to one of the parties. Di Pietro went further. He appeared to be genuinely without political side. What is more, he seemed not to be intimidated by the political forces who saw him as antagonistic to their vested interests.

Di Pietro's first major case dealt with fraud. It was in the 1980s, and he had noticed that many truck drivers and others who had been in accidents had one thing in common: they had all passed through the same small group of driving schools. In Italy drivers are required by law to attend a certain number of driving lessons before they can sit their driving test. Di Pietro did what no judge had done before. He fed the information he had into a computer and cross-checked it against a couple of government data banks. He established that the cases were the result of corrupt local officials from vehicle-licensing offices passing candidates from the same driving schools, even though many candidates could not drive. Because of his computer skills, Di Pietro was to investigate two other fraud cases. One concerned Lombardia Informatica, the information services company controlled by the Lombardy administrative region, which spent 800 billion lire (£350 million) to put health services on computer file. When examined, large numbers of false names were found on the lists. They included the fanciful Carlo Marx. Other irregularities included the donation to a Socialist Party official of 150 million lire which appeared in the books of neither the party nor the company.

If the *deus ex machina* of Operation Clean Hands was Di Pietro's computer data base, he had other more human associates. He and his main collaborator, Gherardo Colombo, made an unlikely pair. Where Di Pietro wore an ill-fitting dark suit and a white shirt, Colombo wore jeans and open-necked shirt. Colombo, however, had a record as impressive as any young magistrate in Italy. For he had helped untangle that whole messy knot of the P2 Masonic Lodge affair. And he had been working for years on the routes black money took to secret Swiss bank accounts.

Scandals and crises are rarely as they first appear in Italy. The newspaper headlines scream Crisis! nearly every day. Political earthquakes are only marginally less frequent. But most scandals seldom last more than a brief moment, and hardly ever have lasting consequences. And crises describe more the aura of drama than any turning point.

In past corruption scandals, some ministerial heads had fallen, and businessmen had been locked away. It had also been common knowledge that nearly every public works contract was rigged, and that contractors had to pay off some party placeman who awarded the contract. Nor was opposition to the system of party financing so new. Some critics had been calling for an end to the rule by the parties for years. They understood the corrosive effect the parties had on the administration and good government. As far back as 1975, one of the most distinguished commentators in Italy, the veteran editor Indro Montanelli, advised his readers: 'Hold your noses and vote Christian Democrat.'

The hypocrisy and immorality of figures in public life had few bounds. Lamberto Mancini was provincial *assessore* or treasurer in Rome for the small PSDI Social Democratic Party. It was a fine June day. He had just laid a wreath at the tomb of Giacomo Matteoti, the upright Socialist whose death at the hands of a Fascist mob in 1924 aroused a moral revolt in the nation against the brutality of the regime. Mancini had delivered a eulogy, speaking with passion against the illegal practices that were corrupting public life. He then went straight off to meet a contact, and accepted from him a *tangente* or bribe of twenty-eight million lire (£13,000) to ensure that a trade fair would be held. Unfortunately for him, the man who proffered the *tangente* was an undercover police agent. This was not the end of Mancini's disgrace. The crowd recognized him as he was led away in handcuffs, and shouted after him: 'Lock them all up!'

It later emerged that Mancini had been set up by a young, new head of the local branch of Confindustria, the industrialists' association, who had campaigned for his elected post on a platform of combating corruption. He was soon hauled in by Councillor Mancini, who explained that rules were rules. If he wanted to have the 190 million lire (£80,000) contribution of the provincial council to the annual fair promoting manufacturing industry, his cut would be 25 per cent. At first the industrialist refused. At the second time of asking, he balked again. At the third time, he decided to play along. But this time, he informed the authorities.

Shortly before Operation Clean Hands, a film was released to the general viewing public which in many ways gave a flavour of what was to come. Daniele Luchetti's political satire *Il Portaborse* ('The Bagman') was too parochial to have the universal appeal and international success of Italian films such as *Cinema Paradiso* or *Mediterraneo*. *Il Portaborse* was not a great film. The satire was too obvious. But, as so often, it was a work of fiction that expressed many of the truths of the Italian way of doing things. The film narrated the story of a provincial schoolmaster who was plucked from obscurity so that his skills at communication could be exploited by an ambitious young minister. The anti-hero found himself rapidly embroiled in the system of *raccomandazione* and exchange of favours that substitute for political activity in Italy. Petitioners came to him to sort out their problems. There was the official in the interior ministry who arranged to doctor the ballot in exchange for help for his son who had been caught abroad on a drugs charge. There was the local party official who complained that the Christian Democrats were upsetting the accepted system of sharing out the bribes paid to the parties. There were the men who came seeking help with obtaining a disability pension.

When the film was released it was dismissed by Socialist politicians as a cheap attempt to besmirch their party. One official instituted legal proceedings for defamation. What the film portrayed was the way the system worked. There should have been few surprises. In thirty years some 520 requests were made by investigating magistrates for parliament to lift immunity from deputies so that proceedings could be brought. Immunity from prosecution for members of both houses of parliament – the chamber of deputies and the senate, in theory a second, equal house rather than an upper chamber – was one of the more staggering features of the Italian political system. In 485 cases, leave was not granted. Members have been sought by the law for all sorts of criminal activity: from tax evasion to stealing from state funds, commercial fraud to implication in murder inquiries.

Throughout the history of postwar Italy there has been a series of political scandals relating to siphoning off public funds from state-funded projects. Many of these fleecing operations have been dubbed 'Golden'. There was the case of the Lenzuolo d'Oro – the Golden Sheets – when the head of the railways was forced to resign because the contract paid for sheets on the overnight sleepers was so inflated the sheets could have been spun from cloth of gold. Then there were the Carceri d'Oro, the Golden Jails, so named because the newly designed or rehabilitated penal institutions were so overpriced it was said the bars could have been made of gold. Di Pietro himself had handled the case, and deciphered the computer records of the architect Bruno De Mico in the Codemi affair, the key company in the Golden Jails scandal. The architect had actually designed his own briefcase, which could take half a billion lire, not a penny more not a penny less, for the payment of commissions. What finesse! De Mico began to reveal the names of his political contacts because he was in financial difficulties. A minister, Franco Nicolazzi, of the Social Democrat Party was accused by De Mico of taking 1.5 per cent of each contract. De Mico also told investigators that another minister had demanded fixed sums for awarding the contracts.

Without doubt the greatest example of the misuse of government funding and political fraud and graft occurred in the aftermath of the earthquake that struck Irpinia in the region of Basilicata on the evening of 23 November 1980. Some 3,100 people were killed, 7,651 injured, and 200,000 made homeless. Ten years later, parliament was officially informed that the government had spent 51,000 billion lire (£23 billion) to repair the damage. Yet more than a third of the victims were still living in prefabricated huts. Since the earthquake struck the South, the debate over how to rebuild was buried in a mountain of proposals about how it should be used for the development of an area that was traditionally economically depressed. A massive programme of development was announced. Generous financial incentives were offered. Yet very little was spent on productive enterprises. Much of the money was diverted into the hands of the Neapolitan Mafia, the Camorra. One of the main beneficiaries was the family of the one-time prime minister Ciriaco De Mita, on the left of the Christian Democrat Party, and the local potentate around Avellino, one of the areas most devastated by the earthquake. His brother Michele won many of the contracts to build roads.

Other Christian Democrat ministers from Naples were active in securing funds for various projects, few of which ever got off the ground. Billions of lire were appropriated for the construction of a shipyard at La Morra, halfway up the mountainside.

Even the Communists, who prided themselves on their moral rectitude, were to be implicated in the broader bribes-for-party financing scandal, although they were quantitively less guilty . than the other parties.

Italy was not the only arena for the *tangente*. Outside the railings surrounding the Forum in Rome hangs a series of huge mosaic maps of the world. They were erected by Mussolini to depict the spread of the empire of classical Rome. All around this part of the Eternal City lie the remains of Rome's past glories. One could imagine another map at the Farnesina, the imposing marble-clad building constructed in the Fascist era to house the foreign ministry behind the Olympic stadium. Vast areas would be shaded in different colours. Great swathes of the Middle East and North Africa would be coloured Socialist pink. Most of Latin America would be a Christian Democrat white. Except for Nicaragua, an appropriately Communist red (the Communists were also allocated Angola and Mozambique, although this was later split with the Socialists because of their success in arranging the end to the conflict there). The colouring would not reflect the political hue of the country itself, merely the affiliation of the ambassadors Rome appointed to those countries. In effect, every country in the world became one more area where party political jobbery could be indulged. So, for example, since the Socialist Party controlled the energy sector, most ambassadors to oil or gas producers would be Socialists, but not in Libya, which was a fief of the Christian Democrats, as were China, the Philippines, Chile and Brazil. Tanzania, South Africa, Vietnam, Cambodia, and the North African countries were all Socialist Party 'provinces'. Bettino Craxi had his holiday home in Hammamet in Tunisia.

The practice was no secret. I gained an inkling of the system on a visit to the Algerian embassy in Rome before the whole Operation Clean Hands exploded. A manufacturer of agricultural machinery from Emilia-Romagna was applying for a visa to go to a trade fair in Algiers. He was indiscreetly bemoaning the costs of doing business in Algeria. It was easy enough to find an Algerian ministry official to bribe to sell his products, he confessed, but the onerous part was paying off the money men in the Italian ministry who controlled the financing through aid and trade deals and arranged the export credit guarantees.

Other countries' diplomatic representatives have become accustomed to acting as ambassadors for their manufacturing industries. Few, however, act in effect as agents for filling their own party coffers. The system reached its apogee – or nadir, depending on one's point of view – under the tutelage of Gianni De Michelis, when he was foreign minister. He rode roughshod over the diplomatic norms of promotion, putting his appointees into places he favoured over the heads of more senior diplomats. Ambassadors had to act as businessmen, and political counsellors as scouts for the best club, in whichever spot the minister landed.

In the absence of a vigorous foreign policy, or armed forces to project it, Italy found a substitute in a comprehensive policy of development aid to the Third World. Massive assistance programmes were initialled and signed. Yet little of this aid went to the needy. The huge aid programme was merely a mechanism for the parties to extend their reach worldwide. *Tangentopoli* was truly a global village, with the grasping hands of the parties extended to the ends of the earth. Greed replaced need. Vast sums of state funds were cynically taken from the mouths of the starving to feed the voracious appetites of the Italian political parties. Now in Italy it was not illegal to pay bribes or commissions abroad to secure contracts. It was, however, illegal for government officials to demand payment from businessmen.

The ravages of Italian rapacity can be seen in the devastation of the Horn of Africa, where, for historical reasons, Italy has always had a special interest. Mussolini invaded Abyssinia in 1935 and incurred the first use of economic sanctions imposed by the world community. In modern times, the Horn has been divided along party lines with Ethiopia awarded to the Christian Democrats and the former colony of Somalia, a satrapy of the Socialist Party. In Somalia between 1981 and 1990, Italy backed 114 projects whose total cost exceeded $1 billion. Yet few projects got off the ground. A 400-kilometre highway was pushed across the desert at a cost of $250 million, despite the fact that only wandering tribesmen used it. A further $40 million was spent on a spanking new hospital south of Mogadishu. This was jammed with the latest high-tech equipment and operating theatres. But the Somalis lacked the technical training to run it and it quickly fell apart. Italian aid accounted for nearly half Somalia's GNP – yet there was little to show for it in terms of economic development and alleviation of misery.

The Socialist Party's interest in Somalia dated from the coming to power of Siad Barre. He had adopted Socialism as a way of transforming a pastoral society into a modern state. At first he was sympathetic to the Italian Communist Party. But after he broke with Moscow, the chosen interlocutors in Italy were the Socialists. In 1978, an Italian–Somali chamber of commerce was set up in Milan to promote the activities of Italian construction companies and engineering concerns. Its president was Bettino

Craxi's brother-in-law, Paolo Pilliteri (yes, him again). In the years that followed, many of Italy's major construction firms engaged in projects in Somalia funded by the Italian state. But, as in Milan, these contracts were awarded on payment of commission. Reports of the amounts in play emerged in 1989, when General Mohammed Farah Aideed, a former aide to Siad Barre, began litigation against the Italian–Somali chamber of commerce. In his suit he maintained that an arrangement existed whereby 10 per cent of all contract prices were payable as commission. This commission, he maintained, was to have been split fifty-fifty between him and another Somali.

Besides Somalia, Tunisia, Sudan, Indonesia and Bangladesh were countries where the parties saw opportunities for financial advancement. Again it was in road construction that the largest amounts could be siphoned off. The ambassadors of several Third World countries were recalled by their governments to investigate their collusion. The Italian officials in charge, including officials at SACE, the export credit guarantee agency, were soon being investigated.

The scheme was like an engine which, as it aged, needed more and more oiling to ensure it ticked over. Italy's democracy was among the most representative in the world. Because its electoral system was one of the purest forms of proportional representation, no single party ever commanded enough seats to form a government by itself. Government coalitions were formed by the Christian Democrats with a combination of the other smaller parties: the Socialists, the Social Democrats, the Liberals, or the Republicans. Thus nearly all parties had a slice of the cake, a share of the spoils. A change of government would reflect the changing balance of power between different parties within the coalition, or more usually reflected the shifting weight of the various *correnti* or factions within each party. Italians called this 'moving the chairs in the *salotto*'.

Real power lay not with the prime minister of the day, but with the party leaders. A 'president of the council of ministers' had powers less than the chief executive in other systems, whether the US or French president or a British prime minister.

Formally, his main job was to chair cabinet meetings. He could not hire or appoint a cabinet: this was achieved through horse trading with the party leaders. For several years two of the most powerful political barons in Italy had no ministerial office: Bettino Craxi and his counterpart as secretary-general of the Christian Democrats, Arnaldo Forlani.

If a change of government was comparable to musical chairs, a metaphor for the exercise of cabinet government in Italy is the administration of the one area many Italians are familiar with: the *condominio*, or residents' association. The *condominio* is the smallest form of association up from the family group. It is a mechanism whereby residents in blocks of flats determine how to manage the common parts. Like national government, it is beset by indecision and arguments about who will pay for repairs to the plumbing and which month the heating will go on. The major causes of dispute are over repairs to the lift, with residents on the ground floor understandably less willing to pay their share. Managing the *condominio* requires great reserves of charm and tact, two attributes of which the Italians enjoy an abundance. It also requires resoluteness and determination, which are frequently rather less evident in Italy.

Real power lay in the *sottogoverno*, a sort of parallel government that devolved from the *palazzi* or headquarters of the political parties in Rome. Over the course of the forty-five-odd years after the end of the Second World War, the *sottogoverno* permeated nearly every nook and cranny of Italian life. The acknowledged masters were the Christian Democrats, who were so accomplished that party, government and state became barely distinguishable. They were able to transform the huge bureaucracy of the state, and the hundreds of thousands of jobs in the public-sector industries, into the largest field for patronage in any Western country. In time, however, as the Christian Democrats found their dominant position weakened, they had to share some of these spoils with the other parties. The Socialists in particular exploited their pivotal position to extract maximum gains, inserting themselves increasingly into this *sottogoverno*, which they milked brazenly for the funnelling of state funds to the party treasurer. The *sottogoverno* in turn was operated by what came to be known as the *partitocrazia*, or rule by the parties. It was the parties who divided up the spoils of office, placing their men by a strictly calculated formula known as *lottizzazione* or allotment. Possession of a party membership card often became a prerequisite for a job as a driver, a secretary or a clerical assistant. It was not long before the critics of this way of running the country drew the parallels with the old Soviet Communist Party and dubbed these lucky men the *nomenklatura*.

It was a junior Christian Democrat minister Massimo Cencelli who in the early 1950s worked out, according to a complicated mathematical formula, the dividing up of not only the key cabinet and junior ministerial portfolios, but many other official posts according to the electoral strength of a party or faction. Each post was ascribed a numerical value according to political weight. So critical was the need for fairness, so delicate was the balancing act, that the Cencelli manual came to be like scripture. It could take weeks for a government to be put in place. The system meant that when a minister left the government he had to be replaced not only by a member of the same party, whatever his or her qualifications, but also of the same *corrente* or faction.

Sottogoverno, partitocrazia, lottizzazione, nomenklatura – what these four words added up to was a multibillion-pound enterprise of patronage from the civil service to hospitals, from university lectureships to the huge state-owned industrial holding companies, which in turn controlled two-thirds of the banks, the main radio and television channels, La Scala and the Venice Biennale. The key posts in all of these were *lottizzati*, that is, they were allocated according to party affiliation. So for example, by the early 1990s, the huge IRI (Institute for Industrial Reconstruction), founded in 1933, was a Christian Democrat preserve. ENI, the main gas, oil and chemicals giant, had become a fiefdom of the Socialists. The patronage worked both ways. The party leader would in effect choose the captains of those industries or concerns which accrued to him.

In return, these heads of industry could serve the interests of the party. This was not a simple case of mere prestige or of promoting a certain policy. Their function came to be one and one alone: to fill the party coffers. So it was, for example, that ENEL, the state electricity generation company, would pay ENI, the state energy supplier, commission to win contracts which would be diverted to the Socialist Party account. Likewise the state helicopter producer, Agusta, whose senior executives were under investigation for payment of commissions to the civil defence authority as an inducement to buy.

The state-run TV channels were perhaps the most obvious examples of *lottizzazione*. The three channels reflect the political bias of the three main parties: Rai 1, the Christian Democrats, Rai 2 the Socialists, and Rai 3 the Communist Party (later the Democratic Party of the Left or PDS). Rai 1 would stress family values and report the daily doings and pronouncements of the Pope, Rai 3 would uncover evidence of government corruption or maladministration, and Rai 2 was a vehicle for promoting the political aspirations of Bettino Craxi. All three were, however, meant to be politically impartial. This fiction was maintained until Bruno Vespa, the director of Rai 1, admitted editorial control rested with the headquarters of the Christian Democrat Party. Calls were immediately made for the disinfestation of the channel (Vespa means wasp in Italian), and shortly afterwards disaffected journalist staff forced him out because they felt the channel was too *lottizzato*.

The consequences of political patronage guiding economic ventures could be seen in myriad areas. A quintessentially Italian tale of clientelism was the case of Federconsorzi, a co-operative of suppliers of agricultural goods. Early in the summer of 1991 it went bust, owing nearly 5,500 billion lire (£2.6 billion). Or, at least, it was allowed to go bust. For as a para-state enterprise, it had always been able to turn to the government to cover its deficit. But the then agriculture minister Giovanni Goria was not prepared to bail out the consortium. He proposed the voluntary liquidation of Federconsorzi. Foreign creditors, including UK, Japanese and German banks, were not happy. They argued that the consortium was in effect a state-run enterprise. The farm minister retorted that it was not.

The confusion was simple. Federconsorzi was a typical Italian combination of party politics and business. It was set up under the monarchy to help farmers sell crops and buy supplies. At first it worked well. It was big enough to operate a near monopoly. Federconsorzi could get good prices for its members' products, and secure low prices for its supplies. After the Second World War, like so many such government agencies, it became a puppet of party politics. It supplied tractors to the farmers, and was a vehicle for scooping up votes for the Christian Democrats. Farmers were traditionally Catholic and conservative. The Federconsorzi had a role in ensuring that its nearly 400,000 members voted for the party. So long as they could be encouraged to stay on the land, they were likely to continue to do so. The inducements were considerable. Fertilizers and farm equipment were provided on favourable financing terms. State-controlled banks in turn lent to Federconsorzi at favourable interest rates. But Federconsorzi over-reached itself. Sometimes farmers could not repay loans offered. Federconsorzi would then buy the farms or the food-production companies which were in difficulties. But, typically, those which went to the wall were the least efficient. So Federconsorzi ended up with considerable assets, few of them profitable. Federconsorzi was also a cash cow for other less legal operations. One scam was to produce bogus receipts for surplus produce destroyed, for which the government was paying compensation. The debts grew. And grew. Until Mr Goria – himself a Christian Democrat, but a young turk opposed to the old guard – said, Basta! Enough!

Many of the problems lie with the political class itself. Piero Rocchini was in a better position than most to learn some of the innermost secrets of the Italian political class. For nine and a half years he was the in-house psychiatrist for the Chamber of Deputies – until he was summarily dismissed after speaking in the most general terms about some of the findings during his tenure. He was later to publish these in a book, *Le Nevrosi del Potere* ('The Neuroses of Power'). I went to see him in his clinic in central Rome a few days after it was published.

One study he had made was of the types of people who went into politics, and the problems they had encountered there. Politics were too important, he said, to be left to the uncertainties of parliament. He described with gentle irony how it was in the interests of the real power brokers in party headquarters to fill parliament with deputies who were malleable. 'I have made a comparison with the Anglo-Saxon countries. There, if someone is successful in life, he or she is likely to wish to transfer that success into the political sphere, by assuming an active political role. It is a form of continuation, part of a process of growing up.

'With us, by contrast, those with some personal inadequacy, and fear of competition in daily life, are chosen to enter politics. I have described a party which such a person joins as having the characteristics of a Mamma Party. It provides for everything. It gives one a position or sense of power, and demands in return an absolute lack of independence.'

Italian parliamentarians are some of the most cosseted in the world. Not only are they paid well – a salary in 1992 for a deputy was 130 million lire (about £60,000) – but they also receive free first-class travel on the railways, for life, and free use of telephones. And, of course, free psychological counselling and psychiatric help.

There were several new parliaments in Piero Rocchini's nine-year tenure, during which he reckoned that some 200 deputies sought the comfort of his couch. Senators had their own psychiatric counselling service. His practice had tripled in size in those nine years. Initially, he worked alone; by the time he left, the team included two psychologists. The biggest increase in calls on his time and professional advice came during electoral campaigns, a time of maximum stress. In the elections of April 1992 there was an enormous increase. The reason, Rocchini said, was the change to the electoral system. It was a tiny technical change to the system of the single preferential vote. Yet it actually introduced an element of competition within the party itself. A survey he made of the deputies who came to him showed that 41.3 per cent saw their opponents in other parties, but as many as 30.8 per cent saw their enemies within their own parties.

He noticed a great rise in stress after the suicide of Sergio Moroni, who was being investigated by Judge Di Pietro. Moroni, former secretary of the Socialist Party for the Lombard region, and a member of the chamber of deputies, had killed himself ten weeks after receiving an *avviso di garanzia* that he was under investigation for corruption and illegal financing of parties. He was the fourth suicide, the first senior party official, who also left behind a valedictory which was as much an apologia for the whole tacit complicity in a system of officially sanctioned grand larceny as it was a rejection of any personal responsibility for what he had done. In a letter to the speaker of the chamber, the veteran left-winger Giorgio Napolitano, Moroni wrote: 'I committed the error of accepting the "system". But I cannot allow myself to be called a thief because I personally never benefited from a single lira. For many years a great vehicle of hypocrisy, shared by all, disguised the parties' way of life and their methods of financing themselves.'

Moroni conceded that the parties would have to change, but in the meantime 'it is not fair that the wheel of fortune should pick out individuals to be the sacrificial victims.' Until that time, even those under investigation remained at heart convinced they could not be prosecuted. Di Pietro shook that cosy confidence. He showed that they were no longer untouchable. So their image of themselves was given a jolt. They had always regarded themselves as the chosen class. Chosen in the sense they were elected by the people. But chosen also in the sense that they were above the ordinary laws of ordinary mortals.

'From that time on many deputies, including those who had no reason to have a guilty conscience, began to have nightmares. One of the more common ones was of the knock on the door in the middle of the night, and the police coming in. This is something a lot of deputies told me about. It was a very severe anxiety.' Dr Rocchini dubbed this condition, with little hesitation, the Di Pietro syndrome.

I asked him, given all the very considerable crosses the average politician had to bear, where best should he seek an outlet for his worries: the confessor's box, the psychiatrist's 'couch or the mistress's sheets?

'It depends on what we are talking about. If we are trying to get them to overcome their own lack of self-confidence and autonomy, then without doubt the best is a psychiatrist. If we are looking to transfer to other types of dependence, then without doubt he should try other outlets. Let us not forget that with confession there is a very good system of control – the confessor is sworn to secrecy – while with a girlfriend or lover, not only in Italy, there is a less certain guarantee of discretion.'

The fact is that those elected as representatives of the people broke the very laws which they themselves had drafted, debated, and put on the statute books. Many reasons are given for the lack of respect the law enjoys. In part, the Italian way of doing things entails finding any way possible of achieving the required result. It is deeply engrained in the culture to try to get round laws, to try and improve on them. *L'arte d'arrangiarsi*, finding a way, is what it says: an art form.

A literature has arisen that not only describes and analyses everyday corruption and venality in Italian life, but demonstrates how much a part of life it is. Enzo Biagi, doyen of Italian newspaper and television journalists, and by no means a subversive figure, wrote a book entitled *L'Italia dei Peccatori* ('Italy, Country of Sinners'). The business magazine *Il Mondo* gave out complimentary copies of a booklet entitled *Il Denaro Facile* ('Easy Money: An A–Z of Corruption in Italy'). And Franco Cazzola, a Torinese sociology professor who taught for twenty-one years at Catania University before moving to Florence, had made the study of political corruption his academic speciality. His book *Della Corruzione* ('On Corruption') came out in 1988; *L'Italia del Pizzo* ('The Italy of the Backhander') in 1992.

For Professor Cazzola, there were two main factors in the corruption of public life. First was the huge growth of the party machines in the 1980s and their transformation into enormous apparatuses of grey figures who devoured vast sums of money. The second was the condoning of corruption by the political classes in the succession of scandals in the early 1970s. Because the culprits went unpunished, this set an example to the rest of the country, where the 'thieves were favoured over the *galantuomini*' and a culture of legalized illegality was allowed to flourish.

He felt that the whole tangle had started to come apart less because of a new moral climate than because the numbers relying on the spoils of office had grown too large and unwieldy and differences arose between them.

Professor Cazzola's second book was not about political corruption, but the corruption of everyday life. In *L'Italia del Pizzo* he noted which ways citizens had to pay, in cash or kind, to obtain services which should have been their right, but which in much of Italy had become privileges granted conditionally. It included such trivial matters as getting a residence permit, without which you cannot register a car or sign on in the local USL health care centre. In Italy you need a certificate of civil status to make a job application, or a penal certificate to demonstrate good conduct. Italians and resident foreigners spend an inordinate amount of time dealing with the *anagrafe* or registry of births, deaths and marriages. In his research Professor Cazzola found that the most common abuse of power, of exchange of favours, was in obtaining a driving licence or a permit to build an extension to a house. Local government officials, in short, were seen as primarily corrupt. Virtually no service was regarded as given without an exchange of favour, be it financial or in cases with, say, girl students, sexual.

No area of life was sacred, not even death itself. Some of the greatest scandals surrounded the fees charged by funeral directors. Around Naples, many were controlled by the Camorra. The ingenuity of the Italian bureaucrat knew no bounds. So in the late 1980s with the arrival of hundreds of thousands of immigrants, mainly from Africa, opportunities were presented for financial advancement in exchange for a *permesso di soggiorno*. Doctors were open to bribes to get *figli di papa* or daddy's boys off doing their military service. Dentists bought false papers so that they could extract teeth and separate huge sums from their unknowing patients. Money did not always change hands. A favour would often require a reciprocal one, sometimes years later. Everyone was corrupted, everyone needed a patron, or a friend, or merely 'saints in heaven' to help them.

The Italian press daily records the incidence of such abuses of public office, from the provision of oats for horses for the carabinieri to the bribes paid to ensure the contract for the costumes of actors. Such abuse was widespread because of the lack of sanction against it, and because of the pervasive climate of exploitation of the system. Some 8,262 people were entitled to official cars, the famous *auto blu*, at a cost to the treasury of 1,400 billion lire (£500 million) a year. In one of the more blatant cases of abuse of ministerial privilege, a minister requisitioned a fire brigade helicopter to take him from a relative's christening to a football match.

The problem was not the lack of laws. Italy has huge numbers of them: its two chambers are among the most prolific in the world. The problem is applying them, and obtaining the popular consensus for their observance. It is widely believed that Italians hate laws. They do not. They desire the comforting structure laws can bring, even if they expend most of their intellectual energies getting round the law. Some laws and regulations are so absurd they are an invitation to be broken. In an attempt to crack down on shopkeepers not declaring their till receipts, which were liable to value added tax, the authorities issued a decree stipulating that customers not having a receipt for a purchase up to 100 metres from the point of sale were liable to a fine. Absurd cases arose. In one notorious example, a four-year-old boy was pounced on by the guardia di finanza and fined for not being armed with a receipt for a chocolate bar. Italians are as ambivalent towards the law as they are towards strong government. They admire the efficiency a strong government like the German one can bring. Yet they regard with horror the idea of another authoritarian ruler like Mussolini.

The governing class, however, makes little effort to sell itself to the public. Some of its inexplicable and, this being Italy, never explained stipulations only serve to confirm the lack of faith the state enjoys from the citizenry. Bureaucratic and administrative directions abound to illustrate the point. In the early summer of 1992, an announcement was made – by whom, it was never quite clear – that a central register was to be drawn up of all rare animals and their products. The edict specified that every crocodile-skin bag, every ivory billiard ball, every tame leopard, every coat made of the hide of a beast deemed rare, had to be registered on pain of being seized or impounded by agents of the guardia di finanza.

Now Italy has a tradition of Third World activism and humanitarian concern. Its Green Party is a growing political force. But in terms of concern for furry little animals, the conscience of Italian womanhood is decidedly underdeveloped by northern European standards. According to industry sources, some 7.7 million Italian women, or one in three, own a fur coat. Many of these have more than one. Every smart young woman seems to have an elegantly cut short mink. Furriers in Rome told me that 85–90 per cent of coats were bought by the wearers themselves – although they did not always sign the cheque. For a Mediterranean country that glories in the sun, it is a staggering figure. It is, of course, part of the cult of *la bella figura*, of showing oneself off to one's best advantage. For fur is not worn just for warmth. The sweltering heat of midsummer does not prevent Roman matrons, for whom the expression mutton dressed as lamb could have been coined, from wearing minks over their shoulders when they go to the open-air opera at the Baths of Caracalla.

The announcement, therefore, that furs were to be registered came as something of a shock. Which furs? The authorities from the ministry of agriculture stated that the register was only for the skins, tusks or products of some forty endangered species. Italy is the largest consumer of animal products. It re-exports more reptile skins than any other country. It imports one million reptile skins a year to turn into bags, shoes, purses, belts and wallets. Worried owners were given a week to register their armadillo, lemur, mandrill, chimpanzee, gorilla, orang-utan, wolf, panda, otter, cheetah, puma, ocelot, jaguar, leopard, tiger, seal, whale, Indian elephant, zebra, rhinoceros, ostrich, condor, parrot, tortoise, turtle, alligator, boa constrictor or sturgeon. The move was a hasty attempt to conform to a twelve-year-old international directive that had only come into force in Italy a few months before. Where the Italian authorities differed from other countries was in placing the onus on the individual consumer, rather than on the importer, to ensure implementation of the law. Those who had inherited a tiger-skin rug from a gamehunter grandfather, or an ostrich-feather hat from a great-aunt, were given a week to go down to the forestry division of the ministry of agriculture. Citizens concerned they would be put behind bars for wearing their grandmother's sealskin coat had to penetrate the concrete urban jungle of Milan or Turin to reach their local branch of the forestry division. The bush that big-game hunters penetrated to bag their prey was nothing compared to the thicket of legalisms which passes for the rule of law in Italy and which sprang up overnight to entangle those who possessed rare and exotic skins. The penalties for non-compliance were high. A 400 million lire (£180,000) fine or three months in prison. It all seemed a little excessive. Yet no official from the ministry would appear in public or on television to explain the new measures to a confused country. In Naples, home town of the practical joke, a lawyer made a monkey of them by phoning the forestry department to register some mythological animal. He was told it was duly recorded – as it was. The lawyer taped the conversation and played it back to the mayor and the magistrature to widespread merriment.

In time, officials announced their reasons. A ban on protected species had come into force in 1980. But no penalties had been laid down for violation of the law. The new measures were intended to correct this anomaly. Within two days there was an about-turn. A crisis meeting was held. Senior officials met from the ministries of environment, agriculture, interior, justice and finance. There had been an error. Overzealous officials had initially misinterpreted the regulations. There was no longer any need for individuals to register the objects themselves. This indeed was a job for the wholesalers and traders.

As usual it was the honest citizens, the law-abiding ones, who wasted their time in this futile endeavour. Some 8,000 went and queued. The whole sorry affair once more illustrated the law was an ass. Italy showed again that it could behave like a Third World country: imposing draconian measures for petty misdemeanours while major crimes go unpunished. On the one hand there is too much bureaucracy and petty administration. On the other, the state and political class frequently demonstrate their complete venality and total indifference to the concerns of the citizens.

Of course, there had always been people who spoke out against the corruption and indifference of the political class. Milan was blessed with an archbishop who had never been afraid, unlike many of his episcopal colleagues, to take a lead on moral issues. Cardinal Carlo Maria Martini had long championed workers' rights and excoriated the excesses of capitalism. A theologian, Cardinal Martini is one of the foremost contenders for the succession to Pope John Paul II. Years before the term *tangentopoli* was coined to denote the sack of the city, Cardinal Martini had railed against the dichotomy between public and private virtue. The health of a company depended on the ethical base on which it was run, he would say. He had sensed that dark relationship between politics and business. Everyone knew about it, he said, even though little was being done.

He dated his crusade for probity to the four-hundredth anniversary in 1984 of the death of that great Milanese saint, St Charles Borromeo. Charles Borromeo, a nephew of Pius IV, was made cardinal at the age of twenty-two. Like St Francis of Assisi, he was a man born with wealth and privilege to a princely family who decided to give it up to endow religious institutions. St Charles was thus the antithesis of those Milanese politicians who saw public office as a vehicle for self-enrichment. As Cardinal Martini was carrying the cross with which the saint had warded off pestilence, he determined to launch his campaign to fight against the plague of corruption.

He was asked how the city and country could pull itself out of the moral quagmire it had sunk into.

'The first step is to recognize that our situation is truly difficult. The second is the conviction that things will not change by themselves alone. The third is that to confront this reality and rise up and overcome it requires a great moral desire.'

He called not for vindictiveness against those who had erred, but for hope for the repentance and rehabilitation (in a spiritual and moral sense) of anyone who wished to turn back to the straight path. At the same time he argued that those who had abused their position of public office, even if they should repent, should never be allowed to hold such office again. The next generation of politicians should be guided by a sense of the supreme values of the social doctrine of the Church: of honesty, of justice and the common good. The common good was not the good of one party or another, of one social group. That was an essential precondition. It was an old rule, but it had served well.

Could, should the business community have spoken out earlier? Once again I turned to Romano Prodi. He was not only a man who had a reputation as one of the honest men of the Christian Democrats. He also had practical experience of the moral questions raised by running a major enterprise, Italy's largest, in an environment of corruption and dishonesty. Could he, should he have blown the whistle earlier? No, he replied. The system was so general, so diffuse. Furthermore, he could not see what was going on in an organization as large as his.

Così fan [quasi] tutti. Almost everyone was implicated. Questions about why the corruption scandals were not uncovered before hide the single essential feature of the case: why did they happen at all? What was it in the Italian system or the Italian character that made the country so much more prone to such widespread corruption and abuse of office? Of course, not everyone accepts this premise. Many national politicians I asked on this subject, all of whom were implicated by commission so to speak rather than omission, could not accept that Italians were worse than anyone else. I would be treated to a dissertation on the prevalence of corruption in France, in Spain, and in Germany, as though this were a pan-European disease which, sadly, Italy's lax border controls had failed to keep out.

Jesuitical justifications were provided for why what these people did was not actually wrong. One senior Christian Democrat in Milan said he thought there was a very clear distinction between stealing for the party and stealing for personal gain. One was merely breaking the law on the financing of the parties; the other was corruption. It was a question, above all, of need. The local parties did not receive much from either central state funds – the entire budget granted by parliament for all the parties, distributed according to their electoral strength, was 200 billion lire (£83 million) – or from their respective party headquarters in Rome. Therefore, they had to make up the difference in their needs from other sources. The man chosen to lead the Christian Democrats after their 1992 electoral setback, Mino Martinazzoli, declared, 'I believe robbery is always immoral but the violation of laws on the financing of political parties is not theft. It is an irregularity which we have made a crime with penal sanctions.'

Only politicians so convinced of the rightness of their own actions, so morally bankrupt and blind to the fact that this process had grossly inflated the national debt, so that they were stealing from generations as yet unborn who would have to pay for this 'financing of the parties', could have articulated such a sentiment.

And Martinazzoli was regarded as personally unblemished! He had once, years before, given his reasoning why a society produced such scandals: 'because it is made of men'.

I did elicit from the Piedmontese former treasury minister (and briefly prime minister) Giovanni Goria the acknowledgement that accepting bribes for the illegal financing of the parties was not only a crime, but a sin (*peccato*). He understood that the issue was ethical. But this was a rarely expressed point of view. Indeed, the lack of a sense that stealing was a sin, and morally wrong, was in large part due to the absence of a moral lead – Cardinal Martini and a few other like, high-minded prelates apart – by the Church.

An enterprising Italian journalist decided to test for himself the attitude of the Church and its priests towards the paying of *tangenti* or backhanders. He went up and down the country, from Padua and Milan to Rome and Naples, posing as a penitent. He chose especially the churches most frequented by the political and business establishment. Kneeling in the confessional box, he would avow supposed complicity in the *tangentopoli* scandal. He would explain he was the personal secretary of an important Christian Democrat politician. Over the years, he would say, he had accepted and solicited contributions for the party from leading industrialists, in return for contracts. And lest the priest be insufficiently worldly – an unlikely possibility – to grasp the full implications of what he was saying, he would specify that he was talking of *tangenti*. Was accepting them a sin or not?

The responses he recorded on a concealed tape recorder varied in detail more than in substance. He quoted a Milanese priest as saying, 'If we're only talking about a few million lire [a few thousand pounds] I wouldn't bother the judges.' Another confessor was more interested in whether the 'politician's amanuensis' was having extra-marital affairs. Only one of the forty-seven priests to whom the journalist 'confessed' invited him to make a full confession before he was prepared to grant absolution. Other priests gave absolution for accepting 2 to 3 billion lire (more than £1 million) in *tangenti* on a scale ranging from three Ave Marias and three Pater Nosters to giving alms to the next beggar he came across.

If the Church as an institution was as amoral as much of society, churches as buildings were also victims of widespread pillaging. The state even had to declare a national emergency because of the thousands of works of art being daily plundered from the country's 100,000 churches and religious institutions. In the space of three years, the amount stolen was expected to be enough to fill seven museums. Besides the celebrated theft of major works of art was the removal of silver and plate which could easily be melted down. The most eloquent testimony to the climate of pilfering was the theft from the Franciscan cathedral in Padua of a reliquary containing the jawbone of St Antony. St Antony is the patron saint of finding lost things. He showed he could still work the old magic when his jawbone was eventually found in a warehouse near Rome airport.

The ease with which the law could be broken, the books fiddled, taxes avoided, politicians bribed, contracts bought, all helped ensure that large sections of the community acquired great riches, and lived happily on the proceeds. And the country could afford it because for so long it deferred payment simply by increasing the public debt.

Even if the Church kept mum, there were voices enough raised against the immorality of the politicians. The liberal-left press, from Eugenio Scalfari's *La Repubblica* to *Manifesto* and *Unità*, had long railed like Old Testament prophets against the iniquities of the ruling class.

Back in 1982 Italo Calvino wrote a lament for his country about shared – and therefore diffused – responsibility. Entitled *Apologo Sull'onestà nel Paese dei Corrotti* ('An Apology for Honesty in the Country of Corrupt Men'), it was a savage indictment of the Italian system.

Once upon a time [he wrote] there was a country which was based on illegality. It was not that there was a shortage of laws. Not that the political system was not based on principles which more or less everyone said that they shared. But this system, posited on a large number of centres of power, needed excessive amounts of financing and these means they could only obtain il-legally.

At the same time, no centre of power felt in the least guilty about this way of financing its activities. Because in its sense of right and wrong, what was done for the good of the group was legitimate, even desirable, as every group identified its own power with the common good.

From time to time, some magistrate or another would take it upon himself to apply the law. This would cause minor tremors in some centre of power, and even the arrests of people who until then had regarded themselves as protected, unpunishable. In these cases the widespread feeling, besides that of satisfaction that justice had been done, was the suspicion that in fact we were dealing with a settling of accounts between one centre of power and another.

There are millions of Italians who for years have been clamouring for justice and fairness in public life and who see the removal of a whole political class as a sign of the strength of their peculiar form of democracy, that same democracy which brought them to this sorry pass. To them too, Calvino had spoken.

Should one resign oneself to extinction? No, their consolation was to think that as there had always existed in the fringes of every society down the centuries a whole self-perpetuating counter-culture made up of rogues, bagsnatchers, thieves and tricksters, a counter-culture which never entertained any idea of ever becoming 'society' itself, so too might the counter-culture of honest people succeed in surviving down the centuries, on the fringes of the mainstream, without any desire other than to live apart and feel different from the rest.

It was an expression of hope for a better moral climate. There were signs that, ten years after he wrote this, the mood for a moral renewal would remove some of the excesses of the past. Excesses, though, which were not universal. For there were parts of Italy that had always functioned better than others.

Note

At the time of writing, few of those arrested or under investigation for corruption had come to trial. Still fewer had been convicted and sentenced, or acquitted. But there is a new climate in Italy and it seems that those who are aquitted of criminal culpability are unlikely to enjoy the fruits of public service again.

FOUR

The Italy that works

If there is a single spot in Italy that encapsulates that glorious combination of a place where people prosper, and know how to have a good time, where they have achieved a very high standard of living without sacrificing quality of life, it is Bologna. Bologna is the Italy that works. Few travel agents advertise holiday trips there. No church groups beat a pilgrims' path to its gates. Yet by many criteria, Bologna is heaven on earth. Its paradise is no Garden of Eden, of innocence before the Fall. Posters pasted on the pillars of the ochre arcades in the historic centre brazenly showed off the city's reputation. 'The art of the culture of seduction in Bologna' they proudly proclaimed. A poster of a half-naked diva, breast exposed, set upon a table piled high with rich meats and exotic fruits, flaunted Bologna's fame as a city whose citizens zealously pursue the pleasures of the flesh. The city's huge fairground – where else? – was the venue once more for the annual exhibition entitled Erotica, an attempt to give an umbrella of scholarship to an exploration and celebration of the sensual.

Bologna has long enjoyed a reputation for hedonism. Not for nothing is it known as 'Bologna la grassa', 'Bologna the fat'. For it is not only the capital of the richest agricultural and industrial region of Italy, after Lombardy, dull, old, honest-to-goodness Lombardy, it is the gastro-erotic heart of Italy. Even the names of the streets proclaim it. There is Vicolo Baciadame (Lady-kisser Lane), and the enticing Via Fregatette (Rub-tits Street). By repute, its pleasures are specifically oral. Casanova, de Sade and Boccaccio all confessed their normally insatiable appetites well satisfied by the erotic inventiveness of its womenfolk. Its tongue-wagging burgesses pace up and down the Piazza Maggiore by the cathedral discussing the plight of Kurdistan or the political intrigues in Rome.

Bologna openly parades its abundance and pleasures. In the old centre, emporium after emporium shows off racks of cooked meats, huge hams hang overhead, and vast arrays of prepared vegetables are set out in shop windows to entice the onlooker. Entire shops are given over to different varieties of the cheeses for which the region is world-famous. In the restaurant Diana, where you will see the more successful of Bologna society indulging their hearty appetites, a typical meal starts with plates of salami and cold meats. Then come the famous stuffed pastas such as tortellini – in the shape of the navel of Venus – agnolotti and ravioli. Then wild boar, and game, thick steaks or other meaty fare, accompanied by produce from the market gardens of the surrounding Emilian plain.

It seems the Bolognese conform to every accepted image of the pleasure-loving Italian. But Bologna's delights are not only of the flesh. It stimulates the mind too. Its university is the oldest in Europe, some say in the world. It is a centre of scholarship, as well as a magnet for young people from the region around. The Bolognese are rightly proud of their university, and it is well integrated into the life of the city. It has leading medical researchers. The city boasts a rich cultural and musical life. Its economic and scientific study centres are of the first rank. The jovial and irrepressible Romano Prodi has his economics research institute Nomisma there.

Like many Italian cities, it is an architectural gem. It has an almost perfectly preserved medieval area of harmonious soft red brick. The miles of arcades run like a leitmotif through every twisting alley, replicated in every modern apartment block, sheltering the shoppers from the ravages of winter and the harsh summer's sun (for Bologna, alas, is not blessed with the best of weather). And if Bologna does not have the treasures of Florence or Venice, none the less its Pinacoteca Nazionale houses an important collection of Giottos and masterpieces of Reni and the Bolognese school, which would do any metropolitan museum proud elsewhere in the world.

Within Italy, Bologna's reputation is something much more than a place whose citizens enjoy a high standard of living. Time and again, Bologna comes top in tables of the best-run city administrations in the country. It is a pioneering city. It was the first to introduce pedestrian precincts, to permit gay couples to apply for communal housing, to ban smoking in public places.

Bologna, it has long been noted, is one of those teasing paradoxes. Bologna is radical chic, showcase of Communism and windows and womenfolk dressed in full-length mink coats, Third World causes and stolid bourgeoisie, big cars and a left-wing campus. It is the largest city in the country's red belt, the area across North-Central Italy which turned to the Communist Party after leading the resistance against the German occupation in the latter days of the Second World War. Since 1945 the city council has been run by Communists, either alone or in coalitions. There is no contradiction between a left-wing administration and highly successful capitalist enterprise.

Every aspect of city life is ordered for the benefit of its citizens. Public transport is quick and cheap. The Communist administration set up chemist's shops throughout the city, including less well-off neighbourhoods. Health care is the best in Italy (Italy has one of the highest doctor-patient ratios in Europe but the standard of hospital care, particularly in the South, is lamentable). And the bureaucracy that hinders so much of everyday life in Italy? You can cut right through much of the red tape. Even a birth certificate, that essential document in Italy for securing a whole range of services, can be obtained at the touch of a button from a computer dispenser in the centre of town. The elderly are well protected, with special low-rent accommodation, free taxis, home help, and subsidized holidays on the Italian Riviera. At the other end of the life cycle, from the moment a Bolognese enters the world, he or she is mollycoddled by an indulgent welfare system.

The day-care centres of Bologna and nearby Reggio Emilia achieved national and international prominence when an American news magazine voted them the best in the world. By 1993, Bologna had forty-five day-care centres, catering for infants from after they had had their anti-polio inoculation (administered in Italy at ninety days) until the age of three. Some 2,000 young children went to these subsidized centres. Parents paid up to 3 million lire (£1,400) a year, whereas the true cost was 15 to 16 million lire (approximately £6,000). The aim of the scheme, when started twenty years before, was to allow mothers to go out to work. It also gave a better start to children of lower social classes. There were very few one-parent families. At three, the child goes to the nursery school (80 per cent run by the *comune*, 20 per cent are religious foundations) until the age of six.

But the reality is less than uniformly Socialist red. The day-care centres only covered 30 per cent of all children, who were selected according to means tests. Middle-class parents had the choice of only one or two very expensive private day-care centres, or nothing. Since most of the day-care centres were in the suburbs, the already diminishing numbers of professional people living in the historic centre could afford less and less to have children.

Bolognese Communists temper ideology with pragmatism. Their brand of Communism is a mere overlay for their real historical determinism, their native entrepreneurial spirit. They run co-operatives to produce the best cheeses in Italy (Parmesan from Parma, Reggiano from Reggio). They quickly condemned the Soviet invasion of Czechoslovakia in 1968. And it was Bologna that hosted the extraordinary congress of the old Italian Communist Party in 1990 when it decided on its historic course of self-dissolution, to emerge later as the Party of the Democratic Left.

Bologna's success was essential to the national Communist Party, to demonstrate that it could provide a credible – and desirable – government for the country at large. It was destined to be flagship of a fleet which was never launched, and was shrinking while the blueprints were being drawn up.

It was also the first Communist administration to adopt the revolutionary step of privatizing certain social services. It sold off the city abattoir and a number of the pharmacies it had itself started. And it farmed out the cleaning and maintenance of schools and the provision of school meals to mixed private–public concerns. The cold wind of the late 1980s, of financial retrenchment, forced a radical rethink. The central government was no longer so willing to grant the city generous sums to run its affairs. Bologna had to make do with less. By 1994, a third of the city's employees will have been transferred to the private sector. Less bureaucracy, more efficiency was the slogan. Other cities in the North tackled the same problems, but none so well.

Selling off the family silver? In part. The pharmacies could go because health insurance was now universal, and the poor could get cheap medicines. The aim was to raise income to pay for capital investment in priority areas. These included creating accommodation for the two sectors of the population whose growth had changed the demographic balance: the old and immigrants. For Bologna also has the lowest birthrate in a country that, despite the general perception of huge Catholic families, had actually achieved the distinction of having the lowest birthrate in the world. The city's population was ageing. And the only new blood came from outside, from immigrants from North and West Africa.

Bologna has become an object of study in its own right. In every survey it comes out top or near the top in terms of wealth, savings, provision of services, quality of life, standard of living. The Bologna model has been documented, examined, commented on, almost universally praised, and in many attempts imitated.

For years, Walter Vitali, the city's long-serving budget director – before he was elected mayor – was much sought after to lecture city administrations in Germany and elsewhere on the Bologna experience. All around, other towns have replicated the same mix of wealth and seeming enjoyment of life. Their townsfolk have got rich quick, without losing those qualities of life, of everyday intercourse, that underlie the Italian genius for the art of living. Parma, Modena, Reggio nell'Emilia, Ferrara, Fidenza, Piacenza and Faenza are smaller versions of the successful provincial town at which the Italians in the North excel.

Bolognese, however, say that some of the shine has come off their city and that it is showing signs of age, like a favourite mistress who turns to the face powder to cover the wrinkles. It has experienced many of the social ills of other less well-off cities: drug abuse, human decrepitude, physical dilapidation, an increase in juvenile crime. In that sense it has not escaped a national trend.

Even after the fall of the Berlin Wall, and the decision of the Italian Communist Party to change name and direction, Bologna's leftist city council prided itself on being shopwindow and laboratory in two other aspects of administration. It liked to consider itself an island of clean government in the sea of corruption which washed most of the rest of the country, although few believe the magistrates will not find some areas to investigate even in Bologna.

'The fight against corruption is one of the main planks of our administration,' Mayor Vitali told me. The city was in the forefront of putting into practice the changes afoot to have mayors elected directly by the people, rather than be chosen in the backrooms of the party organizations.

The mayor also rejected the old saw that in medieval Bologna could be found the future of Communism, an island of real Socialism. Italian Communism was *sui generis*. 'Bologna is not the last bastion of Communism,' Vitali emphasized to me. 'We simply have a good, left-wing, social democrat administration.'

Bologna was in a much better position than other Italian cities because it simply husbanded its available resources better than most of the other 8,000 *comuni* in Italy. Local government could not levy local taxes or set tax rates for businesses. At least half its funding came directly from central government, worked out according to a complicated formula based on population and acreage. Because Bologna's population was shrinking, its inputs were also diminishing. Furthermore, the state was devolving more and more responsibility for raising revenue, rather than spending it, to the *comuni*. By 1993, the state's contribution to the budget for current expenditure had fallen from 70 to 50 per cent. The *comune* had to raise half the 700 billion lire (£300 million a year, or £700 per man, woman and child) through charges for refuse collection, revenue from advertising hoardings and traffic fines and the like. Local *comuni* were about to increase their revenue by collecting property tax direct, where previously it was levied by central government.

The other important policy orientation was concern for the environment. This was part of a wider national debate, although Bologna was simply more advanced in applying specific policy measures. The mayor said this was not normally a left-wing issue. The former left-wing parties had promoted polluting state industries. There was a clear example of Bologna being more green than red shortly after the break-up of the Soviet Union. I went to an exhibition in the fairground where the old state military industries from the ex-Soviet Union were seeking buyers for their now redundant products, from jet engines to space capsules, to titanium church bells to bulletproof glass for banks.

There were a number of curious visitors, but few actual customers. The next hall by contrast was thronged with people, young and old, for a special display of ecologically friendly agricultural machinery and its green products.

Bologna, like so many cities of Italy, has somehow managed to preserve its historic centre more or less intact. The challenge of the 1990s was the continuing degradation and erosion because of pollution, and the high cost of repairs. But the fact that there was still a historic centre to maintain was more by default than design, according to Giuseppe Campos Venuti, brought in from Rome in 1960 to draw up the plans for the development of the city. An urban planner with an international reputation, he was in demand across the world for his expertise. His office in a palazzo on Via Maggiore was neat, functional and modern. He spoke with the American twang he picked up as a runner for the Office of Strategic Services, during the closing stages of the Second World War.

He qualified in architecture after the war, and like many of his generation went to study at first-hand the advances being made in urban planning in Great Britain, in the new towns being built around London. Such a discipline of town planning did not exist in Italy, where cities spread like oil slicks, without any control. Although Italy is now considered a rich and developed country it was then far behind other countries once thought more backward, such as Spain. The first underground railway was built in Milan in 1964. In Madrid the first underground began running in 1899.

The rapid expansion of postwar cities was largely unplanned, Venuti said. 'The quality of the Italian suburbs, the periphery, is the worst in Europe: the lack of green spaces, of transport systems, too much high-density living.

'You must recognize that historic centres in Italy have been preserved because, by the time of great economic development twenty or thirty years ago, the cultural maturity of public opinion was strong enough to prevent a very total dissolution.'

His policy was simple: to safeguard the historic centre; to protect the hill on the outskirts of the city, which has a special place in the affections of the Bolognese; and to decentralize service industries, to prevent them taking over residential accommodation in the centre. The so-called central business district was not central at all, but in one of the suburbs. The other idea was to build suburbs, a 'new kind of periphery where housing and green spaces and social services were mixed and not the kind where the periphery was not integrated into the rest of town'.

Yet Bologna today has to run to keep still, to change so that nothing changes. The current chief planning officer for the city, Mauro Bertocchi, was frankly gloomy about its prospects. He said the plan drawn up for Bologna in the 1980s was now being overtaken by events. The major problem was that new legislation had been passed to restrict noise pollution. Bologna made its own arrangements for controlling traffic flow then found these overtaken by central government legislation. New laws came in because other cities had bigger problems. But the laws also forced Bologna to rethink its policies for controlling noise levels and environmental pollution.

The other challenge to Bertocchi was that lobbying and pressure groups had suddenly become an issue. Thirty years ago it was possible to build a road, and no one would raise a finger. Now, the local residents would form associations to fight any such moves. For that reason a plan to widen the ring road had been blocked. This was also one reason why the airport remained so small, thwarting Bologna's desire to have truly international communications. It occupied a central place in Italy, as a major road and rail junction between North and South, East and West. But flights to and from the rest of Europe were few.

Indecision meant that Bologna still did not have a high-speed transport system. Those living and working in the city centre could travel around by bicycle. But this was not a satisfactory mass solution.

Heaven? Or hell? The epicureanism and licentiousness of the Bolognese provoked an anathema from Pope John Paul II. He condemned Emilia-Romagna as the most degenerate province of Italy, where divorce and abortion rates were highest. He lamented the death toll from Saturday Night Fever – the weekly curse on the highways, when the lives of young people are sacrificed on the roads after all-night dancing at the pleasure domes and hyper discos of Rimini and the Adriatic coast, fuelled up on a high-octane mix of rock and roll, alcohol, Ecstasy, speed and Papa's fast car. The region bore the 'stigmata of illness and death', he said. 'Satiated and despairing', the Archbishop of Bologna, Cardinal Giacomo Biffi, described the Emilians. 'Society has lost the capacity to distinguish between good and evil.'

The veteran journalist Enzo Biagi shared this pessimistic assessment of his native city. 'The list of evils has everything. Fall in population, suicides, drugs, Saturday night killings. It is true there has been a loss of values. They appear satisfied and prosperous, but they are unhappy. Always seeking instant gratification, with no longer-term vision.' But he questioned whether, in the class list for perdition, Emilia-Romagna was really heading for hell. According to the national statistical agency, there are more abortions in Puglia, more drug overdoses in Lombardy, Piedmont and Lazio, and more suicides in Trento. Emilia's receipts from the entertainment industry are greater than those of any other region.

The counterposing arguments about whether Bologna was Sodom or Paradise came to a head at one of the three gates of the city, the Porta Saragozza. It was a prime site, and when in 1982 the municipality leased this national monument to ARCI-Gay, the national gay rights movement, the Church was up in arms. It was not only that the practice of homosexuality ran directly counter to Catholic dogma and the whole sacred family unit. It was that this particular site was the arch through which each year the Cardinal passed in procession to celebrate the feast day of the Madonna of San Luca. How could Franco Grillini, president of ARCI-Gay, have an office whose outside wall carried the dedication to 'Our Lady of San Luca, supreme protector of Bologna'?

Bologna was a laboratory for social experiments with the gay community no less than for other groups within society. Besides the request to apply for communal housing – a principle granted, but never put into practice – Bologna was the first place in Italy to have a special Condomeria, a shop dispensing prophylactics and advice on safe sex (it had to close for lack of funds).

Homosexuality has never been illegal in Italy. An attempt was made in 1933 by Mussolini's justice minister to outlaw it. But this only drew attention to it. Both before and since that time the policy of the government, of the establishment, has been to ignore it, not to draw attention to it. The issue first came to public prominence in 1986 after the anti-homosexual anathema pronounced by Cardinal Joseph Ratzinger, the German theologian who was the Vatican's chief hardline ideologue on faith and doctrine. The only restrictions on gays are non-statutory. Presidential decree (number 41,B 1008/85) of 1985 provides for exemption from compulsory military service for 'sexual deviation'. Although not specified, this was intended for homosexuals. A decree of the health minister of 15 January 1990 forbade homosexuals to donate blood, as a means of protecting against the spread of AIDS. Otherwise Italian homosexuals may engage in sexual acts at the same age as heterosexuals: sixteen.

Despite the absence of legal restrictions, Franco Grillini said that considerable social stigma attached to the gay community. His association had 15,000 members – more, he said, than the Republican Party, which had won 3.5 per cent of the national vote at the previous elections – but gays were reluctant to come out. It was still very hidden, with some notable exceptions. 'One of the few good things of public life in Italy,' Grillini declared, 'is that not a line about the private life of public figures ever appears in the newpapers.' It was true: people gossiped about this minister's mistress, or that one's penchant for little boys, but this tittle-tattle seldom appeared in the press.

Although Milan had the most gays, it was only right that Bologná should be the seat of the national movement. This was because Bologna was on a 'European level' in its free-thinking attitude, Grillini said. 'The European level': it was a theme that appeared again and again. Bolognese were proud that in some aspects of civil society they could match the best of Europe. It was a constant reminder of the sense of inferiority Italians feel, of their desperate desire and need to be regarded as truly among the comity of modern nations.

For Bologna prides itself on its tolerance (although it can afford to be tolerant, say, of Southerners: it just never encourages their migration as cities like Milan and Turin have). According to Luciano Pignotti, a Roman who had lived in Bologna for twelve years, its openness is a form of conformism. Bologna was very bourgeois in the way it conformed, very provincial. The Bolognese prided themselves that they were open-minded. So everyone had to be open-minded. When the sun came out, the old men went round the square, and put the world to rights. 'But then they go home, and they close the door, wham, they re-enter the total privacy of their home. The difference between Bologna and Rome is that Bologna is a *salotto*. You can relax among friends, but you have to obey certain rules. In Rome, you can do as you want, but you cannot relax. Bologna is on a more human scale.'

A Sicilian friend said that in two years of living in Bologna he made many friends – but not once was he invited to visit any of their homes. People tend to meet at cafés or outside.

There were clouds on the horizon. For his part, the mayor spoke frankly about the weaknesses of the city. He was very aware that the Bolognese, who had struggled over the previous forty years to achieve what they had, needed new challenges to avoid complacency in order to maintain a high standard of living. His major concern was the continuing de-industrialization of the city. Throughout the 1980s and early 1990s, the city had maintained an enviable record of full employment. Bologna actually lived out the prescription in the constitution that Italy is a republic based on work. The city worked. So did its citizens. In 1993, 42 per cent of the population was employed, a labour force of 171,000. Of these 26 per cent were self-employed. The greatest change over the previous ten years had been in the move out of manufacturing and into commerce and the service industry. Bologna had nine companies per hundred head of population, the highest ratio in Italy. It was a typically Bolognese trait: the desire to be one's own master, to run one's own company. At the same time, these family-run companies had grouped together in co-operative associations, which helped them market and promote their products. This in turn helped weave the particularly tough fabric of Emilian society. Sports clubs, *circoli* or social clubs abounded, reinforcing the attachment of the people to their city and region.

The mayor's worries about de-industrialization were a microcosm of the more generalized trend within the Italian economy. Many family companies set up after the war were now experiencing a problem with succession. As the founding fathers of these companies reached retirement, some discovered that their own sons were not suitable to take over the running of the company. Other concerns were too small to compete in the international market. The option was merger with other Italian companies, or being taken over by a large multinational. Some of Bologna's best-known industrial names had already been swallowed up, including Buton, the drinks manufacturers who made Vecchia Romagna brandy, the motorcycle maker Ducatti, and the rubber company making condoms. The Bolognese were suspicious that the new style of international management would not always be in the city's best interests.

The mayor, despite his move towards privatization, still believed in intervening to help keep small businesses from closing down in the city centre because of high rents and other costs. Costs could be reduced, he said, by more efficient running of public services. The number of residents in the city centre had gone down by a third in the previous ten years, as the pressure of banks and large financial institutions seeking office space forced rents up.

What is the secret of Bologna's success? Conservative businessmen like Guidalberto Guidi, vice-president of the regional confederation of industry, believe the answer lies in the extraordinary desire and ability of the Bolognese to make money through productive enterprises. They have none of the crotchets of the British middle classes about trade, and making money through industry. At their annual dinner I met one of their most distinguished elder members, Dr Gazzoni, who had read politics, philosophy and economics at Oxford after the war. Whereas his British contemporaries pursued more respectable but less productive careers in banks or the professions, he had entered the family firm of food processing. His sons, with degrees from Italian and foreign universities, were following him into the business. Italians, in the North at least, have large disposable incomes because they work hard – I was always staggered how many seemed to work on Saturdays – and have no problems about working in the manufacturing industry. With no natural resources, including energy, and no international financial centre to create wealth, Italy relies on its manufacturing sector.

Guidalberto Guidi was proud of the achievements of Bologna and Emilia-Romagna. 'We have the highest standard of living in the world. I have travelled worldwide. I think the style of life you can enjoy in Bologna, in Emilia-Romagna, if you exclude a quarter in New York, between Fifth and Madison maybe, and maybe twenty-five square metres in London or in Paris, I think it is the highest in the world.

'Why? One reason is that the people work. Then there is the quality of our entrepreneurs. We are very flexible. I managed companies in the USA, in France, in Caracas, in Mexico. But my companies in Emilia-Romagna can change a system of production, of network sales, in minutes. The quality of our workers means they want to produce good work. Also, if they don't want trouble, they don't make it. But today there is another reason. The feeling in the trade unions is changing. Then there is the link with the factory. We like to make things. Not only to deal in finance or shuffle paper, but to take pieces of metal and turn them into something else. Personally I can only do this kind of job. I cannot do any other kind of job.

'We are sure and we are confident we can continue to live in one of the best places in the world. Bologna is successful because of the Bolognese. It is a big mistake to think it was the Communist administration. In Italy you can find quality of life like that of Emilia-Romagna in Veneto, but it is different. It 'is a very strange situation, because here 50 per cent of the people in the past were Communists, 50 per cent were Catholics. Both religions were against profit, but one hundred per cent of the people live for profit.

'It is a strange region. The people of Emilia-Romagna don't want to be rich because they like money. They like money because with money you can live well. They spend money. Not too much. Because we don't sleep soundly with debts. But money equals goods. With these kinds of goods you can live normally with your family. Bologna has changed. It is not the same as ten or fifteen years ago. But the difference is relative. It has changed less than other towns. The Communist administration. They are honest. They were and are honest. That is the difference. Personally honest, because they always had a special interest in the co-operative movement. The administration is relatively efficient. It was better in the past. The hospitals and so on. But it still isn't bad. If you are sick,' he said with a chuckle, mindful of the horror stories of patients going into hospital elsewhere in Italy for a check-up and having limbs or organs removed by mistake, 'you can go to hospital and you have some possibility, not much, of getting out again.'

The engine for economic development in this part of Italy has been the 45,000 small- and medium-sized enterprises, above all in manufacturing, in food production and processing. If the city of Bologna was a paradigm for successful urban administration, the surrounding region of Emilia-Romagna became a model for regional economic development. Each town has its own speciality. Reggio for cheese; Parma for ham and meat products; Modena for Ferrari cars and machinery.

The particular strengths of this form of regional industry could be seen clearly in the ceramics industry. This was centred on Sassuolo and Fiorano Modenese, two towns on the flat plain south-west of Modena, beneath the foothills of the Apennines. There was talk of increasing competition from Spain, or Brazil, where costs were lower. Or of new production lines in the emerging democracies of Eastern Europe. But when I visited the headquarters of Iris tilemakers, the mood was upbeat. They had just launched a tile made with granite dust guaranteed for thirty years, and another for one hundred years. How could they possibly hope to guarantee a product when industrial pundits were predicting that the whole system of small- and medium-sized industries on which the region's wealth was based was rapidly being outmoded and outstripped by the bigger conglomerates in Germany and the rest of Europe? Romano Minozzi, president of Iris, which he founded in 1960, was brimming with self-confidence. He stressed the importance of tradition. 'I don't agree with this hypothesis of decline. We have undisputed world leadership in ceramics. What is more, we have tremendous entrepreneurial spirit. You cannot make entrepreneurs. We have entrepreneurs not only in the making of ceramics, but also in the support industries all around. In other countries these are outside the area of production. Here they are all together.'

Indeed, the ceramics industry around Sassuolo, producing bathroom tiles for flats in Dortmund, and hard-wearing floor tiles for shopping malls around the world, was cited as one of those peculiar success stories in a case study by the Harvard Business School. One reason for their success was their skill at marketing. Although they built tiles to last, the bread and butter of their sales was for bathrooms. In Italian homes, the woman nearly always chooses the tiles and, with an eye to fashion, will demand frequent changes. The Sassuolo tilemakers maintained their position as world leaders because of their superior design and their technological innovation. For all around were the small machine companies designing and making the equipment specifically for the industry. These machines could be sold to competitors abroad, but the manufacturers around Sassuolo maintained the technological lead.

The strength of the Sassuolo-based industry, with 250 different companies all producing similar products, may have been in its versatility and flexibility in producing products to order. In other industries, the Italian model of small- and medium-sized companies could become a disadvantage. Bigger companies have the advantage of economies of scale, and greater resources for research and development in new products. Italy spent less on research and development than its industrial competitors. In the tilemaking industries, the key has been the ability to reduce a major component of their costs – labour – to affordable levels through greatly increased automation. Such a transformation was less easy in the labour-intensive knitting industry, for example. There, Italy's high labour costs were likely to force manufacturers increasingly to the luxury end of the market, leaving mass production to countries with lower costs. For the time being, Italians of what has been dubbed the Third Italy, between the industrial triangle in the North and the underdeveloped South, are confident they can adapt to any changing economic circumstances with their accustomed flexibility and ingeniousness. But at the same time the chill winds of international competition are exposing the growing gap between the North and the South.

FIVE

Regionalism and pasta sauce

It is a cliché to describe Italy as a country made up of several quite different countries: geographically, topographically, culturally, economically. It is one of those fortunate countries blessed with diversity in climate and landscape, where you can ski in the mountains and swim in the sea, virtually in the same day. Because it is long like a boot, it passes through many different temperature zones. The history of the peninsula, too, accounts in large part for why the North feels closer to Middle Europe, and the South seems more part of the Levant.

The regional variations of Italian life find fullest flavour in the cuisine. One of the most celebrated writers on the food of Italy, Marcella Hazan, states without any leavening that:

> the first useful thing to know about Italian cooking is that as such it actually doesn't exist. 'Italian cooking' is an expression of convenience rarely used by Italians. The cooking of Italy is really the cooking of its regions, regions that until 1861 were separate, independent, and usually hostile states. They submitted to different rulers, they were protected by sovereign armies and navies, and they developed their own cultural traditions and, of course, their own special and distinct approaches to food . . .
>
> Tuscany's whole approach to the preparation of food is in such sharp contrast to that of Bologna that their differences seem to sum up two main and contrary manifestations of Italian character. Out of the abundance of the Bolognese kitchen comes cooking that is exuberant, prodigal with precious ingredients, and wholly baroque in its restless exploration of every agreeable combination of texture and flavour. The Florentine, careful and calculating, is a man who knows the measure of all things and

his cooking is an austerely composed play upon essential and unadorned themes. Bologna will sauté veal in butter, stuff it with the finest mountain ham, coat it with aged Parmesan, simmer it in sauce, and smother it with the costliest truffles. Florence takes a T-bone steak of noble size and grills it quickly over the blazing fire, adding nothing but the aroma of freshly ground pepper and olive oil. Both are triumphs.

From the introduction to *The Classic Italian Cookbook*

Mmm. Other countries have even greater regional differences, ethnic and religious as well as culinary. Yet France, for example, has a stronger sense both of the centralized state, and of a shared history as a nation. In Italy, most people express loyalty more to a town or village than to the state or even the administrative region. In an area like Tuscany, historic rivalries persist between different towns. Pisa and Florence, for instance, or Florence and Prato (now more or less merged within Florence itself). You are more likely to hear someone say they come from Ferrara or Parma than from Emilia-Romagna, the region in which the two towns are. Most Italians take pride in dividing and subdividing their countryfolk according to their geographic origins. It is easy to point to differences of character: the arrogant Florentine; the pigheaded Sardinian; the joyless Milanese; the exuberant Neapolitan; the smug Bolognese; the cold Piedmontese. A Roman told me, only part tongue in cheek, that another man in the room was not really Italian since he came from the island of Pantelleria, off Sicily. Milanese transferred to Rome often feel they are being posted to a foreign country. They feel more at home in Berne or Munich.

My neighbour in Rome was from Calabria, married to a Milanese. When he drove around in Milan in his wife's car, no one took any notice of him. Yet when he was behind the wheel of his large Volvo estate with Reggio Calabria licence plates, he was for ever being cut up by young louts brandishing their fists, screaming *Terrone* (Southerner) and abusing him for hopeless driving.

There are sound reasons. Any journey round Italy will reveal how different one region is from another, how distinct one town is from the next. Whereas in Britain and elsewhere in Europe towns and villages have lost their distinctiveness as the same homogenizing chains of shops establish branches in each one, in Italy most towns maintain their separate identity. They have preserved their own small shops and kept out intruders such as foreign supermarket chains because in Italy the local chambers of commerce, rather than planning officials in local councils, issue the licences for new enterprises. Whether it be a different variety of grape, another way of making cheese, or sweeter-flavoured tomato, townspeople can express pride in their special particularity. This is often expressed as *campanilismo*, the sense of loyalty to one's own *campanile* or bell-tower. Banks and newspapers are often highly localized. A major national daily newspaper like *La Repubblica*, whose headquarters are in Rome, has separate editions in Bologna, Naples and Milan. Each edition contains an entire section of local news that is, in effect, like a mini-newspaper in its own right. *Campanilismo* has its most extreme form in Siena where twice a year seventeen different quarters of the city compete in the renowned *palio*, a horse race round the main square.

That regions are different because of their histories is not contested. The great fault line has always been between the North and the South. Where this fault line lies is a matter of often heated discussion. Some place it along the Germans' Gothic line of defence against the Allied advance, between Rome and Florence. Northerners will joke that Garibaldi did not unify Italy, but dismembered Africa. Does Egypt begin (they ask) at Rome, or Orvieto, or Florence?

For a thousand years, the South was under a succession of authoritarian rulers or kings. In Sicily the Norman kingdom was established over the foundations of Byzantine and Arab governments. This Northern European regime controlled Sicily and in time Apulia and Calabria. The man who in 1130 united Sicily with Southern Italy, Roger II, took on many of the systems left by the previous rulers for the efficient administration of these territories, including tax-gathering. Over the next century, the centralized, autocratic state was perfected. For the proper administration of the kingdom, a trained administrative class was required, for which purpose a university was founded in Naples in 1224, the first state university in Europe. Sicily flourished. Ports and harbours were built. A merchant fleet was launched, and a navy to protect it. By the end of the twelfth century, Sicily was the richest state in Europe. But the absence of free enterprise, and the state monopoly of most commerce, later proved the kingdom's undoing. For, in the course of time, it could not compete with the maritime city states that were rising up elsewhere in Northern Italy.

The Normans had unwittingly laid the foundations for the type of centralized, autocratic rule which was to dominate the South until the unification of the country. After the death of the great King Frederick II, the power of the centre diminished and that of the barons increased. The barons in turn evolved into a feudal landowning aristocracy. The mass of the population were wretched peasants. A class of intermediaries, of professional notaries and administrators, was caught in between.

The South's wealth was always based on land. This was the case right up to the *latifondi* or large estates that survived until the land reforms after the Second World War. The system remained autocratic and feudal. By the eighteenth century, the Kingdom of Naples, which included both Sicily and the Southern mainland, was the most populous in Italy. It had five million inhabitants, but they were also the worst administered. For nearly all the population lived in some way off the state, as employees of the royal court, servants, or priests. Neapolitans frequently blame their ills on centuries of subjection to foreign rule, as the French and Spanish, the Habsburgs and Bourbons, vied for control.

By contrast, in the North, from Tuscany through Emilia-Romagna to Lombardy, self-governing republics or *comuni* had been established by the Middle Ages, in what were effectively experiments in community living and rule. Elsewhere in medieval Europe, the main system of government was feudal, between lord of the manor and serfs. In these towns and city states, men were allowed to take part in the making of laws and decisions and the running of their own affairs. Of course, by twentieth-century standards the enfranchisement was limited. Only a small minority of the population were full members of the *comune*. Yet the success of these liberal systems of government could be seen in the rapid expansion first of manufacturing, then in trade and the development of finance.

Most of those differences between North and South carried over into the modern period. It did not matter that in many cases there might have been several centuries without the kind of community rule that had been widespread in the North in the twelfth to fourteenth centuries. What mattered was that some feeling of participation in government in its broadest sense existed in the popular consciousness. When the intellectual and economic movements of progress started wafting across Europe in the latter part of the eighteenth century, these Northern parts of Italy were more receptive to them. As a result, after the establishment of regional government in Italy, some were efficient and served the needs of their citizens. Others were hopelessly inefficient and corrupt. The reasons for the greater success of some regions than others has been the subject of research for years. The recent study by Professor Putnam (*Making Democracy Work: Civic Traditions in Modern Italy*) stated baldly that the seeds of regional government planted in fertile soil in the North flourished and grew. Those planted in the barren soil of the South withered and barely survived. The soils varied greatly, from the ardently Catholic in Campania round Naples to the militantly Communist in the red belt of Emilia-Romagna. It made hardly any difference which parties ran the regional governments. Nor was affluence in itself the key (the richest region was Lombardy, but the best government was found in Emilia-Romagna). The not altogether surprising conclusion was that where there was a developed civic sense, where there were community associations, be they libraries or choral societies, church groups or old people's homes, good government would follow. Where there was little sense of society, but only reliance on cronyism and hand-outs from the bosses, then the growth of good local government was stunted.

The analysis had a fatalistic conclusion. For it suggested that in terms of local government, Italians were very much hostages to their past. For those regions such as Calabria where a civic sense was either very underdeveloped or non-existent, then there was little hope of improvement. The regions in the South would remain mired in the poverty trap. No matter how much in financial resources was transferred from the North to the South, these would be misspent and diverted into the hands of corrupt politicians and organized crime. It was a circular argument, but events proved this contention depressingly correct.

On an administrative level, the region is more a political division
than one which inspires local loyalty. By the time the constitution
was drawn up, some regions furthest from the centre already
enjoyed various measures of autonomy: Sicily, Sardinia, the
French-speaking Valle d'Aosta and Trentino-Alto Adige. This
situation of special regions was later enshrined in the constitution,
while the rest of the country was divided into fourteen (later
fifteen) ordinary ones. The policy makers thus balanced their desire
to avoid the centralization of the Fascist state through devolving
power to the regions, without losing sight of the aim of a unified
state. Despite the failure of regional government in Sicily, by the
late 1960s it was felt desirable to extend the regional system of
government throughout the whole country. In 1963 Friuli-Venezia
Giulia was also granted special status, because of the peculiar
position of the Slovene-speaking population in the hinterland
above Trieste, whose status as a cultural minority was accepted in
the 1954 agreement with Belgrade. In 1970 the remaining regional
governments came into being, to bring the total number to
twenty.

A look at three areas or regions – the mixed German-Italian area
of Alto Adige (Südtirol), Calabria and Naples – shows how
they differ not only in history and culture, but also in their
dealings with the central government in Rome. Italians stress these
differences incessantly, yet over the passage of time they have all
become more recognizably Italian. Politically and economically,
the gap has widened between the North and South. Culturally,
thanks to better communications, and the near-universal use of the
Italian language diffused through television, those differences are
less than most Italians are prepared to acknowledge.

Bolzano is part of Italy, but hardly Italian. Several generations
after it was ceded from the Austro-Hungarian Empire, it still looks
and feels Austrian. The people are fair-haired. Chalet-style houses
climb up the steep hillsides. Window boxes prim and neat adorn
the balconies in the winding alleyways. Yellow and green glazed
tiles decorate the cathedral church off Piazza Walther. Even the
banks have no bulletproof security doors, as though they are
immune to the affliction of bank robberies that is endemic in the

rest of Italy. Through the narrow winding streets of the town centre run cycle lanes, those late-twentieth-century indicators of civic society and concession to the environmentalist lobby more commonly found in Northern European cities. Drive in from the North, from Austria, and you may feel you have not left one country for another, except that the road signs are written in both German and Italian. In the surrounding villages, brass bands and the local mayor will bless the arrival of the new fire engine. Today, the Dolomites are popular tourist weekend resorts for skiers and hikers from towns and cities of Northern Italy, Southern Germany and Austria.

Bolzano, a town of 100,000 inhabitants, is capital of the province known to Italians as Alto Adige (Upper Adige) and to German-speakers as Südtirol. It is a curious anomaly whose history is part of the history of central Europe of the twentieth century, a history of competing nationalisms and big-power rivalry. Today, its solution to the knotty issue of ethnic minority rights is being touted as a model for minorities in the new Europe of the regions, of a Europe without national or state boundaries. The Italian foreign ministry even took the Alto Adige model further afield, to the disputed enclave of Nagorno-Karabakh, as a way to show how minority rights might be protected.

At the October 1991 census, the population of the province of Alto Adige was divided as follows: 270,000 German-speakers, 130,000 Italian-speakers and 20,000 speakers of Ladino, a dialect of Rhaeto-Romanche that is spoken mainly in the valleys. The proportion of German-speakers has grown in recent years, due mainly to a high birth rate, and the return of Italians on retirement to their original homes be it the nearby Veneto or faraway Campania in the South, but also because some Italians registered as Germans to help obtain jobs in the public administration, under the strict quota system.

The Italian presence in Bolzano stemmed from a secret commitment made between the government in Rome and the Allies – Britain, France and Russia – in 1915. Until then, Italy had been a member of the Triple Alliance, with Germany and Austria, but when war broke out in 1914, Italy remained neutral. Italy agreed to side with the Allies in exchange for a promise that, in the case of victory, it would receive the territory up to the Brenner Pass. For the Italian military command had insisted on the necessity of strong defensible frontiers, even if geography disregarded the linguistic and ethnic complexion of the population.

In 1919, when the Austro-Hungarian Empire was carved up and dismantled, the Tyrol – previously a single region – was duly split. The Southern part was ceded to Italy, along with the province of Trento, then as now 98 per cent Italian-speaking, the payment for Italy's betrayal of its former ally Austria. After Mussolini's rise to power in 1923, a major push was made to Italianize the population of Alto Adige (Südtirol). Il Duce tried to do the same with those Slovene areas of Trieste and its hinterland, also incorporated into the state after the First World War. In Alto Adige (Südtirol) he used a number of devices. He suppressed manifestations of German-speaking culture, banned the instruction of German in schools, forced the German-speakers to learn Italian, and in many cases obliged them to change their German names for Italian ones. German was no longer permitted as a medium for legal transactions. When the Austrians protested, they were told this was an internal matter. It was a response that successive Italian governments have made until this day. At the same time he sought to change the demographic character of the area by swamping it with Italian-speakers from the Veneto and the south of Italy, drawn by very generous incentives. They filled the newly available posts in the expanded public administration, as well as jobs in industries he established. Most of these Italian immigrants therefore were concentrated in the main towns, Bolzano and Merano.

Mussolini was convinced that the German-speaking population would prefer the benefits of Italian Fascist rule to old irredentist feelings of German nationalism. In 1939 he decided to hold a plebiscite in Alto Adige (Südtirol). The population was offered the option of going to live in post-Anschluss Germany. So confident was he of the success of his policy of Italianization that he offered to buy up the property of any who chose to go to Germany. He was doubly shocked at the result. First, he had to pay millions in compensation to those who chose to leave. And the tenuousness of his claim that he ruled with the consent of the people was exposed when 80 per cent voted against his brand of Fascism. About 212,000 chose Nazi Germany over Fascist Italy;

34,000 preferred to remain. In the event, only 75,000 were resettled in Germany, because of disruptions caused by the outbreak of the Second World War.

After the war an agreement was quickly reached between Italy and Austria to settle their rival claims to the area. Known as the Paris Peace Treaty, this agreement was signed in 1946 by the Italian prime minister Alcide De Gasperi and the Austrian foreign minister Dr Karl Gruber. De Gasperi was personally acquainted with the problem: he had served as a member of the Austrian parliament for Trento. In essence, the Austrian government renounced its territorial claims to the area, on condition that Italy respected the cultural identity of the German-speaking minority through regional autonomy. Austria was to have the status of protector.

In 1948, the two provinces of Trento and Bolzano were united into one region known as Trentino-Alto Adige, with its own regional government and parliament. It was a form of gerrymandering to make sure that the new administrative area – the region – would have an Italian-speaking majority in the larger regional administrative structure. Austria complained that the change was a violation of the Paris Peace Treaty, since the five-to-two predominance in favour of Italian-speakers in the enlarged region simply obviated the promised autonomy.

From the late 1950s, through the 1960s and into the 1970s, right-wing extremists perpetrated a number of attacks against military and other targets in the region. Bombs were planted against electricity pylons, and soldiers were targeted. The incidents served to increase tension between the two governments, and between the two communities.

The United Nations was invoked, and in 1960 and 1961 a number of resolutions were passed by the general assembly. In 1964 the governments of Austria and Italy agreed on a package of concessions, which gave more powers to Bolzano to protect the rights of all language groups, and established a commission to monitor implementation of the measures. The *pacchetto* was formally adopted in 1969, with considerable reservations, by the Südtiroler Volkspartei (SVP), the South Tyrol People's Party. The *pacchetto* was linked to an operational calendar. It was not until 1992 that the Italian government advised the Austrians that they had enacted the 137 provisions, which would lead in effect to the settlement of the outstanding areas of dispute. This was achieved largely through the offices of the outgoing prime minister Giulio Andreotti. He had been imbued with the same European vision as his political mentor De Gasperi and had understood better than most the aspirations of the Südtirolese.

Austria remains the nominal protective power for the German-speaking inhabitants of Alto Adige (Südtirol), in accordance with the Paris Peace Treaty. But, in effect, with Austria's membership of the European Community only a matter of time, and Europe evolving into a Europe of the regions, this role will decrease.

The region's buildings reflect its convoluted history. As in many towns in Italy, the Fascists left in their municipal architecture permanent monuments to their grandiose concept of Italian power. In Bolzano it is found in the new town, built on the west bank of the River Adige to house Mussolini's Italian immigrants. Victory Monument is a focus for Italian nationalist demonstrations held by the neo-Fascist Movimento Sociale Italiano (MSI) to oppose any more autonomy for the Südtirolese. The bombastic law courts bear the vainglorious exhortation PRO ITALICO IMPERIO VIRTVTE IVSTITIA HIERARCHIA VNGVBVS ET ROSTRIS.

The architecture, however, is merely a façade. The solid stone buildings stand instead as testament to the permanence of human vanity. Their triumphal proclamation of the superiority of Italian Fascism has been deflated by its political failure and eroded by demographic changes. Look more closely, and you see that the river does not divide the two communities quite so neatly. In the new town, attached to the pillars of Fascist buildings, are the name plates of German-speaking lawyers. In the old town, in Piazza Walther, you see Italian designer shops. Sleek Italian businessmen and local officials disport themselves after their morning cappuccino. In effect, the two communities are topographically and geographically less segregated than might appear.

Politically, too, they are not so sharply divided. The old stereotypes no longer hold. Not all Italian-speakers are MSI neo-Fascists, voting for the party whose first leader had brought them there, and convinced that their interests can be protected only by the continuation of Italian rule. Nor are all Südtirolese *lederhosen*-wearing conservatives. There have been a number of distinct trends recently, all pointing to a lessening of these divisions. On the one hand, there has been a slight decrease in the Italian-speaking population. Between the censuses of 1971 and 1981, there was a 3 per cent fall in the Italian-speakers, against a 3.4 per cent increase among German-speakers. The previous census figures provoked a genuine fear among Italian-speakers in Bolzano that they were an endangered species, and that they would shortly be eradicated. However, the census of 1991 showed that the decline had slowed, and that the fears of the previous ten years had been misplaced. That said, many of the Italian-speakers face social and administrative disadvantages. They were never landowners. Mussolini never brought in peasant farmers. They are concentrated in the towns. For example, Bolzano town is 70 per cent Italian-speaking, while Italian-speakers are a minority in the province of Bolzano as a whole. The Italians are the true minority, and many have failed even to learn properly the second language which would enable them to compete more easily with their German compatriots.

By contrast, the Südtirolese are pulling in opposite directions. In the villages in the valleys, an increasing number of the young people are not taught Italian, as a reaction by their parents against their own forcible instruction in Italian. On the other hand, in the towns, there is greater mingling on a social and cultural level between the two communities.

That does not mean that they are integrated in any meaningful sense. The whole history of the *pacchetto* has ensured the separate development of the German-speakers and Italian-speakers, with all the loaded implications of that term. So extreme is the cultural divide that the SVP repeatedly vetoed proposals for Italian schools to teach German, which in turn reinforces and perpetuates those divisions. This creates problems in all aspects of life, for example, for parents in the small number of mixed marriages. I met such a couple who were debating whether to register the child they were expecting as German- or Italian-speaking, for this would determine which school system he or she would go through. There was no possibility of transferring from one to the other. The German-speakers have been so intent on preserving their status through rigid application of the quotas that when, for instance, a vacancy occurs for a hospital surgeon, and there is no German-speaker to fill it, it will remain unfilled, even if there are dozens of otherwise qualified Italian-speakers, or even foreigners, who could fill it. They have rigidly insisted on their quota: 67 per cent of jobs in the public administration for the German-speakers, 30 per cent for the Italian-speakers, and 3 per cent for the tiny minority who speak Ladino. The Ladinos have a reputation as entrepreneurs. However illiberal the German-speaking policy is, it is the hardline reaction of a minority which seeks to maintain its dominant position within its own province. For the German-speakers are more usually bilingual; few Italian-speakers can speak German well enough to secure jobs. When I first went to Italy to learn Italian, the adjacent class was filled with Bolzano German-speakers perfecting their Italian so as to be able to sit the *concorso* competitive exam for a job in the civil service.

The political obstinacy of the SVP was a rearguard action. The party's power was based solely on ethnic fear. It reacted like a porcupine raising its spines against a threat, real or imagined. Now with most minority rights protected, the SVP had to find other targets so as to satisfy its more hardline nationalist faction on the right wing that it was standing up to Rome. Political tactics rather than substantial grievances lay behind last-minute demands by the newly elected leader of the SVP, Senator Roland Riz, to raise in autumn 1991 the requirement for an 'international anchorage' for the *pacchetto*. The Italians pointed out that this was an internal matter.

The general elections in April 1992 revealed quite how far public opinion had changed. What emerged was a greater sense of common purpose among the Italian- and German-speakers. Each moved away from the parties representing their more extreme nationalist ambitions. Among Italian-speakers, the vote for the neo-Fascist MSI declined for the first time. Among German-speakers, only 3 per cent voted for the most extreme nationalist Union Für Südtirol, which seeks self-determination, the codeword for reunification with Austria. Others broke the taboo and for the first time deserted the parties of their ethnic minority, voting for the

Northern League as a generalized protest against government in and from Rome, or for the Greens, the only other party or movement which has no ethnic colour.

Some of the more forward-looking German-speakers decried the obstinacy of their older political leaders. The Green Euro-deputy Alex Langer wrote against the *pacchetto*. He said it reinforced those divisions which they should be trying to break down.

If Bolzano is part of Italy, how Italian do the people of Alto Adige feel? It was chic in the 1960s for radical Italian-speakers to describe themselves as Südtirolese of Italian mother tongue. Bolzano Italians are unique in having no specific dialect of their own. Some preserve the dialect of the places from which they migrated. This explains why a few oldtimers still frequent associations for migrants from Friuli or Rovigo. Yet I met younger natives of Bolzano whose parents had come from Naples and Calabria, and they simply defined themselves as Italians, from Alto Adige. Ask liberal German-speakers today how they view themselves, and they will probably respond that they are Italians of German mother tongue. Many, however, prefer to call themselves simply 'Europeans'. Calling themselves European obviates any need to define themselves narrowly as in one community or another. It is an understandable emotional and intellectual position. But it is not acceptable within the law. For the laws in Alto Adige (Südtirol) require one to be either German-speaking or Italian-speaking. There are no half-measures.

The area has produced its distinguished citizens. Lilli Gruber was an atypical sex symbol. She had none of the classic Mediterranean voluptuousness of an Alba Parietti or a Sophia Loren. Yet in successive surveys of the amorous fantasies of Italian males, the diminutive television journalist was pronounced Ideal Woman. She was not just a pretty face. As a presenter she coolly handled the production glitches that dogged Italian television news broadcasts. As an interviewer, she fired questions with an Anglo-Saxon directness. And during the overthrow of the old politically controlled regime at Rai 1, she was among the leaders of the rebels. Yet as her name suggests, she was an Italian whose mother tongue was not Italian but German. A native of Bolzano, like the world's top climber, Reinhold Messner.

Alto Adige (Südtirol), culturally apart, linguistically different, is an anomaly even by the standards of the regional variations within the Italian state. Yet its relationship with Rome provides more generalized lessons about how the periphery deals with the centre. The province has played its cards well. It has not hesitated to cry out when deemed necessary that its minority population was being discriminated against. So keen have successive governments in Rome been to avoid conflict that they have bowed to nearly every demand. As a result, the German-speakers of Alto Adige (Südtirol) are the best-protected minority in Europe (better protected than the Slovene minority in Austria) and cosseted with a 4,100 billion lire (£1.9 billion) annual grant from central government. Thus each baby born in effect receives a 100,000 lire (£45) gift. Another reason for the lessening in hardline nationalist sentiment seeking reunification with Austria is that the citizens of Alto Adige (Südtirol) are now far richer than their counterparts of Northern Tyrol, and among the richest in Italy. So though these people, in terms of blood and history, are the least Italian of all, the benefits gained from membership of the state now far outweigh the advantages of seeking separation and reunification with Austria.

At the other end of the peninsula in both geographic and political terms is the harsh mountainous region of Calabria, in the deep south of Italy. Calabria is a world apart. Everything visible confirms the failure of the state and of central government to influence or have any impact on the daily lives of a whole section of the country. The bleak concrete-box building, dubbed by some wit 'the Calabria unfinished style', the *abusivo* (illegal) construction, the uncompleted roads, the almost total absence of productive manufacturing industry, the lack of any planning have all added to the deterioration of the quality of life in the region. As soon as you arrive at Reggio Calabria airport, far down in Italy's toe, you realize the people do not enjoy a high standing. The men's urinals are fixed to the wall a foot lower than the national level.

Calabria does have its own industrial triangle. It may not rival Milan, Turin and Genoa in terms of manufacturing output and world renown, but it in some way matches them in terms of per capita income. For the three communities of San Luca, Natile and Plati, with that Italian genius for niche enterprises, have cornered the market in a very precious commodity. They form the kidnap capital of the country, and their victims or their families have led to a resource transfer from the North to the South of proportions that any social engineer would be proud of.

You could see the result of this particular form of employment in the town of Bovalino, a coastal resort on the Ionian Sea, which I visited in October 1992. Locals proudly pointed out their own millionaires' row, a street of large and inelegant buildings constructed by a single clan from Saluga up in the hills. They called it Via Borghetti, local pronunciation for Paul Getty: the kidnappers successfully carried out their crime, seizing the oil-fortune heir and holding him for ransom for six months in 1973, and cutting off part of his right ear to prove their intent. They got away with the $750,000 ransom paid for his release. Less fortunate was the local *comune*. Its entire membership was slapped in jail in 1992. They were placed under investigation for corruption in the awarding of the public works contract for the hideous new 4.5 billion lire (£2 million) local council building popularly known as 'Il Fungo', 'The Mushroom', which resembled a poor imitation of the Guggenheim Museum in New York.

The coastal road ran parallel to the railway line, which still carried diesel locomotives. Money had never arrived from Rome to electrify the line. A couple of turbaned Sikhs padded slowly along the tarmac beside the bamboo, part of the growing force of immigrant labourers who took seasonal work picking tomatoes – despite the high local unemployment. Bright oleander trees lined the dusty road, and crimson hibiscus and brilliant morning glory cascaded over the shoddy buildings, buildings whose architectural inspiration owed as little to the humanist ideas of the Florentine Renaissance as any in the Third World. It is a place of raw natural beauty, of wild mountains, and stunning beaches strung along the coast, one after another, more tropical than Mediterranean.

The road branched at Bovalino for Plati, a dozen kilometres away in the foothills of the Aspromonte mountains. In Greek, Aspromonte means white mountain, because its peaks are often covered with snow. But it also means the harsh mountain, the deserted mountain. For since the time of Homer it has been a vast emptiness, where only the intrepid or foolhardy dare tread alone. Huge olive trees covered the hillsides, riven by dried-up watercourses. At the entrance to the village, a garish orange school bus deposited its charges with their day-glo satchels. They waved at one of their young contemporaries who, like so many in the South, played truant, tending a herd of goats.

Plati was the very picture of abandonment. A village of 3,800 souls – the locals all talked of souls, when they did not talk of Christians – it had been declared ungovernable by the ministry of justice. Its local *comune* had been dissolved, and a commissioner had been appointed by Rome's man, the prefect in Reggio Calabria, who came twice a week to try to run some sort of administration. Furthermore, the recent local elections had been boycotted by all but a few hundred, who voted for the neo-Fascist MSI.

This too was part of an Italy which was among the world's five largest industrial powers, a member of the G7 richest nations, and part, too, of the new Europe of 1992 and beyond. It was not a village which had fallen on hard times. It had never emerged from them. Nature's cruelty had played its part. The earthquake of 1908, and the landslide of October 1951, which carried away homes and eighteen villagers, had taken their toll. The landslide diverted the stream that ran on down the valley at the edge of habitation. It was used as the village dump. From it arose the musty smell of grape leavings from winemaking. Rats scurried their way through the rubbish and the broken chairs and fridges. There had been another flood in 1973. But, above all, the neglect was due to the absence of interest of a government structure to deal with chronic criminality.

At the entrance to the village, a couple of carabinieri stood in their bulletproof vests with sub-machine-guns slung in front of them. This was as far as they – or the officers of the state and officials of the central government – would normally go. For Plati was in effect a no-go area, a place that the ministry of justice had deemed ungovernable, and had therefore left to its fate.

Large cars, the latest Land Rover Discovery and various Japanese four-wheel-drive vehicles, moved through the narrow streets, with young men in dark glasses peering out from behind tinted windows. Plati had a secondary reputation as a major drugs distribution point for the area and beyond. Youths went down to travel agents in the nearby towns like Bovalino to buy day-trip tickets for the flight to Milan or Turin, arriving in big cars and paying cash. Despite the huge amounts of money they were generating, they tried to reduce costs: the younger couriers would ask for the under-eighteen fare.

In the Idamos café-bar in the village, children who should have been at school played pool and pinball machines. The barman limped behind his bar, one of the minority whose disability pension was genuine. On the shelf behind him was pinned a spoof electoral list for what he called 'the Drunks' Party'. He did not encourage close examination: the names on it were a roll-call of the major Mafia clans in Plati, including the infamous Barbaro and Trimboli *cosche*.

He would not talk about the Mafia, but alluded to the pastoral employment of most of the fathers of the community. 'In a flock there is always a black sheep.'

'The only good thing here is the air,' one stocky old peasant declared. 'There's nothing else.' So why didn't he leave? He shrugged. This was home, there was nowhere else for him to go. Like so many he dismissed Plati's notoriety as a kidnap centre. 'Every time the kidnappers released a victim, they were found here, at the nearest point off the mountain. That's why they say we did it.'

Italians of the North find it hard to explain how the phenomenon of kidnapping as an organized industry perpetrated by the Anonima gangs persists into the end of the twentieth century in Calabria and Sardinia. Open letters have been written decrying the 'degenerate subhuman race of San Luca'. 'You are the shame of Italy, you are the bubonic plague of our country,' read another. Kidnapping is a practice which thrives on the complicity of the population. The teenage schoolboy Cesare Casella recounted how during his captivity a lone shepherd stumbled on his underground hiding place on a mountainside. He shouted at him, screaming to alert him of his predicament. The old man hid his eyes with his hands, and went on his way. As help failed to arrive in the next hours, the kidnapped boy realized that his fortuitous discoverer had told no one, had not even made an anonymous call to the police, paralysed by the ancient code of *omertà*.

According to the police, a typical kidnap band could count on fifty members, with twice that number who would cover up the traces. The kidnap industry continued for two simple reasons. First, because despite the laws banning the payment of ransom money few Italian families were prepared to sacrifice the lives of their loved ones for such a point of principle. And second, because the authorities were so inept at pursuing their men. In more than one case, when the government in Rome risked losing electoral support, every effort was made to release kidnap victims, with rapid and notable success. The daughter of the industrialist Ghidini in the city of Brescia was quickly recovered because the Christian Democrats feared the affair would lose them votes to the rapidly growing Lombard League.

In Plati village square, a poster advertised without irony a meeting of the Association of the Blood Donors of Locride. How many in this sanguinary culture were not volunteers? The village school was closed, its doors padlocked. On its outside wall was painted a vast mural, a mix of primitive style and social realism. It was an evocative depiction of childhood fantasies and grim realities. There were the usual idealized scenes of idyllic pastoral life: cows grazing in green fields, clean tarmacked streets, a happy married couple emerging from the church porch, water flowing from the pump. But the mural had not survived intact. The heads of the policemen had been defaced. Other policemen were portrayed firing their weapons.

Scrawled on the roughcast walls of the council building, slogans in red paint enshrined past and present concerns. 'Down with the mayor.' 'We want a sports field.' 'We want work so as to eat, not to pay taxes.' 'We don't want carabinieri and police' – this last painted over with regulation police blue paint.

Halfway up the village, up a potholed narrow alley that had never been metalled, stood a cluster of houses which looked out over the sloping mountainside. I had gone with a contact from Reggio Calabria to meet Bruno Trimboli, member of a family under investigation for a series of child kidnappings. We entered warily, with a tray of cakes taken in the naïve hope it might somehow show the right spirit of offering and grant us protection.

'There was really no need to bring the cakes,' Trimboli declared. 'As though it would make any difference.' It was uttered not as a threat, but as a welcome, to show we had almost questioned his own hospitality in a culture where it is renowned – notwithstanding other less noble aspects of social intercourse such as brutal and violent settling of scores.

He was a good-looking man of around forty, with pale green eyes which fixed you when he spoke. His cracked fingers were stained dark red with grape-juice from winemaking. Four or five of his children – the eldest was fifteen – gathered round, pretty, unassuming pictures of innocence. It was hard to believe this man had made his living by inflicting the utmost barbarities against children unknown. One of his young daughters made coffee in a tiled, newly fitted kitchen grand beyond the means of the ordinary peasant farmer this man insisted he was. No mere goatherd, however adept at cheating on the EC agricultural funds, could have built such a home.

Like others in Plati he complained about how little the government had done for the village. He pointed to the unmade roads, the shortage of running water, the absence of the most basic services. His story was that of a leading family in the kidnap business. He had six children; his father had had fourteen. Now his father and two nephews were being held by the authorities for investigation for a series of child kidnappings. His father was suspected of being the watchman at the hideout where they held Cesare Casella, whose mother travelled south from Pavia and chained herself to the railings in Locri to protest against the failure of the authorities to obtain the release of her son. He was eventually released the following year, as well as two other kidnap victims, Patrizia Tacchella and Carlo Celadon, freed in 1990 after twenty-seven months in captivity after the crack Alpine Brigade was deployed in the Aspromonte. Trimboli and his family were, of course, all innocent.

Did he know the Barbaro family?

'Barbaro? Never heard of him.'

'Yes. Yes, Papa, you do know,' one of the daughters prompted.

'No. Don't know them.'

It was a wholly unconvincing denial, but one which did not in the circumstances invite contradiction. On the recently dissolved town council were Antonio Barbaro and Pasquale Barbaro, as well as Domenico Trimboli and Paolo Trimboli. All were members of the Christian Democratic Party. A few months previously, the carabinieri had impounded the assets amounting to 30 billion lire (£14 million) of eight people suspected of being members of the Barbaro Mafia clan, including Pasquale Barbaro. Some members of the Barbaro clan had also been implicated in the murder in March 1985 of the mayor of Plati, Domenico De Maio, struck down as he was walking with his nine-year-old daughter. The following year another ex-mayor, Francesco Prestia, was killed by persons unknown.

Plati had more than local notoriety. In 1977 an Australian politician named Donald MacKay had been murdered in the town of Griffith in New South Wales. His body had been found down a pit. He had been campaigning against drugs trafficking and organized crime. Two years later the official Australian report into his murder concluded it had been carried out on the orders of Mafia clans who came originally from Plati. The mafiosi were accused of belonging to six clans, one of which was the Barbaro. Up to a third of the population of Calabria emigrated to Australia in the years after the Second World War. Many whole communities simply packed up and left. Others departed and continued to sustain their families left behind with money from their new homes. As MacKay discovered, not all that money was legally generated. In New South Wales they had been farming on an industrial scale the novel crop of marijuana. Subsequent investigation by Australian and Italian police established that the seed money for this drugs farming had come from a series of kidnappings in Italy. The drugs profits were in turn ploughed back into legitimate businesses in Calabria. The carabinieri report cited by the leading sociologist of organized crime in Italy, Pino Arlacchi, in *Mafia Business* linked Domenico Barbaro with Francesco Trimboli.

This area of Calabria has the highest murder rate in Europe, higher than Sicily. The province as a whole had on average one murder a day, yet few murderers were ever found, still fewer brought to book. Yet villager after villager protested against the hostile media for tarring them all with the same criminal brush. Again and again they would say that it was wrong to criminalize an entire community. At the offices of a local newspaper in Reggio Calabria, the former Communist mayor of Plati gave his reasoned analysis for its current predicament. It was a discourse that combined all the worst elements of Italian verbosity and bombast with prolix Marxist historical dialectic. Although Francesco 'Ciccio' Catanzariti had resigned from the then Italian Communist Party in 1985 for what he called its failure to address the Southern Problem, he could still master the jargon. It would be hypocritical to deny there were problems in Plati, he conceded, but what were the causes? It was the key question. Were the Calabrians victims of their own culture and history, and incapable of development and resistant to any form of government? He stated absolutely not. He defended the integrity of his fellow Calabresi. Some had had distinguished careers. The carabinieri commandant in Piedmont, who had served in Valle d'Aosta, was from Plati, he proudly proclaimed, as though one senior official in the forces of law and order from among the sons of Plati somehow made up for the remaining lawlessness. Plati, he said, was a place which had for a long time suffered an almost feudal system of government. It had been weakened not only by the earthquake and landslide of October 1951, but also eroded by emigration. In the first census, in 1881, the population was given as 9,980. There are now said to be between 40,000 and 45,000 sons of Plati around the world, in Canada, the USA, Argentina, Australia and northern Italy, especially Turin and Milan. Now the population was about 3,800.

After the *comune* had been dissolved, because of Mafia association, many local people were visited by carabinieri at home. The village had a high population of *pregiudicati*, people with criminal records. The schoolteacher, a young girl from the city who had not learnt the value of prudence, was more outspoken than Trimboli. 'You go into their homes, and you know they are all mafiosi. Everyone knows who the bosses are but they won't speak out.'

The sense of neglect, of inferiority, left a great feeling of despair in the province. Calabria was one of the poorest regions of

Western Europe, with the highest levels of unemployment, and an almost complete absence of industry. Even state-owned industry had avoided investing in the region. IRI, whose companies employed hundreds of thousands in the rest of Italy, had only a handful of jobs in Calabria. Calabria accounted for only 2 per cent of the country's GDP, yet had 3.6 per cent of the population. Billions of lire had been poured into the region, mostly for public works contracts in roads and railways, controlled by organized crime. After the government decided in 1970 to place the regional capital at Catanzaro rather than Reggio Calabria, serious urban protests broke out. And as a sop to local sentiment, plans were announced for the building of a steelworks at Gioia Tauro. Olive and citrus groves were cleared. A huge port was built. The local Mafia used the proceeds from the kidnapping of Paul Getty to purchase a fleet of haulage trucks. These were then employed for transporting the materials needed for the construction of the complex. But the steelworks were never operational. Of all the cathedrals in the desert, this was the most spectacular. It was being built at a time of a glut of steel on the world market. When it was planned, Italian steel plants were already producing at only two-thirds capacity. The coming of the project spawned substantial rake-offs for the Mafia. It also led to a spate of murders related to the carving up of the contracts for the project. The project failed in a number of ways. It ravaged an area of natural beauty and highly productive agricultural land. It wasted billions of lire from state funds in the pursuit of political ends divorced from economic requirements. And the steel plant's failure to open torpedoed the whole industrial strategy of the state, a strategy which was intended to bring private investment in its wake. As a result of this and other such failures, the South is largely bereft of industry. No wonder industrial giants like Fiat and Olivetti have been so reluctant to invest there. Not only must they cope with the Mafia and the corruption, they also have to deal with the different cultural attitudes towards work, of higher than average absentee-ism, a low skill base and greater labour friction.

The widening gap between the North and the South poses a serious problem for central government. If the region is abandoned to itself, it will deteriorate even further and become totally ungovernable. Crime and corruption will rule absolutely. But if Calabria continues to be supported as it has been, then aid will go on being passed through the hands of the Mafia-controlled politicians.

Calabria holds some more infamous records. With a population of two million, it has the dubious reputation of having had the highest number of local councils dissolved by order of the justice ministry. There are some ten thousand police, carabinieri and guardia di finanza garrisoned there. Such, however, has been the shortage of magistrates willing to assume posts in these dangerous places that Locri had to take on three newly qualified women lawyers. While their qualifications were not questioned, the then president Cossiga pondered whether more experienced magistrates might have been available to volunteer.

One survey showed that at least 90 per cent of building and public-works contracts were controlled by the 'ndrangheta, as were 40 per cent of the transport sector, 20 per cent of credit and finance, and 15 per cent of trade. Pino Arlacchi, himself from Calabria, declared that the region was a disaster to beat all disasters. He recalled that when he was growing up Calabria was even poorer, but people had some hope of change or of an improvement. The new steelworks, the university at Cosenza, the economic development plans, all gave a boost to Calabrian self-esteem. But the hopes evaporated. The steelworks collapsed, the university was never a major centre, and organized crime increased rapidly to penetrate nearly every aspect of life.

There is not even equality of misery in Italy. The Neapolitans endure a type of depressing poverty quite different from that in Calabria. You notice it as you arrive at the railway station: the outstretched hands of beggars in the former capital of the southern kingdom where soliciting handouts from the haves – the Church, the king (formerly), the state – has for generations been the accepted alternative to productive enterprise. Naples is an enigma. Everywhere there is movement. People rush to and fro. Yet it remains desperately poor. It is less a cash economy than one of exchange. At the same time, after portable phones were introduced in Italy in time for the 1990 World Cup finals, the Campania region around Naples quickly had the highest number in the country.

The greater Naples conurbation is the most populous in Italy. Huge tenement blocks rise up around the wide sweep of the bay with that brooding peak of Vesuvius towering behind. It is one of those myths that the Northerners live in cities, and the Southerners in villages. In fact, the opposite is true. The South is more urban than the North. In 1986, 51 per cent of Northerners lived in towns or villages with fewer than 20,000 inhabitants, whereas only 42 per cent of Southerners did. At the same time, 15 per cent of Northerners lived in cities of more than 250,000, as opposed to 22 per cent of Southerners.

For sheer bleak hopelessness, it is hard to beat the ghastly concrete slums of Secondigliano. It is an area where the city's own sense of victimization, and its feeling of being discriminated against by the outside world, do not seem misplaced. The sprawling housing estate was built on the outskirts of Naples to take overspill from the crowded city centre. When I visited it, it resembled a war zone. The most notorious blocks were known as the Sails and the Towers. In one of the Sails the lifts had long since stopped working, after a woman was killed when a door failed. The stairs were littered with the syringes of the junkies that abound. Young men hung around the corners of the buildings, eyeing strangers threateningly. Between the buildings, waste water lay in fetid pools. Some of the residents had tried to make the most of their surroundings and had built chicken runs out of old wire. The only legitimate economic activity seemed to be the water-melon seller proffering his produce from the back of a cart at the entrance to the estate.

Crime was rife. Most was petty crime, associated with drug abuse. It was the mothers who were the main pushers, according to some of the children. The presence of the state was nowhere visible. Volunteers from a church charity who took me round explained how little hope there was for children growing up in this environment. Yet even Naples was changing, demographically. There were nearly 900,000 children in Naples and the surrounding province. One-third of the population of the city were under fourteen, a quarter under nine. The population profile was very different from Northern Italy. The urchins of folklore still ran round the streets. A third of children did not complete their compulsory schooling. The national average was 9.6 per cent. The repeat rate, of pupils having to do a year's schooling twice, was twelve times higher than in Florence. For most, the only real school was the school of knocks, the street. They ended up illiterate, often unable to converse in anything but dialect, and were therefore prey to the sole employer who would take them on, the Camorra, the Neapolitan Mafia. In 1989, some five thousand minors were charged with criminal activity, of whom 920 were jailed, mostly for selling drugs. While Neapolitans constantly assert that children are their hearts and souls, the level of abandonment is much higher than among families in the centre and North of the country. Volunteers from a church community were trying to encourage young children to go back to school, to get some qualification, any qualification, to break out of the cycle of violence and despair that was otherwise their lot. It was a noble effort, but a drop in the ocean.

Children were no longer dying of starvation, or running around barefoot. For some time there had been no major outbreak of infectious disease such as cholera, as had occurred in the not so distant past. Yet infant mortality in some of the poor, overcrowded areas of the city centre was double that of cities in the North. Children were not the only social challenge. Another, according to the church voluntary organizations, was the old. There was little or no state provision for them, and families were less willing to look after aged and often infirm grandparents and relatives.

Naples is a Third World city. It is a place that excites strong feelings of like or dislike among those from the North. It is only 180 kilometres from Rome, little more than two hours by train. But it feels a different world. It has long been dubbed the only oriental city without a European quarter. It provides many of the old stereotypes of the Italians: the voluptuous women (Sophia Loren); the bag snatching; the appalling public services; the noisy Vespas. At the same time, it has one of the country's top universities, and its foremost school of oriental studies. It has the leading museum of ancient Roman and Greek sculpture. Neapolitan intellectuals and dramatists have made a disproportionate contribution to Italian arts. Pipo Daniele, Italy's nearest thing to a rhythm 'n' blues star, is the best-known of a galaxy of Italian entertainers who have melded foreign, mainly American, influences with traditional forms. Its satirists are acknowledged to be the best. Humour is particularly regional in Italy. But Naples in modern times has provided many of the comedians who have achieved national fame such as Eduardo De Filippo, and, in the case of Dario Fo, an international reputation.

Hundreds of thousands of people in and around Naples owed their livelihoods to one of two bosses: the local political barons whose networks of patronage extended to every area of economic activity in the city, or the Camorra, the Mafia organization which far more than the Sicilian Cosa Nostra still provided a role model for the young and opportunities for personal enrichment. Naples more than anywhere in Italy was a city where the citizen had no rights. The only way for the mass of the population to survive was by going cap in hand to one or other of these bosses, and selling themselves for a chance to get a leg up. It was a combination which held a high risk of an explosion. For should any concerted effort be made by the authorities to clean up the rampant political corruption or combat the drugs traffickers, then the city's two main employers, indeed almost the sole employers, would in effect be removed from the marketplace. Unless the state were to step in, risks of social tension would be very high.

Are the differences so great? A native of Bolzano of Neapolitan origin feels Italian. It became a cliché to say that the only thing that united the Italians was the blue team, meaning not Belladonna and Garozzo – the world-champion bridge players of the 1960s – but the national football squad. How much was done to integrate Sicily into the national consciousness by the starring role of the busy little Sicilian striker Toto Schillaci, top scorer in the 1990 World Cup finals played in Rome? This also in the year when the official government map of Italy for its presidency of the European Community excluded both Sicily and Sardinia.

Regional differences, on a cultural level, have lessened greatly since unification was achieved in 1870. The single most important unifying factor has been language. The founding fathers of Italy were confronted in many ways with a challenge similar to those of countries founded on immigration such as the United States, Australia or Israel. That is, how to forge a common sense of belonging to a shared culture and national identity when most did not speak the same language, and so could not understand each other. A measure of this was the fact that many of those who led the struggle to establish the unified state did not speak Italian. Most, being from Piedmont, spoke French. The first king of a united Italy, Victor Emmanuel, never mastered the language. Modern Italian itself is a literary language which has evolved out of Tuscan, although the modern Florentine accent, with its 'c' rendered like a guttural Spanish *jota*, is not current elsewhere.

At the time of the start of the process of unification in 1861 fewer than one in ten – some say only 2.5 per cent – of the population spoke any recognizable form of Italian. It was a literary language of the educated classes, and spoken by only a small number. Most spoke dialect, were it Venetian, Neapolitan, Lombard or Sicilian, or those different languages such as Sard.

By the 1990s, however, only about one in seven spoke no Italian, but only dialect. These tended to be among the old, and in places where truancy from school was high, such as Naples and the South. Various factors had pushed the standardization of language: Mussolini's drive to promote Italianness, the *leva* or military service, where dialect was forbidden (though in practice merely discouraged) and the internal migration of Southerners to the North to man the great industrial plants of Milan, Turin and Genoa. It was first radio and then, more importantly, the advent of television in the 1950s that had the greatest impact. Newspapers, too, even in regions of Sicily and Naples where dialect is still widely spoken, are written in Italian. Purists lament the price paid, in terms of a progressive impoverishment of the everyday vocabulary. Yet Italians of all backgrounds generally have an articulateness and fluency that few other people can match.

Regional variations persist. In a politically inspired move to resurrect Babel in Italy's green and pleasant land, on the eve of the formation of the single European market, Italy's chamber of deputies approved a bill to allow minority languages to be taught in nursery and primary schools. Italian democracy already allowed every sector of society a voice. It was now prepared to allow them to speak in their own tongues.

The initiative was a further step away from the centralizing, Italianizing inheritance of Mussolini. The languages and dialects would be permitted to be used in government offices, at first in conversation rather than in written documents. Access was to be given to state-run broadcasting. Street names, Italianized under Mussolini, could revert to their original spellings. Of course, this already was the case in some areas: the names of villages around Trieste were given in Slovene and Italian; and in Alto Adige (Südtirol), in German and Italian.

The designated languages included Provençal French (in Valle d'Aosta and Turin); Friulano (in Gorizia and Udine, in the north-east); Ladino (in Bolzano and Trento); Occitano (in Turin and Cosenza); Sard (in Sardinia); Slovene (in Trieste, Gorizia and Udine); German (in Bolzano and elsewhere in the North); Albanian (in Palermo, Foggia and other places where Albanian communities had settled in the past centuries); Catalan (in Sassari); Croatian (in Campobasso); and Greek (in Lecce, near Homer's birthplace, and Reggio Calabria).

The bill was passed despite a last-minute appeal by a group of Italian intellectuals to the Socialist and Communist Parties to cast a no vote. 'We appeal to you to vote against the bill that represents a blow against the cultural unity of the Italian nation,' the intellectuals wrote, 'which threatens to plunge the country into that provincialism that has always accompanied the darkest moments of our secular and pluralist society.' One academic complained that the bill would 'force children to learn two languages, when they have few facilities to master one'.

The bill's proponents said that it enshrined in law respect for different cultural identities, a source of rich diversity in a country such as Italy. There was also a political motive. They were attempting to undermine support for the regionalist Leagues, particularly the Lombard League, by borrowing from its vocabulary. The League had long emphasized the legitimacy and respectability of dialect as part of its separate cultural identity. It had made some half-hearted attempts to promote Lombard songs and poetry recitals, but with limited success only. Yet opponents feared that the bill's provisions would merely accelerate the very centrifugal process it was seeking to arrest.

Language is only one unifying factor. Morality, or the lack of it, is another. The eminent journalist Enzo Biagi (born in Bologna, but based in Milan) asked in his book *L'Italia dei Peccatori* whether Italians sinned equally in the North and in the South. The work of a Southern magistrate in Milan revealed that corruption and venality were as extensive in the North as in the South. The attribute of *furbismo*, of sly cunning, is a national characteristic. Why else have foreign companies shied away from doing business in Milan as readily as in Messina, in Genoa as readily as in Gela? The excuse given was the difficulty for outsiders in breaking into the local market, or their inability to do things the Italian way. This was barely concealed coded language for saying they could not do business in a climate so corrupt that they had to pay bribes at every turn.

The differences between the people in the different regions are, of course, huge. How could they not be, given their greatly varying histories and racial inputs and cultures? You see it immediately in the body language and in the disparities of wealth between North and South. Yet the similarities far outweigh the differences. It makes little odds whether an Italian comes from Reggio Calabria or Reggio Emilia, from Rome or Rimini, so many features are unmistakably and uniquely Italian. The warmth, the vivaciousness, the importance they all place on human relationships, whether in business or other day-to-day dealings, all these are common throughout the peninsula south of the Alps.

It is certainly harder to define what constitutes being Italian than to define, say, the characteristics of Sicilians or Sardinians. That is why Marcella Hazan asserted that Italian cooking as such did not exist, only regional dishes. Every region has its specialities, as the names of dishes suggest: ragù alla Bolognese, saltimbocca alla Romana, risotto alla Milanese, fegato alla Veneziana, bistecca alla Fiorentina, pizza Napolitana and so on. Yet these are variations on a theme. From an outside perspective, they do not appear so dissimilar.

Each pasta dish may have its regional sauce. But every Italian eats pasta. From the Alps to a point in Sicily, which lies south of

Tunis, the basis for the daily dish of pasta is durum wheat. And every Italian eats it.

A Milanese might feel himself closer to a Bavarian in culture and outlook than to someone from Calabria, which is definitely further away. Yet, in many ways, a Milanese and a Calabrian have much more in common than either would care to admit. Italians, in short, are like tesserae, the pieces of a mosaic. All separate, and of different size and colour. But the pieces add up to a recognizable whole. And this, when all is said and done, is greater than the sum of its parts.

SIX

Myths and mysteries

Carlo Mazzantini was a man with a mission. A mission to explain. We had met once before, when he invited me to a dinner party at his farmhouse to celebrate the selection of his novel *In Search of a Glorious Death* (*A Cercar la Bella Morte*) for *The Independent*'s monthly award for foreign fiction in translation. Carlo lived near Tivoli with his Irish wife, the painter Anne Donnelly, and he worked in central Rome on the Italian encyclopedia.

We arranged to meet near his office, in the Piazza Venezia. Under the balcony. *The* balcony? I asked half-jokingly. Yes, he insisted. Well, where else? After all, it was a precise spot, which everyone knew. It was a balcony as celebrated as Juliet's in Verona. For it was from this balcony that Mussolini had harangued the mob below during his twenty years as supreme leader.

Carlo's book was remarkable in two ways. It was one of the few works of Italian fiction to attempt to explain how it was that young men in the summer and autumn of 1943 had ignored the calls to join the advancing Allied forces, after they had landed in Southern Italy, and instead headed north to join ranks with the Fascists. It was therefore rare in not glorifying the heroic exploits of the partisans and the resistance. And it created scarcely a murmur in Italy.

Carlo Mazzantini's thesis, broadly speaking, was that Italians had never really come to terms with their past. His view of current events was that the failure to acknowledge and atone for the sins of the past had led to the present situation. The Fascist period had simply been swept under the carpet. Yet, he maintained, Fascism had sprung from a fertile Italian soil. Mussolini was not an aberration, but the prototype of the virile new man. With his bombastic rhetoric about patriotic sacrifice and dying for noble causes totally at variance with reality, he was archetypically Italian. And most youths of Mazzantini's generation, born after Mussolini's 1922 march on Rome – which, of course, never took place – who had been exposed to social and cultural influences that were exclusively Fascist, could not help but be Fascists themselves.

In his book, the protagonist is also called Carlo, and speaks in the first person. When on 25 July 1943 Il Duce's powers are taken away by the Grand Council, Carlo's father suffers a moral collapse. At this moment Carlo chooses to run away from home to join a Blackshirt battalion. Some 6,000 or 7,000 enlisted, in a vain attempt to defend the honour of Italy as they saw it. Theirs was a brutal war. They were not deployed to check the advance of the Allied forces, but sent to Piedmont in the north to fight in what became an increasingly bitter and bloody civil war. Italians were fighting Italians. In one village square Carlo witnesses the death by firing squad of a group of captured partisans. One nobleman refuses to die. After he is shot, his right foot continues to shake. He is despatched with a second volley. At some point Carlo is captured in his turn by a Milanese mob. He is kept in a temporary prison for a few days, then released by his partisan adversaries, who show more humanity than he does. The book is not told as a straight narrative. Wartime experiences are mixed with accounts of later encounters, of meetings with former comrades-in-arms, many of whom try to forget the past. It is a book whose purpose is not to justify but to explain.

Mazzantini's was only one aspect of the war. Between 1945 and 1947 more than one million Italian soldiers, who had been sent abroad in defence of the *patria*, returned home to an Italy which wanted to forget, and wished them to expunge the memory. Every effort was made to stop the formation of veterans' associations, lest these became too strong as they had after the First World War, in which Italy fought alongside the victorious Allies. The Second World War was a trauma for the country itself. Italy was made smaller, after it was forced to cede territory in the Istria peninsula to Yugoslavia in what are now Slovenia and Croatia.

The political system that arose out of the ashes of defeat in the Second World War was one of consensus, where compromise and the ability to reconcile seeming opposites took precedence over promoting a strongly argued policy line. The postwar political settlement was an attempt to avoid a repetition of the past, to prevent a Fascist dictator assuming power once more, through a series of checks and balances, without addressing the problem of what it was in the Italian people, rather than the system, that permitted Mussolini's hijacking of the institutions of the state.

In the half-century since the Italians signed an armistice with the Allies, Italian leaders have tended to romanticize the role played by the resistance in the overthrow of Fascism. At least fifty institutes, libraries or special archives were set up to record the glorious exploits of the resistance. (As a corrective, two centres have been set up, one in Pisa and the other in Rome, to study the manipulation of history by politicians.) The resistance became like the civil religion of the state. To declare oneself an ex-partisan had the same political cachet the former resistance fighters enjoyed in France. Nearly 70 per cent of the resistance sprang from the ranks of the Communist Party. Among other resistance figures who were not Communists was the veteran political figure Ugo La Malfa, whose Partito d'Azione was made up of Liberals and Democrats. Those trumpeting the importance of the Italian resistance point to Germany where there was none of significance at all. Yet at its height the Italian resistance probably numbered no more than 100,000, scarcely enough to have a major impact on the course of the war. The Christian Democrats only joined after the removal of Mussolini by the King on 25 July 1943.

In truth, Mussolini was not swept away by a groundswell of popular feeling from below, but summarily dismissed in what was essentially a coup d'état from above by the man who had appointed him twenty-one years previously, King Victor Emmanuel III. Furthermore, only part of the country took part in what was variously seen as an armed liberation struggle or a civil war. The whole of Sicily and the South were liberated by the Allies before the partisans started their operations. Accordingly, the South was unable to claim it took part in what became the founding myth of the republic, that the republic was born of the resistance. It immediately set the South at a disadvantage.

In 1992 a researcher at Turin University, Romolo Gobbi, published a slim volume entitled *Il Mito della Resistenza* (The

Myth of the Resistance). It was dismissed by serious historians like Claudio Pavone as a scurrilous tract. But it made some attempt to debunk some of the unchallenged myths of Italian postwar history. Gobbi noted that the absence of any serious acts of revenge against known Fascist sympathizers was the strongest indication that, in fact, most people were sympathetic to the Fascists. He wrote that the need to create a new national myth after the Second World War and following the twenty years of Fascism led historians and politicians to make up a credible one, which would absolve Italians from any sense of blame for being Fascist and having sided with the Nazis. Whole sections of the political parties were named Martyrs of the Resistance. Resistance songs acquired popularity. Echoing Mazzantini he wrote that 'the anti-Fascist front, which it was necessary to maintain at all costs, prevented the formation in Italy of a real alternating system between government and opposition.'

Some historians have tended to look at the series of strikes at Fiat and other factories in the North in March 1943 as the first internal challenge to Mussolini's grip. Yet it is debatable how much effect such strikes had on the regime. As for the resistance, no one knows how many victims there were. Official figures list 44,720 partisans who fell during the war (other figures speak of 31,000, as well as 400,000 other Italians killed). No account was kept of how many of these were killed in accidents or through their own inexperience. And in 1991 an episode was recounted by an ex-partisan in his seventies which put the resistance in a less pure light. The Communist partisan confessed publicly for the first time to killing the parish priest of San Martino in Casole a year after the end of the war on 4 July 1946, for his supposed collaboration with the Fascists after the 1943 armistice.

The Catholic historian Pietro Scoppola, whose political role in the 1990s is in seeking to establish a bridge to the left, has argued that, on the contrary, Italy has produced a mass of research on the Fascist period. He contends that Fascism is the point of reference for the study of contemporary history. One could not come to terms with the problems of the country without making a judgement on Fascism. For Italian democracy was in its nature anti-Fascist. Anti-Fascism could only be achieved by first defining what the Fascist past represented, and furthermore what it was in the Italians that made them renounce the Liberal experiment at the beginning of the century in favour of Mussolini.

Many Italians, however, have taken a rosy view of their past. They contrasted the Fascist experience favourably with the brutality of the Nazis in Germany, glibly overlooking the violence of Mussolini's regime. I once overheard an elderly gentleman at Bologna railway station – yes, Bologna the Red – bemoaning the fact that the trains were running more than an hour late. 'It wouldn't have happened before, during the time of . . .' His wife cut him off with a swift jab in the ribs (it was equally a myth that Mussolini made the trains run on time, although he did improve the service). Many Italians also failed to appreciate to what extent Italy's postwar problems were due to Fascism. It is true that Mussolini created several of the strategic industries which were to survive into future generations. But he also reduced what could have been a leading political force in Western Europe into a backwater.

The Fascist past lives on. It is faced in travertine in the architecture of courts of justice up and down the land. It survives with dubious legality in the neo-Fascist party the MSI. Dubious because the law bans Fascist parties, yet the MSI regularly obtains 5 per cent of the vote, and twice that number in Naples. It was an absurdity of Italian public life that Alessandra Mussolini, the granddaughter of Il Duce, could sit in parliament, while the ban remained on any descendant of Italy's monarchy, the House of Savoy, from setting foot once more on Italian soil. Italy had not been well served by its monarchs, it is true. Victor Emmanuel III, as already noted, both entrusted Mussolini with government and then dismissed him. His predecessor, Victor Emmanuel II, was a symbol of national sovereignty in the process of political unification, the Risorgimento, after 1861. Yet in that process, too, Italians only managed to secure a unified state for themselves with the help of outside powers, and Italians fought on both sides of the conflict. The struggles to build and preserve Italy have never enjoyed the total support of the population on the peninsula.

Italy's Fascist past is seen outside the country more in terms of its international implications, especially Mussolini's alliance with

Hitler, than of what it meant domestically. Inside Italy, the legacy of the Fascist experience was to drive the country to seek compromise and accommodation in foreign policy as well as in national political life. Since the end of the Second World War, Italian foreign policy has stood on three main legs: support for Nato; membership of the European Community and pursuit of European integration; and encouraging relations with Middle East oil and gas producers on which Italy is heavily dependent. Italy has always regarded itself as an essentially European country and it was only natural that it should be a founder member of the European Community. The benefits were huge, the costs small. At one stage, Italy received 60 per cent of all funds for development from the European Investment Bank, although by 1993 this had fallen to 25 per cent.

In the first years after the war, Italy turned eagerly to the United States for financial and political support, first for the reconstruction of the country, then for monetary handouts for the Christian Democratic Party. Italy also played a key role in Nato, less as a provider of costly front-line troops than as a supplier of the bases where others could be stationed. Italy knew that the benefits in terms of relations with the United States far outweighed the possible domestic political risks of being too closely identified with Nato. Despite the strongly pacifist streak in Italian Catholicism, Italy joined Nato in 1949. Thereafter it successfully behaved as the most reliable US ally. When General De Gaulle pulled France out of Nato's military command in 1967, Italy was happy to welcome the transfer of the US Sixth Fleet in the Mediterranean from Villefranche to Naples. When the Spanish decided in a fit of nationalist pride to close the Nato frontline air bases, Italy popped up with a replacement at Crotone, in the south. When the US was obliged to redeploy theatre nuclear weapons and Pershing II missiles in response to the Soviet deployment of SS20 missiles, they found a home in Italy. It was a policy which cost nothing and paid huge dividends, political and financial. The air base in Crotone was, in the event, never completed. Congress scrapped it for budgetary reasons. And money paid for initial work to contractors who had signed the necessary disavowal of any association with organized crime was largely diverted to the Mafia gangs.

On several occasions, however, Italy did assert its national sovereignty and refused to accede to US requests for military assistance on the grounds that the issues did not fall under the ambit of Nato. The first was a refusal to allow bases in Italy to be used for the resupply of arms to Israel during the 1967 Arab–Israeli war. The second was in 1985, when US fighters had intercepted the Egyptair plane carrying Abul Abbas, the Palestinian mastermind of the hijacking of the *Achille Lauro* cruise ship, and forced it down at the joint US–Italian base at Sigonella. There was an armed confrontation on the tarmac between US and Italian troops. Prime minister Bettino Craxi stood firm and Abul Abbas went free. Neither this action nor Italy's close ties with North African hydrocarbon producers – Italy imports 90 per cent of its energy requirements – prevented an attack by Palestinian gunmen on the check-in counter of the Israeli airline El Al at Rome's Fiumicino airport on 27 December 1985 in which sixteen people were killed.

Then US and Italian forces clashed over method and approach when both were deployed in the UN peacekeeping force in Somalia in 1993. The dispute was portrayed as Machiavelli versus Rambo, with the Italians believing in negotiation and dialogue to avoid bloody confrontation with the complex warring factions in Mogadishu, and the United States using force to impose their will.

The close relationship with the United States has provoked a new school of study, to which all can subscribe, known as the 'secret history of the Republic', or 'Italy of the mysteries'. Such writing of history is the polar opposite of the history of the Fascist period. Then the facts were known but the national myths were subsequently woven around them. More recent events, those of the past twenty-odd years, have not been satisfactorily explained, for lack of evidence. The history of modern Italy is run through with intrigue and enigmas. It is a history peopled with subversive secret-service agents, terrorists, the Mafia, corrupt bankers, Free-masons, and outside powers. Few satisfactory or conclusive explanations have been formulated for a series of violent acts in the 1970s and 1980s. Newspapers regularly print the list of these unsolved mysteries.

The first such incident took place on 12 December 1969. A huge bomb exploded in the lobby of the Banca dell'Agricoltura in the Piazza Fontana in Milan. The explosion killed sixteen and wounded eighty-eight. Two other bombs went off simultaneously in Rome. On 22 July 1970 a train was derailed as it was passing Gioia Tauro in Calabria, killing seven. Other incidents followed. On 28 May 1974, eight people were killed and ninety-four injured by a bomb thrown at an anti-Fascist rally at the Piazza della Loggia in Brescia, in Lombardy. A couple of months later, on 4 August, the Bologna to Munich express, known as the *Italicus*, was hit as it was leaving a tunnel at San Benedetto Val di Sambro. In this, twelve were killed and a hundred and five injured. A similar explosion ripped through train number 904 on 23 December 1984, killing fifteen.

Ghastly though these incidents were in terms of loss of life, they pale before the carnage of the bloodiest single terrorist incident in Europe up to that time, the bomb in the second-class waiting room at Bologna railway station at the height of the tourist season on 2 August 1980 which killed eighty-five people.

There were, of course, other incidents. For in the climate of revolutionary change that swept Europe after 1968, Italy was subject to the kind of terrorization by ultra-left-wing groups that afflicted other countries. Most of those attacks in Italy were associated with the Red Brigades, culminating in (though not ending with) the kidnapping on 16 March 1978 and murder fifty-four days later on 9 May of Aldo Moro, secretary-general and therefore highest-ranking member of the Christian Democrat Party. Moro was snatched as he was about to attend a session of parliament to vote on the new government, in which in a historic compromise the Christian Democrats were to have the support of the Italian · Communist Party. It was the first time that the Communist Party was to be 'in the area of government'. Moro's five escorts were killed in the ambush. During his captivity, Moro wrote a series of anguished letters to his former party colleagues, begging them to negotiate his release. The government stood firm, and Moro's bullet-riddled body was found in the boot of a car eight weeks later.

The Red Brigades grew out of Italian universities and quickly began to embrace factory workers and post-office workers mainly from northern Italy. They were united in the idea of striking at the heart of the state. Other organizations of the revolutionary left included Lotta Continua, Prima Linea, Nuclei Armati Proletari, and Autonomia Operaia. For more than a decade, Italy was plagued by *gli anni di piombo* (the years of lead). Northern industrialists still recall the fear with which they would go to work each day, scared that they would be kneecapped, or worse, by these would-be revolutionaries. The state was not prepared to forgive these urban terrorists easily. Their leader, Renato Curcio, was not allowed temporary release from prison until 1993.

It has never seriously been suggested that the Red Brigades were behind any of the unsolved mysteries. But they provided one side of the historical context in which they took place. It is not my purpose to seek to identify the perpetrators of any or all of these massacres. The Italian magistrates have failed to secure any convictions. It would be impudent and imprudent to point a finger. But it is worthwhile to consider what Italians themselves think about these incidents, and why.

The most popular spectator sport in Italy, more so even than football, is *dietrologia*. Roughly translated, this means looking at the facts behind the facts, seeing who is doing what to whom and why. Once upon a time it was easy. To the byzantine Italian mind, these unsolved outrages had a logic of their own. The left always saw the CIA and the Italian security services behind the 'black terrorism'. The right would point to the hidden hand of the Bulgarians or the Czechs working through the Italian Communist Party. No one would accept the simplest, most obvious solution, nor would they contemplate that a magistrate could possibly be conducting an investigation except under orders from his or her control. The end of the Cold War has rather spoiled the game, and changed the rules under which *dietrologia* works. As in so much of the Italian *modus operandi*, the players are waiting eagerly for the formulation of a new set of rules.

The conspiracy theorists, however, have accumulated a huge amount of mainly circumstantial evidence to demonstrate that the security services, working under the tutelage of the Americans and co-ordinated by the P2 Masonic Lodge under their Venerable Master Licio Gelli, had been behind the 'strategy of tension' in the 1970s. When P2 was uncovered in 1981, it was found to constitute an entire network of anti-Communist forces. The lodge membership lists found in Gelli's possession included senior officers from all branches of the military, top secret-service chiefs, two score members of the two houses of parliament, cabinet ministers, judges, journalists and prominent figures in industry and finance. P2, according to Tina Anselmi, the head of the parliamentary commission which looked into its activities, 'tried to influence and condition political life in our country above all by acting through the security services, which it controlled for many years.'

The supposed purpose of the strategy of tension was to create such panic in the population that they would shy away from voting Communist, at a time when the party's electoral support was growing to the point where it might in time have been able to form the government. Some more extreme elements went further, and aimed to bring down the democratic system and replace it with an authoritarian regime.

The result cannot be refuted: eight otherwise unsolved bomb attacks over fifteen years which claimed nearly 150 lives. (The plane crash off Ustica was a mystery, but of a different sort.) The courts have in the end had little success. In 1988 the Bologna assize court convicted four right-wing terrorists of planting the bomb at Bologna railway station. They were sentenced to life imprisonment. Licio Gelli was sentenced to seven years' imprisonment for his role – a part he strenuously denied. Two years later the convictions were overturned on appeal. Then a Bologna court also quashed the convictions of two neo-Fascists who had been sentenced to life imprisonment for the 1974 *Italicus* train bombing.

In February 1989, a Florence assize court convicted three members of the Neapolitan Camorra and two of the Sicilian Cosa Nostra of the 23 December 1984 bombing of train number 904. The court ruled that the five had worked with right-wing terrorists to give the impression that political violence was still an issue, and so divert attention away from the fight against organized crime. Most prominent of those convicted was Pippo Calò, a major figure in Cosa Nostra. Two years later the Court of Cassation overturned the guilty verdict for lack of evidence. A retrial was ordered. Finally, in February 1993, the Supreme Court confirmed the sentence against Pippo Calò and his Mafia accomplices.

The corpus of circumstantial evidence that the secret services, or elements within them, were behind the 'black terrorism' came with the official confirmation of the longtime existence of a special covert force set up in Italy by Nato. This was Gladio, named after the short double-edged sword used by Roman gladiators. Anywhere else, the acknowledgement that the Italian authorities had secretly maintained a specially trained force for the defence of the realm after a possible invasion by Warsaw Pact forces would have been greeted as reassuring evidence that they were truly concerned about the fundamental duty of any state to protect the integrity of the country against external threats. Not so in Italy. When prime minister Giulio Andreotti confirmed in 1990 what had been widely known, many other questions were asked. Was its purpose merely to resist an external agressor? Or was it rather to fight the enemy within, as they were perceived in some quarters, namely the Communists? Had either Gladio, or members of it, been behind the spate of terrorist incidents which had at the time been pinned on the left?

Andreotti announced that Gladio was a small force of between 600 and 1,000 specialists organized in forty independent cells, responsible for intelligence gathering, sabotage, running escape routes and guerrilla warfare. They had been trained by American and British secret service experts at Cape Marrargiu, on the Northern tip of Sardinia. They had set up 139 arms dumps around the country, mainly in the North-east near Gorizia where any Soviet invasion was expected to pass. Since then, according to the prime minister, 127 had been recovered, ten more had been built over, and two were unaccounted for. Could these, it was asked, have been used either by rogue elements within the secret services, or Gladio members, for the perpetration of these unsolved attacks?

The catalyst for the revelations about Gladio was the inquiries made by a young investigating magistrate in Venice, Felice Casson. He and his colleague Carlo Mastelloni were delving into two unsolved mysteries. One was the death by a booby-trapped car of three carabinieri in 1972 in the Veneto village of Petreano. The other was the mid-air explosion aboard a military aircraft, the Argo 16, on 23 November 1973.

Two neo-Fascists were eventually convicted for the Petreano bombing, the only bombing in which an individual actually declared his complicity. Vincenzo Vinciguerra, who was sentenced to life imprisonment, went further. He told a magistrate that all the bombings after 1969 were linked to an 'apparatus belonging to the state'. Was he telling the truth? If so, was this Gladio?

Two other cases deepened the mystery about the purpose of Gladio. In 1967 it came out that during 1964 the head of the carabinieri, General Giovanni De Lorenzo, had been planning to put into effect Piano Solo (Operation Solo). General De Lorenzo had earlier been head of SIFAR, the domestic intelligence agency of the time, when he built up more than 100,000 files on Socialists, Communists and trades unionists, indeed anybody who might be seen as a possible subversive. Was Piano Solo really a dress rehearsal for Gladio? A parliamentary commission later ruled that General De Lorenzo had breached the constitution but had not actually been planning a coup d'état.

Then in 1970 a second bid was made to subvert the democratic authorities, in a coup attempt by Prince Valerio Borghese, a former Fascist navy commander who founded the right-wing Fronte Nazionale in 1968. The aim of the coup was to seize control of the interior ministry, as well as the foreign and defence ministries, the broadcasting station, and parliament. Left-wingers were to be rounded up and transhipped to islands off Sicily. The coup attempt fizzled into farce. And in the fullness of time those implicated and convicted of taking part were all acquitted on appeal. The full story, however, has yet to emerge. At least one Mafia *pentito* has declared that the Cosa Nostra was approached about joining the coup.

In the early 1990s, rumours of a coup being plotted by the carabinieri and the security forces circulated with the frequency normally associated less with a modern European state than with a comic opera. But, as so often, warnings of possible impending coup bids hardly coincided with the reality: the carabinieri or undermanned army were neither willing nor able to take control and put tanks on the streets. The warnings were merely the soundings off of one political faction seeking gains at the expense of another.

Dietrologia reached its zenith with the case of Ustica. Ustica is a small island that lies 160 kilometres north of Sicily. It was off Ustica that on 27 June 1980 eighty-one passengers and crew aboard a DC-9 airliner perished when it plunged into the sea. Flight IH-870 of the now defunct domestic airline Itavia had left Bologna two hours late on a routine flight to Palermo. At 8.56 p.m. it disappeared from radar screens. No Mayday was ever picked up. No satisfactory explanation has been forthcoming for the families of those who died in the crash. The plane is widely believed to have been brought down by a missile.

Many of the grounds for suspicion derive from what is considered the evasiveness and misleading information supplied by the Italian armed forces and their intelligence wings. Seven air-force generals were charged with lying about what happened. Why was it that the air-force radar stations had no record on tape of the flight? Transcripts of conversations by Italian pilots omitted the crucial hours around the crash.

Twelve years on, investigating magistrates were expressing their belief that the plane was brought down by a missile, probably fired by a Nato fighter. Yet they were making their assessment at a time when only a tiny part of the wreckage had been recovered. Much still lay on the sea bed. Some had been recovered, first by a French company, then by a British one. But much more evidence lay under water.

Whatever happened that night, the attitude of the authorities to the inquiry has strained further the relationship between citizens and the institutions of the Italian state. Hence the distrust expressed towards the secret services, and the fertile imagination of the conspiracy theorists. Various theories produced are:

- the plane flew into a huge aerial dogfight and was shot down by mistake
- the plane was mistaken for one taking the Libyan leader Colonel Gadafi back from a meeting in Yugoslavia and was shot down in error
- the plane was carrying arms for a coup to be engineered by Libyan dissidents in Tobruk and it was shot down by the Libyan air force
- a missile exploded outside the plane
- a missile passed through the plane
- there was a bomb on board

- the plane crashed at sea and was then sunk by frogmen from a Nato submarine to bury the evidence
- it was shot down by a sea-to-air missile from a French submarine

The story sheds more light on how Italians view the institutions of the state than on what really happened. One leading journalist for whom Ustica has become an obsession confessed: 'Any serious journalist in Italy must confront the question of Ustica. And when you do, you find yourself questioning everything. The trouble is that *dietrologia* is infectious. Was Falcone killed by the Mafia, or by the security service? Of course he was killed by the Mafia. It's crazy even to ask such a question. But you don't know what to believe any more. You can't be sure of anything any more.'

It was the lament of one who had seen every attempt at reform or renewal in Italy since the war confronted by an eruption of unexplained or at least unsolved acts of violence. It was widely believed in society as a whole that the perpetrators of these acts of violence lay within the apparatus of the state and not outside it. And it was in part because of this mistrust of the state and some of its agents that people as always fell back on the one institution in which they had implicit faith: the family.

SEVEN

Family matters

When Beppe Severgnini returned to Italy after a five-year stint in London as correspondent for the daily newspaper *Il Giornale*, there was nothing more natural than that his father should offer him one floor in his house. And nothing more natural than that Severgnini should accept. It was not only the poor who lived in an extended family, although financial constraints were the principal reason for staying at home. Nor was living at home necessarily more common among more traditional communities in southern Italy. Severgnini's father was a professional man, a lawyer. Severgnini's parents were both Northerners. It was for him primarily a question of personal preference. He felt at home, well, at home. There were none of the conflictual tensions that so often mark the relationship between children and parents in northern Europe, and none of the social stigma of living under the same roof. There were benefits too. His mother would cook lunch for his wife and him whenever they wished. It was an offer his wife took up several times during the week. Not only was it simpler, but the family actually enjoyed each other's company.

Family in Italy means much more than grown-up children taking round their tray of cakes, freshly purchased and specially wrapped, to the parental home for Sunday lunch or major holidays. The family represents more than the great occasions, the weddings and the christenings and the first communions, which are celebrated with such evident gusto. Family provides the network of the deepest and most important relationships of Italian society. Now the same could be said of most other societies, but in Italy the family has a hold on loyalty which is so strong, so tenacious, so resistant to the evolution of other norms of behaviour that it can still rightly be called the basic building block of society. In every decade commentators have remarked that despite the apparent changes in Italian society, the shrinking birthrate, the growing numbers of divorces, the greater social mobility, the family unit is virtually impregnable. Luigi Barzini in the 1960s and Peter Nichols, *The Times*'s veteran correspondent in his *Italia, Italia* in the 1970s, had warned against overemphasizing apparent assaults on the ascendancy of the family. Nadio Delai, director of the social research institute Censis, told me in 1992 that 'Families are smaller, there is more divorce, and there are fewer children. The traditional large family no longer exists. But the great strength of society is still the family. The family has changed. But the family linkage is still very important.'

The family history of a friend of mine illustrates perfectly how the institution had seemed to change dramatically in appearance, yet in substance remained fundamentally the same. He had seven brothers and sisters. His wife had six brothers. All of their brothers and sisters were married. Each and every one of them had precisely one child, with one exception, a brother who had none. Each of them in other words, despite their own family histories, had seen fit to have just one child. They all fell short of replacing themselves. My friend had also done things very differently from the norm. He and his wife had paid for their own wedding. They had received no money from either of their parents to buy a flat to set up their matrimonial home (it was very common for a bride's father to give a wedding gift of an apartment to his daughter). My friend seldom went home to his or his wife's parents for Sunday lunch. They did not have a grandmother living near by who could help with the babysitting. Yet my friend was quite categorical: 'The basic institution of the family has remained unchallenged. Just because it is smaller does not mean it is weaker.' Within the family there had been only some adjustments to the traditional roles. He would cook, but not often. He would bath their daughter, occasionally. As for washing the dishes, well, they had a cleaning lady who came twice a week, and the plates piled up.

Often Italians are best able to articulate what they consider special about their own lives when they have lived abroad. I asked an Italian journalist living in London what he considered to be the main differences between bringing up children in Italy and bringing them up in Northern Europe. 'There are two levels,' he stated, 'the socio-cultural and the practical. On the socio-cultural level, the Italian family is better designed to cope with bringing up children. On a practical level, it is difficult in London to find nursery schools and playgroups.'

In other words, the family might have shrunk, but its centrality has not diminished. No longer will classic Italian films portray screaming children living all on top of each other in a single room in a Naples tenement, with father arriving late, drunk, and grandmother dressed in black mumbling to herself in the corner. The family's change in size has inevitably affected its role, and the balance of relationships within the family. The father and mother of ten children cannot spend as much time with each child as the parents of a single boy or girl. As a secondary result, the relationship between husbands and wives has changed, and the links between brothers and sisters too. On one of those television chat shows, a woman from Naples rang to seek advice on what to do about her first child, who showed great jealousy after the birth of her second child. The chat-show host turned to the resident child psychologist in the studio audience and said, 'You must come across this kind of problem all the time. What do you think?' 'Not at all,' the doctor replied. 'So long as Italians have only one child, the incidence of sibling rivalry is non-existent.'

If Italians are rich and happy, or appear so, it is not because of great independent institutions, of a wise government, of sound investment policies or the provision of lavish social services, it is because of the family. It is the family that is the father of economic success. The family, through its regard for itself, has created and husbanded enormous national wealth in little more than a generation. It is the family that has allowed Italians to raise their standard of living to among the highest in Europe. At the same time, it is the family rather than the state that has ensured that the quality of life in Italy remains so high. The family does not make the sun shine. Nor is it responsible for the natural beauty of the country. But it is truly, and indisputably, the genetic determinant for making the Italians some of the most attractive men and women in the world. Family too is the progenitor of the Italian way of living, of close and warm human relations. The charm and cheerfulness of the Italians comes, above all, from the security which an Italian family brings. As for Italy itself, others have observed, it is not really a country, but a mosaic made up of ten million families.

The hold of the family on its members is not regarded as a form of tyranny in Italy. Rather, as the Catholic Church has long encouraged, the concept of family is the strongest expression of solidarity in Italy. The Church's magazine *Famiglia Cristiana* ('The Christian Family') is one of the most influential and widely sold. Even in post-Catholic Italy, where only a minority are regular churchgoers, family matters. For all sorts of historical, social and cultural reasons, the family has remained paramount. It was the family that was forced to look after itself in the absence of help from a welfare state. It may have been the state which led the economic boom of 1958–63 with its massive investment programmes, but it lagged behind in the provision of social services. Families as always would turn inwards, and rely on themselves, using their newly acquired wealth to provide for health care, nursery schooling, pensions, and a new car given the lack of efficient public transport. Even now, when patients whose beds are crammed into the corridors of overcrowded hospitals in Naples find that kitchen staff are on strike, it is their families who bring them food and change their sheets. And the absence of family today still means the absence of provision. A young mother I knew had no social security from the state, and no help from her ex-husband, nor did she have any recourse in reality when he failed to keep up his maintenance payments.

This almost Third World reliance on the family is not only the source of the strength of Italian society but also its weakness. Italy is a country where the sense of civic responsibility remains very low. The family has reinforced the tendency of Italians not to contribute to the building and maintenance of civil society. The cult of *individualismo*, which means me-firstism rather than originality, has only slightly been tempered by the rise in the numbers doing voluntary work (four million by the early 1990s), a sign perhaps of the emergence of a more caring society. For just as many see the family unit as its strength, because of its human size, and the cohesiveness of its internal relationships, so too others have seen its limitations as the main reason why Italy has a blocked democracy. The building of a modern society needs more than bricks. It needs the framework, reinforcing rods and crossbeams which only properly functioning social institutions can provide, and which in Italy have remained for so long underdeveloped. Some blame the Church for putting private virtue before public virtue. Others blame the party system, yet others the historic mistrust of the state. For their part, the Communists did try to put the collectivist ideal above narrow family interests, but with limited success only.

The family, however, is changing. The typical family in the economic boom of the 1960s and 1970s would have several breadwinners. Every able-bodied member would have a daytime job, usually as an employee of a company or government department, on which he or she would pay tax at source. Then, typically, each would have a second job, in a shop or a bar, or selling goods in the black economy which would escape the taxman.

The generation of this income in time led to the accumulation of wealth. Families would pool their resources to invest in property, or high-interest-paying state bonds. They might buy a garage or a workshop. Most bought their own homes. Some 60 to 70 per cent of Italians – depending on whose statistics you trust – own their own homes. And 14 per cent have a second home for weekends. People would still have two or maybe sometimes three jobs, but increasingly families generated wealth from assets rather than earned income.

Most of the great success stories in Italian manufacturing industry, as we have seen in Emilia and the Third Italy between Bologna and Rome, have been family-run concerns. In the largest private company of all, Fiat, control passes dynastically through the Agnelli family. And even when companies are not the creation of a family combining its human and financial resources, often the founder will seek to make it a family firm. In 1990 Leonardo Del Vecchio declared to the authorities the highest taxable income of any man or woman in Italy. Not bad for someone who had come from nowhere. For Del Vecchio was brought up in an orphanage in Milan. His father died five months before his birth in 1935. In fifty years he built up his company Luxottica into a world leader in spectacles manufacture, making glasses for all the top designers, from Armani to Byblos, Yves Saint Laurent to Valentino. By 1991 turnover was 460 billion lire (£200 million) and he employed 3,500 workers. Although he started without any parental help, he was going to ensure that his children made the most of the advantages given them. All three worked in the firm, and his eldest son would take over from him in due course.

It is worth considering how one highly successful company exploited ties of blood to run as an efficient business unit. Many of the great fashion houses of Italy are family concerns. The Palazzo Feroni-Spini in the centre of Florence, with its austere Renaissance lines and vaulted ceilings painted with mythical scenes, oozed old money. One of the largest, grandest and finest of the palazzi, it sits imposingly at one end of the Via Tornabuoni, which runs down to the River Arno with the fashion houses dotted on either side.

Appearances deceived. For its incumbent was not some noble scion of an ancient line. Rather, she was the heir to an upstart industrial empire with feet firmly on the ground, feet shod, but always, in the finest leather shoes that craftsmen of the house of Ferragamo can make. It may have been new money that allowed the acquisition of this palace but the same principle of lineage that had kept the palazzo in one family for centuries was destined to ensure the health of this family firm.

Signora Ferragamo was a matronly figure, who dressed with modest and understated elegance. A woman of means – the family empire had a turnover of 217 billion lire (£100 million) in 1991 – no bauble, no gem would be beyond her. Yet the one piece of jewellery she wore was a simple gold chain around her wrist from which dangled eighteen gold dog tags, marked with a name and a date, one for each of her grandchildren. 'And there's another on the way,' she explained with touching pride. But hers was an exception to the trend of small families.

The rise of the house of Ferragamo is one of those mythical stories of rags to riches that is an archetype for so much of successful Italian enterprise. Signora Ferragamo's late husband Salvatore was born in the small village of Bonito, 100 kilometres east of Naples, in 1898. Family lore had it that he was only nine years old when he made his first pair of shoes, a pair of white slippers for his sister's first communion. His parents were poor, and he was obliged to go out to work at a very young age. He was apprenticed to the village shoemakers, then when he was eleven moved to Naples where he was taken on by a fashionable shoemaker.

But, like so many young Southern Italians with drive in those desperate days, he knew his destiny lay elsewhere. He already had four brothers in the United States, working as shoemakers. And in 1914 he sailed to join them. Then began his meteoric rise to become shoemaker to the stars, first in Santa Barbara and then, when the film industry moved, in Hollywood. The customer list for his creations came to read like a Hollywood hall of fame: Rudolph Valentino, Douglas Fairbanks Junior, Marlene Dietrich, Greta Garbo and later Audrey Hepburn, Marilyn Monroe and Sophia Loren.

Ferragamo discovered that he could not find the craftsmen he needed in the United States and in 1927 he returned to Italy. His home area of Naples is renowned for its tailors, glovemakers and other leather workers, but it was to Florence with its long tradition in the leather industry that this uprooted Neapolitan came. He restarted with a workshop with sixty craftsmen, and within a short time had made his first shoes for export to some of his old customers and many new ones in the United States. He also widened his sales area to include Italy. In 1938 he managed to purchase the Palazzo Feroni-Spini.

When Wanda Ferragamo inherited the business on her husband's death in 1960, she knew next to nothing about running the company and the youngest of their six children was only two. She had no knowledge of shoemaking: her father had been the district doctor of Bonito.

It was at this time that the company expanded out of shoemaking into the design and production of other fashion accessories. Yet shoes remained the base of the business. Shoes represented 70 per cent of the entire production, or 60 per cent of turnover. In the difficult years of economic downturn in the United States from 1990 to 1991, Ferragamo was the only such company not to lose money. It registered a 7.5 per cent growth. The company attributed its success to value for money and customer loyalty. 'We have struggled to achieve a good market,' said Signora Ferragamo. 'We don't want to lose it. We suffer when the dollar goes down. Thank God we have a very good structure and very healthy background so we can adjust. The first important thing is not to lose markets. Customers know well the quality of our products.' Another was the tight control the family keeps over all products, steadfastly refusing to give licences to anybody else. There were no signed Ferragamo sunglasses, or watches, or perfumes. Such fripperies would debase the family name, its spokesman said snootily.

Ties of blood were not in themselves enough to ensure employment in the company. The Ferragamo children were not taken on automatically. 'We are not prepared to take them on if they are not well prepared. We have many examples of children who destroyed what they inherited.' Signora Ferragamo did not need to motion in the direction of the house of Gucci across the street, for years riven by internal feuding between heirs of the original empire. 'There is a saying: "When your neighbour's house is on fire, put water on your own."'

Ferragamo is still a family concern. The company is 100 per cent controlled by the family. All six children work for the company. Fiamma, the eldest daughter, is vice-president and in charge of women's shoes and accessories; Giovanna looks after women's ready-to-wear; Fulvia is responsible for silk accessories and scarves; Ferruccio is the chief executive officer (and heir apparent); Leonardo is in charge of development of the markets in Europe and the Far East (the Japanese are great buyers); and Massimo oversees the American market.

Signora Ferragamo was confident that her children would carry on the family labours, and the traditions of making shoes. 'I have been replaced now by my son Ferruccio. He has shown great skill and financial sense. The others concentrate on the creative side or in developing markets. And after them? Then we have the next generation. We borrow very little. Traditions are sacred. Nothing is more important.'

As a general rule, Italians do not lend money, nor do they borrow it. Italy remains a cash society. Credit cards are not widespread.

And people prefer paying cash, which has no trace, to using cheques or bank transactions that might prove of interest to the tax authorities. There are, it must be admitted, loan sharks prowling the shallows of the poorer neighbourhoods to grab those floundering to make ends meet. Yet house mortgages are virtually unheard of. Most Italians only produce wealth by accumulating it, not by borrowing from a bank. Family wealth built up over generations is nearly indestructible; at least it runs little risk of being broken up by easily avoided inheritance tax.

Many Italians flaunt wealth in the way that those who have only recently acquired it often do. In the 1980s they discovered the sea. Or rather, the gin palaces that float around on it. There was no point in putting out to sea if they would then no longer be visible. So many people had luxury yachts that in a futile and unpopular bid to generate more income the government placed a special tax not just on the purchase of boats but on their ownership, payable annually. Boating was the craze even before Italians took pride in Raul Gardini's *Il Moro di Venezia* competing in the America's Cup in 1992. Nor was it politically incorrect for the leader of the former Communist Party, Achille Occhetto, to be seen holidaying at the helm of a spanking ocean racer.

How could they all afford it? The majority of Italians, sailors and landlubbers alike, were BOT people. BOT – government savings bonds – were traditionally the safest means of saving. Since most of the better-off self-employed generally underdeclared their incomes to the tax office, the net revenue for the state was reduced, the need for additional financing for state expenditure through borrowing rose, and, lo and behold, the non-tax payers had more money to lend to the hard-pressed treasury. Italians were the world's greatest savers after the Japanese, saving up to 25 per cent of their income in some areas. The BOT were the most popular vehicle for saving. They offered higher rates of interest than the banks. The Milan stock exchange, capitalized at less than one-eighth of the London stock exchange, and manipulated by insider dealing, was treated, like so many Italian institutions, with suspicion. And even after Italy finally lifted controls on the flow of capital, there was no rush out of lire into US dollars or Swiss francs, there was no run on the lira. Furthermore, because of the fiscal imbalances, the Italian economy did not behave according to the rules of others. Interest rates were high in Italy for three reasons: because inflation was higher than in most other industrialized countries, because the government had to pay a premium to the market to finance the huge government debt, and because the Bank of Italy wanted it high to support the lira. Over 95 per cent of debt financing was generated internally. The state did not borrow on the world capital markets. In other economies, raising interest rates depresses demand. In Italy, because so much government debt is held in family hands rather than in the banking system, this actually increased purchasing power and therefore demand. Italy truly does not obey normal rules.

The amount of disposable wealth in Italy is impossible to assess, given how much is held overseas in secret bank accounts or not declared to the authorities. But one indicator is the incidence of car purchase. For most people a car is the largest item of expenditure other than a family home. According to the Mintel report, 'Quality of Life in Europe 1993', ownership of cars per thousand inhabitants is highest in Germany and Italy and lowest in Spain. Within Italy, the cars become smaller the further south one goes. And more of them are Italian, whereas in the North bigger, often German-made models are more common. The report noted that the car was seen as more than purely a means of transport in Italy. What understatement! Italians may not be the most considerate drivers in the world. They may have scant regard for any traffic regulations, particularly those seeking to restrict what they see as their birthright and others their death wish to drive at speeds only marginally short of supersonic. Yet they must have the best natural feel of any drivers in the world. No other nation can race through the tightest of corners with such perfect judgement of distance and speed. Cars are a national obsession. Car magazines abound. Newspapers regularly carry special supplements on the latest fast cars, though the recent recession saw a drop in sales of Ferraris.

So how do Italians spend their money? Government statistics show that the average expenditure of Italian families varies from region to region. This is hardly surprising given the great disparities in income in North and South. In 1992 the richest families in the North spent on average 3 million lire a month, of which 16 per cent was on housing, 20 per cent on food, 8 per cent on clothes and 16 per cent on transport. Families in the South and Centre spent less, but overall ate better, spending more on meat (157,000 lire a month in the North, 183,000 in the Centre) and fish (34,000 lire a month in the North, 48,000 in the Centre). With an increase in unhealthy Northern diets has come a rise in the diseases associated with developed societies – something Italy had been largely immune to. Some 230,000 people died of stress-induced heart attacks in 1992. The high incidence of smoking also aggravated heart failure.

The general political consensus in Italy that full employment was more desirable than the brutal policies that led to mass lay-offs elsewhere in the Western industrialized world directly led to the government's high borrowing requirement. This was due not simply to a recognizably Italian reluctance to take hard decisions, a desire to avoid confrontation and conflict. The social and economic policy of the Christian Democrat ideology was very different from that of free-market Conservative parties elsewhere. The Christian Democrats were traditionally anti-capitalist and pro-state control. Although the state-owned industries might have become largely vehicles for patronage and for corruption, a strong streak of idealism underlay the support they enjoyed from the political establishment. The struggle of the labour unions in the 1960s and 1970s played a major role in the protection of jobs in Italy, but the Christian Democrats were reluctant to throw people out of work. Uneconomic industries were kept going. For instance, Italy continued to make motorcycles even when they were highly uncompetitive on price and performance: the carabinieri who used to roar on their huge Moto Guzzi through the little piazza where I lived expressed their own displeasure at the government's policy of buying Italian when they complained that their machines were too slow and heavy compared with BMW or Japanese models.

There were other financial and economic costs to these inefficiencies. On average, there are three times more retail outlets in Italy than in Britain, a country of similar population and economy. There are twice as many cafés and restaurants per head of population in Italy than in Britain (257 inhabitants per establishment in Italy against 451 in Britain, 795 in France, 558 in Germany, and 778 in Spain, according to the Mintel report). Yet this overmanning brought social benefits. More people were in work. More owned their own shops. There were more opportunities for distributors. Inner city areas remained vibrant and full of workshops. One never has to go far to buy one's food.

Some cutbacks were forced upon the government. There was no tombstone in the pages of the financial newspapers to announce the demise of the *scala mobile*, yet in a way its passing marked the end of a peculiarly Italian relationship between labour and employers. The *scala mobile* was a form of wage indexing which had been agreed after the war by employers who wished to avoid labour strife with the unions. It became the great single cushion for workers against the ravages of inflation, by providing an automatic adjustment when prices rose. It also pushed up labour costs, and therefore inflation, in a dizzying spiral. It was one of Bettino Craxi's major achievements as prime minister to obtain popular consent through a referendum in 1985 to lower the gearing of the *scala mobile*. And it finally shuddered to a halt in 1992.

The family, however, is changing in shape and size, and more slowly in importance and role too. And the vehicle for change has been the Italian woman. The New Man has scarcely arrived in Italy. Italian men still largely regard it beneath their dignity to wash up, change nappies, do the shopping, help with the housework, or try their hand in the kitchen. They have, after all, been spoiled by their mothers. Modern technological advances have not changed the traditional male attitude towards women. They have merely facilitated the Italian male's dependence on his womenfolk. The acquisition of small portable phones has helped the Italian male with a crucial daily operation. Instead of calling home from the office after carefully calculating the estimated time of arrival, the Italian husband can now ring home en route to give that time-honoured order to *buttare la pasta*, to throw the pasta into a cauldron of boiling water, so that the steaming plate will arrive on the table precisely as he opens the door.

But, as an unspoken part of the social contract and marriage arrangement, the Italian woman has increasingly got her own way. It is she who takes the decision to delay having children, and having done so, to limit the family. Not that the New Italian Woman has exchanged femininity for feminism. Few actually wear the trousers. But she has put mammon before the desire to be *mamma*.

Within marriages or partnerships, the onus remains on the women to make the sacrifices of their careers. They are still expected to look after the home, husband and any children they may have. As a result, few women reach prominence in business or the professions. Besides Wanda Ferragamo, among the most prominent have been Marisa Bellisario who headed the telecommunications equipment makers Italtel, Cecilia Daniele who took over the control of the steel empire founded by her grandfather, and Mariuccia Mandelli, founder of the Krizia fashion house.

One area where women are surprisingly well represented is in organized crime. In Naples the authorities have discovered numbers of women running Camorra clans or activities. Invariably, the reason for their prominence was not because they had climbed up the corporate ladder of criminality but because they were the wives, mistresses or sisters of clan bosses who were temporarily unable to perform their functions because they were behind bars. Their emancipation followed a period when they used merely to play secondary roles, as dealers or messengers. Their rise to prominence was shown in a conversation bugged by the authorities. Police reported that a bug planted in the visiting room of Poggioreale prison in Naples recorded a woman, Elvira Palumbo, giving tactical advice to her lover, Enzo Romano, the lieutenant of the clan boss, Ciro Mariano, of the city's notorious Spanish Quarter. 'Enzo, isn't it better that we send X to do that job? This one you're talking about really doesn't know how to shoot.'

Female gangsters included two sisters, Rita and Anna Esposito, who according to police headed a ring pushing deadly pastilles of cocaine and heroin. Others participated in extortion, smuggling and prostitution rackets. All were shopped, however, by another woman, known only as Cerasella (Little Cherry), who began collaborating with the authorities after her brother was killed by a rival clan and her son was turned by them from a drugs dealer into an addict. She was said to be the first member of the Camorra to become a *pentita* or turncoat.

On the other hand, few women were implicated in the *tangentopoli* corruption scandal. And women have been in the forefront of the campaign to resist paying the protection money to local Mafia criminals. It was a woman, Rosa Stanisci, the young mayor of San Vito dei Normanni between Bari and Brindisi, who mounted such a campaign.

Women's movements remain fairly limited in Italy. They tend to make a point over single issues. When the Pope declared himself against abortions for Bosnian Muslim women who had been raped by Serbian soldiery, the feminist writer and novelist Dacia Maraini called on women to withhold the 0.8 per cent of their taxes that they could specify should go to the Church for charitable works. She decried the 'misogynist' Church, and noted that since the legalization of abortion in Italy under Law 194, the number of abortions had gone down by about 12 per cent. Whereas once women might have had several backstreet abortions, now because of better counselling by doctors and changed social attitudes, as well as the greater availability and acceptance of contraceptives, there were fewer abortions.

According to anti-abortionists, Italian women have one pregnancy terminated for three live births, be it 160,000 abortions against half a million live births a year. Half of the abortions are undertaken for social and economic reasons: women simply cannot afford to have the children, or will not. Abortion is thus used as a form of birth control, rather than for strictly medical reasons.

The vital statistics of the Italian woman are one of the great myths of our time. It is still a traditional view held outside Italy that Italian girls are slim until they marry, but balloon out once they supposedly start having large families. In fact, they fight hard to keep their figures. The shapeliness of Italian womanhood is of greater uniformity than elsewhere. When a foreign company took over one of the largest lingerie makers in Italy, it found that all the bras it made had standard B cups.

Of course, there are bulges in the statistical abstract. A generous figure is still considered an asset. When the entertainer Angela Cavagna accused her rival Sabrina Salerno of having artificially boosted her magnificent bosom with a silicon implant, Signorina

Salerno brought a case for defamation. Her voluptuous shape was entirely the work of Mother Nature, she contended. Leading experts in cosmetic surgery were invoked to give evidence that hers were assets that owed nothing to their skill. The time and money women – and men – spend on their appearance is self-evident. Even in exclusive sports clubs, women spend hours in front of the mirror making themselves look their best after their work-out.

It is figures such as Signorina Salerno's that feature prominently in even heavyweight news magazines, which seem unable to market their rich coverage of the major political events of the week without nudes on the front covers. Public displays of nudity are not proscribed. One of the more popular nightly television shows is *Colpo Grosso*, a kind of striptease game show. The contestants are young women who volunteer to show off their expertise at shedding their clothes, with any assistance needed to unclip that recalcitrant suspender provided by a team of saucy international hostesses. Pornography is widespread. Surveys show that the most common relationship of seven in ten couples is a ménage à trois, where the third member in bed is a remote control device for watching pornographic movies on the video machine.

Since the closure of the brothels in 1958 under a law introduced by the Socialist campaigner Angela Merlin, various attempts have been made to reintroduce them. They remain illegal. Until the Merlin Law, brothels had been licensed like bars. They kept opening hours like bars (closed on Sundays) and strict regulations stipulated the minimum distance from the bed to the basin. The closure of the brothels forced prostitutes on to the streets, where they tout for business quite openly. Many are foreign, or transvestite, or both. Transvestite prostitutes have a long tradition in Italy. When steamers first opened up the tourist trade to Capri, many of the early passengers were young Neapolitan boy-transvestite prostitutes.

In Italy, despite the teaching of the Catholic Church, sex is for recreation, not procreation. For if Italians love children, which is a truth universally acknowledged, then their value increases as they become rarer. Italian children are yet to be listed as an endangered species. Nor is the Italian *mamma* yet extinct. But the fecundity of

Italian womanhood is the lowest in Europe. According to the World Bank, Italian women produce on average 1.3 children, a figure lower even than for industrialized countries such as Austria, Denmark, Germany, Hong Kong, Greece, Luxemburg and Spain (all with 1.5). In France and Britain the average was 1.8 and in the United States 1.9. The same survey gave the fertility of African women as 6 to 8 children.

It is all a great change from the baby boom of the 1960s, when Italians achieved an average of more than a million births a year. By 1988 Italy had attained virtually zero growth, when there were ten live births per thousand head of population. On current predictions the Italian population will fall from 57 to 55 million by the year 2025.

According to the ten-yearly census carried out on 20 October 1991, Italians are growing older, living longer, getting richer, moving out of the big cities, having smaller families and are increasingly employed in the service sector. Sociologists and demographers attribute the falling birthrate to the changing attitudes of women towards having children. Simply, maternity is no longer essential for their fulfilment as women. Having children is restrictive of personal freedoms, and very expensive. 'My daughter is too wrapped up in her work,' is the familiar lament of a father despairing of ever having grandchildren.

To have or not to have children is a topic of debate in feminist politics. When Livia Turco, head of the ex-Communist Party's women's section, had a child (she at least was sufficiently un-bourgeois not to be married), she was accused of betraying her commitment to the principle of women's independence, of fulfilment of womanhood without maternity. It was a criticism she deflected without difficulty. Having a baby was exercising her right to choose, she said. Her (male) issue never became a feminist political one.

The 1991 census showed that the population resident in Italy, including for the first time a sizeable immigrant component, had grown by 0.3 per cent or 167,355 over 1981 to 57,103,833. There were regional variations. Over ten years, the population in the North had shrunk by 1.4 per cent, in the centre it grew by 0.2 per cent, whereas in the South it went up by 2.5 per cent.

The average size of the family shrank from 3 in 1981 to 2.8 in 1991. There were more women than men: 51.4 per cent against 48.6 per cent. The most densely populated area was the North, where 44.8 per cent of the country's population was concentrated. In 1981 some 24 per cent of the population were below nineteen; by 1991 only 18 per cent were. The over-sixties made up 17 per cent of the population in 1981, and 20 per cent in 1991.

The census results established the data for planning for the whole range of social services. Already by 1991 there was a glut of teachers as school populations fell. Of greater concern, however, was how Italy would pay for the pensions and the health care of this ageing population. As in most countries in the industrialized world, Italy was having to cope with the Third Age. Hospital administrators were closing down maternity wards and preparing for more geriatric care. Modern Italy did not, however, have a developed population policy.

It had had under Mussolini. This took several forms: emigration, the colonization of Africa, and internal migration. A concerted campaign was mounted to combat infant mortality. And mothers were given financial and other incentives to have large families. Partly in reaction to this form of social engineering, subsequent governments adopted only barely articulated policies on population, besides offering very limited child benefits, although the Church and its temporal agents the Christian Democrats emphasized the values of the Christian family.

If Italian women really love children so much, why do they have fewer of them? Is it so that they can look after them better? Or do they love themselves even more and wish to pursue their lives without the encumbrance of dependants? Italian law incorporates some of the most generous terms anywhere for maternity leave. But as in so many areas of Italian life, the obstacle to the securing of citizens' rights has been the application and enforcement of the law. The practice is widespread in small firms and workshops in the Marche and elsewhere for women to be hired on condition they do not get pregnant. According to union organizers, bosses have threatened women with a Morton's fork if they slip up: either they would have to submit their resignation or they would be accused of stealing from the petty-cash box and summarily dismissed.

The decline of the extended family has also played its part. As families have shrunk, working mothers have fewer sisters and other family members with whom to leave their children. The increase in women's education has also raised expectations. An awareness of the costs of bringing up children, the lack of services provided by the state, and the small size of flats in which most average families live in urban areas, have acted as brakes on bearing and rearing children. And among the more socially responsible there is a sense that there are already enough mouths to feed in the world. A friend who was already a parent of three and was considering having a fourth found herself regarded as a social leper by the other mothers at her children's school.

The size of the family may have changed enormously, but the ties have not. The most stable relationship of all in Italy remains between mother and son. From the moment a blue ribbon is tied on to the outside of the front door to signify a male birth, a son is the pampered centre of attention. *Mammismo* has none of the connotations of 'mother's boy' in English-speaking countries. It merely means that sons are spoiled by their mothers, which they almost always are. It is such a stereotype of Italian life, but little has changed. 'Men exchange one mother for another when they marry,' the writer Dacia Maraini asserted. Even in the 1990s, few men leave home until they marry. One often meets single men in their thirties who still live with their mothers. In Anglo-Saxon countries young people generally go to university away from their home towns to cut the apron strings. In Italy there is scarcely any provision for student lodging. Most young people simply cannot afford to leave home and tend to go to the local university.

The strength of the mother-son relationship can greatly prejudice the successful fulfilment of subsequent relationships. The model of the Madonna and Child persists as *the* stereotypic Italian relationship. Time and again, when sons sin, in their mothers' eyes they can do no wrong. The Italian mother is the most forgiving soul. When a television programme showed the story of a girl gang-raped by seven young men as she left a discotheque in Lamezia Terme, the switchboard was jammed with mothers calling up to defend the boys' action and accusing the girl of being a provocative harpy.

The feeling is reciprocated. On International Women's Day – 8 March – men give their loved ones sprigs of yellow mimosa. But throughout the year the crooners glorify their mothers. In the last summer of the 1980s, the Neapolitan singer-songwriter Eduardo Bennato sang a rock song to the words '*Viva la mamma*'.

Italian men appear to be quite at ease in the presence of women. Their legendary charm, their ability to flatter and their appreciation of attractive women have all reinforced the myth that they are wonderful lovers. Sexual prowess and the Latin lover are, of course, fundamental to the image of the Italian male. One senior Italian politician was known as 'The Orgasm'. Yet it seems Italian manhood falls short of the myth. The talents of the Latin lover have to be learnt, not inherited. In Trapani in Sicily an enterprising businessman set up a school for the Latin lover to teach techniques evidently not acquired as a birthright.

As husbands, however, Italian men are not always so good. It is impossible to assess the incidence of marital violence in Italy because, as in so many indicators of civil society, Italy was behind other countries in setting up a helpline for battered wives and women who had suffered violent attack. The Telefono Rosa was set up as a research project in 1988 and established as a proper helpline in 1990 to give counselling and advice. A profile rapidly emerged of both victim and aggressor. Some 84 per cent of victims were aged between twenty-five and fifty-four, two-thirds were married, almost all had children. Most of the complaints were about psychological pressure or beatings. Only 7 per cent reported sexual attacks. In 79.8 per cent of the cases the reported aggressor was the husband, and in 82.1 per cent of the cases he was not under the influence of either alcohol or drugs.

Divorce and legal separations are on the increase. There were fewer divorces in the South until recently. But now the more traditional society there is catching up with the rest of the country. In 1991 the number of marriages celebrated was 309,116, down from 312,585 in 1990. Couples still preferred to marry in church: fewer than 20 per cent had civil ceremonies alone. Put in historical perspective: in 1947, 440,000 Italian couples married; in 1970 some 400,000; and in 1987 about 306,000.

Fewer may be marrying, more divorcing, but the family unit is tighter than in France or Britain. Where in France nearly one in three marriages ends in divorce, and in Britain over one in three does, in Italy the figure is between 7 and 8 per cent. Figures were not available for the numbers of *separati in casa*, those who for the sake of appearance or money or both chose not to divorce but lived separately under the same roof. For in Italy, attitudes to marriage and marital infidelity differ from those in the Anglo-Saxon world. It is not simply that people cannot afford to divorce. It is just that to divorce because one partner or both is cheating on the other is not sufficient reason to tear a marriage asunder. Marriage is still seen as a lifelong contract. But marriage is not seen as the provider of all needs, which could be fulfilled by a mistress or lover.

A mistress has a special place in Italian life. Mussolini openly kept his mistress, Claretta Petacci, to the annoyance of his wife, Rachele. Yet it was his mistress who showed loyalty to her man. She tried to shield his body as he was shot down by partisans who caught them near Lake Como. Nowadays, men are even more likely to flaunt their mistresses. One Roman hostess confided to me that when she invited a man to dinner, she always had to ask whether he would bring his wife or his mistress. No opprobrium was attached. On the contrary. It was the norm. It was considered right that a politician should have a mistress. These were not simple affairs. Rather they were long-term steady relationships. More than one writer has written largely autobiographical tales about men who had two families concurrently: one legitimately with his wife, the other with his *amante*. This was in effect a form of polygamy.

When marriages do fall apart, a problem arises with the children. As in other countries, in cases of child custody and division of matrimonial wealth a number of court judgements have tended to discriminate between married couples seeking divorce, and cohabiting couples wishing to split up. Italy does not have a system of common law whereby one judgement can establish a precedent. Yet by the middle of 1992 a number of judgements in personal status cases conformed to a surprising trend: that it was easier for a married couple to divorce than for a couple who were living together in what the Church in its inimitable way calls *more uxorio*.

*

If the average new Italian woman does not want children, or many of them, there are also those unfortunates whose lack of children is not by design. Involuntary childlessness is as big a phenomenon in Italy as unwanted children. Some couples accept this as divine will. However, in a country which has largely turned its collective back on traditional religion, this is not the usual reaction. Some will seek help from modern medical science, despite the uncertainties. A small number of doctors in Italy have pioneered methods to conquer infertility. In the bourgeois Rome district of Prati, a couple of hundred metres outside the walls of the Vatican City, Dr Severino Antinori explained the work of his controversial clinic, the Istituto di Ricercatori Associati Per la Riproduzione Umana (RAPRU). He had earned some notoriety for helping menopausal women in their fifties and sixties to conceive children. He would mix donated sperm and eggs and then implant them in a patient. His oldest patient was a sixty-two-year-old widow from Palermo, who was successfully impregnated with her late husband's sperm, frozen before his death in 1982. The woman had been unable to have children during her marriage. She said she wanted to have a child because of her continuing love for her late husband.

These *mamme-nonne* (mummies-grannies) provoked a furious reaction from the Church in Italy. Catholic teachers of medical ethics decried what they saw as the creation of orphans. How could women of this age possibly hope to raise children to maturity? Dr Antinori utterly rejected the accusation as hypocrisy. 'Why can a man have a child at sixty and a woman not? I call that male chauvinism. Why this hypocrisy? There are so many children who are brought up as orphans, whose parents are separated or divorced, or who never knew their father. These children I am helping are the product of a real love. And look, seventy years ago, many women died at forty to forty-five years old, and their children were brought up by their grandparents. So why is everyone so scandalized? The Church is against the pill, it is against abortion, and now it is against having children. The Church is obscurantist.'

Prospective candidates were given a thorough check-up before being accepted. Longevity of their own parents was a prerequisite, to demonstrate that they were of suitable breeding stock. 'We took great care,' he asserted. Some of his older women patients had even had twins, who were flourishing, Dr Antinori said. He had pioneered the method known as SUZI – subzonal insemination, sometimes called microinjection.

Colour charts of human eggs in the process of being fertilized, as well as a mother and child in pastel shades, adorned the walls. More ominous was a small glass case containing Arab surgical instruments from the tenth century. The waiting rooms of his clinic in Via Properzio were overflowing with hopeful clients prepared to ignore the teaching of the Church against such interference with the reproductive process. There were a couple of young German doctors, coming to study his methods; a Swedish woman, desperate for a child; a Dutch-Moluccan woman, with her husband; and many Italians, men and women, for whom Dr Antinori offered a hope that years of barrenness could be overcome and fruit brought forth.

Infertility was a terrible bane in Italy, he said. He estimated some 20 per cent of couples could not have children. In such cases, 60 per cent was due to the woman, and 40 per cent to the man. I asked whether in test-tube cases he could determine the sex of the child. He said he believed that one could tell the XX from the XY chromosomes about 70 per cent of the time. But he was against interfering with nature. Except for one couple: they had had four girls, and he helped them to have a son.

Round the corner from Antinori's clinic was a shop selling those beautiful clothes that proud Italian parents dress their children in. The shop was called Babies, a marketing device suggesting that giving it an English name was chic and would somehow encourage more people to have children. Times were hard, the assistant said. People were just not having babies any more. Two other shops like hers had been forced out of business because no one was buying.

Of course, Italy is a child-friendly country. Visitors with children are overwhelmed by the openly expressed joy with which their children are greeted and welcomed. No restaurant would have a sign saying 'No children'. Take a child along, and he or she will be swamped with attention from the waiters, the cooks, the owner, and other customers. Children still stay up late, especially on hot summer nights, playing around their parents. Whereas in other countries men are often tongue-tied with children, in Italy they immediately establish a rapport. Men brought up in larger families always had young children around them.

You could argue that with a language as beautiful as theirs they have a sacred duty to mouth it as often as possible. One reason why Italians have such a gift for language, such a fluency with words, is that their whole lives have been trained for this. Their educational system is directed towards verbal fluency. All their schooling is a test of oral skills. Most examinations are oral, rather than written, and test a pupil's ability to spout cogently on a given subject. These examinations need long, elegantly constructed, well delivered answers. Short, concise responses do not work. Generally speaking, Italian education is best at the beginning and steadily deteriorates. The playgroups and nursery schools are excellent. Middle schools provide good, rounded education. At a *liceo scientifico*, a grammar school for more academic students, sciences are not actually taught. Typical subjects are mathematics, technical drawing, English, history, geography, Italian and Latin. And the *liceo classico* will give a superb knowledge of Latin and classical Greek to a standard rarely found in other countries until university level.

School also provides the main place for the formation of lifelong friendships. A class will stay together throughout a school career, often with the same teacher. Schoolchildren hang around in packs, enjoying the security of the group, in their almost identical casual clothes and shoulder bags, induced early into the regimented conformity to the single style of the day which is the substitute for fashion in Italy. School hours are crammed into the morning, and pupils go home for lunch – another factor that acts against working mothers.

It is at university level that the Italian educational system really collapses. Lectures are overcrowded. The entrance requirements are minimal. Vast numbers therefore apply for university and start courses. They are successively weeded out by yearly exams. Many have no intention of finishing, but embark on university courses to defer doing their compulsory military service.

The emphasis on oral skills is shown too in the country's arts. Italian television is quite unlike television elsewhere. The chat shows go on for hours. Since most of them go out live, it is impossible to edit some of the unstoppable torrents of verbiage. But television reflects the national character. The guests are effusive, fluent, quick on their feet and love talking for its own sake. Many of the programmes, like the Maurizio Constanzo show, are required viewing for those following current affairs, which in Italy means almost exclusively Italian domestic politics. Another is the show of Giuliano Ferrara, who has a twin career as a Socialist member of the European parliament. His vast bulk disguises a nimble brain. He can talk fluently and effortlessly on apparently any subject. The written word is also highly valued. At one level, the most popular magazine is a weekly stuffed with crossword puzzles. At another, Italy has over 3,000 literary prizes, many of them enjoying an international prestige, like the Premio D'Italia. Fewer titles are sold each year than in, say, Britain, but a journalist cum political commentator like Giorgio Bocca can sell hundreds of thousands of copies in hardback of a book like L'Inferno, a polemic on the awfulness and intractability of the South. Newspapers, too, ensure that literary trends are accessible to all. The arts are not something for a cultural élite in Italy. Rather they are for everyone. The administration of the arts may be a national disgrace, as anyone knows who has tried to enter a museum after 2 p.m. But galleries are well patronized, and Italians at all levels talk knowledgeably, especially about the visual arts. Indeed, my local greengrocer's wife had recently been to London with other members of a cultural group to see the National Gallery and other repositories of Italian Renaissance art.

Can the family survive? Is society changing so rapidly that it threatens the structure of the family? Will the shrinking of the family lead to the disintegration of society? As I noted earlier, Barzini and Nichols in different generations, and Delai today, have warned against writing premature obituaries for the family. Italy has survived many of the social ills of developed industrial societies in large part because the family provides an economic and human safety net. But it is changing. And those that are suffering are the most vulnerable, the children. The incidence of child abuse, of broken homes, of children in care, may be lower than in other countries. But there is an unmistakable trend. These aberrations – and in Italy they remain aberrations – are on the increase.

I recognize that to devote space to cases of Italian mistreatment of children gives a distorted picture of the reality as it exists today. It is a given fact that Italians are wonderful with children. Children are God. Parents will be given all sorts of unsolicited advice from grandmotherly figures in the street about how a child is dressed, with admonitions about the dangers of taking them in the sun without a hat, or not putting enough blankets on a baby. Children suffer none of the cultural or institutional discrimination of those two countries that have the worst record for the treatment of children, the United States and Britain. However, my intention has been to identify a trend, a small but disturbing one.

During the time I spent in Italy, I was surprised by the number of cases of cruelty and abuse towards children which came to light. The most extreme examples appear in the *cronaca nera*, the crime pages of the press. Besides the cases of child kidnapping – more an expression of a certain kind of criminal activity in Calabria or Sardinia – there also emerge, though still fairly seldom, reports of horrific crimes against children that shatter the idyllic picture of child-loving Italy. In the autumn of 1992, near the village of Foligno outside Perugia, the body of a four-year-old boy was found in a field. Simone Allegretti had been strangled. Later examination showed that before being killed he had been subjected to violent sexual attack.

As noted earlier, it is often to fiction that one must turn to find the reality of Italian life best expressed. The film *Il Ladro Di Bambini* was released just in time to pick up awards at the 1992 Cannes film festival. It was a portrayal of the seedier side of child prostitution in the Northern industrial concrete jungle of Milan. A single mother, transplanted like so many thousands of others from Sicily, offered her eleven-year-old daughter to a local businessman. They were caught in the act. The opening scene was violent and dramatic. Police burst in and bundled the mother and the client off in handcuffs. The girl and her brother, half innocent, half fully aware, were removed almost as an afterthought. No one appeared to know what to do with them, how to handle them. The film was the story of their journey with a carabiniere down to Sicily, there to be put in an institution run by nuns. It was a film of unremitting drabness. There was not a single beautiful scene, no sunsets over beaches, no fine clothes, no handsome buildings. In the starkest neo-realist depiction of a sordid subculture, it touched on one of society's great taboos, loss of innocence, unrelieved by any evocation of Pasolini's ideas of the innate nobility of the peasantry.

Fiction or reality? Cinematographic, for sure, but very close to the reality, according to Ernesto Caffo, professor of child psychiatry. He was in a position to know, as the founder of Italy's first child helpline. 'Our experience shows that there is much covert child abuse in Southern Italy,' Professor Caffo confirmed. He launched the Telefono Azzurro after studying similar projects in New York State. In its sparkling clean premises in central Milan he painted a picture of a child's life in Italy today very different from the popular image. 'Italians all love children, or say they do, but everywhere their actions show they do not care. Some 30 per cent of children do not go to school in Bari, 35 per cent do not go to school in Palermo. Instead, they become common criminals and are inducted into the Mafia.'

There are far fewer cases of severe physical abuse of children than say in Britain or Scandinavia, but there are still – officially – 300 cases a year of infanticide, and officially again some eighty to ninety cases of abandonment, of young mothers throwing their newborn babies into rubbish skips. Many young parents no longer enjoy support from the community. Often the family is small, with only one parent. Big, extended families are becoming less and less common. It was estimated that in 1992 a million children lived with one parent only, who in 80 per cent of cases was their mother.

Another indication of growing unhappiness or desolation among young people is evidenced by the increase in suicides. By the early 1990s, some 800 to 1,000 Italians under the age of twenty committed suicide each year – double the figure for the 1970s. Added to the increasing death rate of teenagers from drug overdoses and car accidents, this has greatly raised the figures for deaths before reaching the age of maturity. Psychologists attribute the increase in teenage suicides to a sense of alienation in a society where the old support system provided by the big family is rapidly being stripped away. Before, a young person would have had dozens of contemporaries in his or her own family, as well as schoolfriends, but probably only one grandparent alive. Now it is the other way round. In the North especially, a teenager is likely to have perhaps one brother or sister or cousin, yet possibly three grandparents still alive. One of the chief reasons for calls to the helpline is the sense of desertion children feel as more and more women go out to work, leaving their children behind.

The issue of the employment of children was so serious, despite it being outlawed by national and European Community legislation, that it became an object of special study of the parliamentary anti-Mafia commission. In its report, it noted how children were suborned into organized crime networks. They usually began with peddling smuggled goods, gradually moving up the scale of criminal activity, through protection rackets, drugs dealing, enforcement, settling of accounts, and finally murder.

There are many reasons why parents should turn against their children, or children against their parents. In Italy, it is rarer than elsewhere. But it happens none the less.

EIGHT

Radix malorum est cupiditas

One day in April 1991 news broke of a crime so horrendous that it immediately opened the sluices to one of those floods of national collective soul-searching, self-examination and self-justification that every society periodically undergoes. In a ghastly frenzy of bloody violence, teenager Pietro Maso murdered both his parents in the family home. He was helped by three friends. All four of them were between seventeen and nineteen years old. On a national level the Maso case was not simply seen as a family dispute. Rather it was seen as an assault on the sanctity of the family. Some, not least the psychiatrist brought in as a prosecution witness, took it as evidence of the moral degeneracy of a whole society.

Historians of crime will attest that the murder of one or other parent in a quarrel is not in itself uncommon. Between 1975 and 1992 some one hundred parents were killed by one of their children in Italy. There have been other very rare cases, too, of the murder of both parents, both before and since. The most gruesome was in 1975 when Doretta Graneris, aged nineteen, together with her boyfriend, murdered her father, mother, little brother and grandparents. Then, shortly after the Maso case, in December 1992, Giovanni Rozzi, a young man from near Rome, was arrested and charged with the murder of both his parents, owners of a pizzeria. He too had an accomplice, the drug-addict son of the pizzeria cleaning lady.

What set the Maso case apart, what shocked comfortable Italian society, was the motive. There was no domestic row. Nor was it the act of a drug-crazed son seeking money for a fix. It was rather the son's calculated and cold-blooded attempt to wipe out people who stood between him and the inheritance which was in any case one day to have been his due. No matter that the victims were his parents. Pietro Maso had to get his hands on the legacy in order to buy a bigger and better car and the fast lifestyle to go with it.

The case quickly became one of the most celebrated in modern Italian penal history and its dramatis personae household names. Journalists flocked from around the world to the trial in Verona in the spring of 1992. Recalling the city's fame as the scene of Shakespeare's star-crossed lovers Romeo and Juliet, they wrote portentously that the proceedings were in effect putting the whole of Italian society on trial. A generation whose only god is money, screamed the headlines.

The case sparked off a heated debate within Italy. Some believed it demonstrated the sickness of a rich, spoilt, degenerate and violent society that had lost its sense of values, where the blind pursuit of materialism had undermined and destroyed human and family relationships. Others argued that someone who killed his parents for money must be mad, not bad.

The case was cast in almost biblical terms. Surely it was a modern parable about the lost soul of traditional Italian society, of the corrupting influence of degenerate cities of the Po Valley plain, that dank triangle stretching between Milan, Bologna and Venice. Evidence was presented in court that exposed the cultural emptiness of these suddenly rich rural villages. There bored young men would not only fantasize about fast cars but could easily acquire them.

It all happened one April night in the village of Montecchia di Crosara, in the foothills of the Alps. Montecchia is typical of those small settlements above the Po Valley. On the edge of Soave country and surrounded by a patchwork of vineyards and by orchards that produce the best cherries in the country, it is a village of some four thousand modest, unassuming and hard-working folk. The village had got rich in a single generation through the agro-industrial revolution. During the cherry-picking season the factories close and the workers go into fields they still own or help their families with the harvest.

Nothing indicated anything out of the ordinary in the village, although it was not unacquainted with more or less violent death. Only a year before, a warrant officer in the air force had died after a dispute over his Southern origins. A couple of locals had been goading him with anti-Southern taunts. His temper boiled – ah, hot-blooded Southerner, of course – and he had a massive heart attack that killed him. Not strictly speaking a violent attack – no charges were pressed – the fact was that a Southerner died as a result of Northern intolerance.

That, however, was a parenthesis. In the village today you will not see posters and memorials at each street corner reminding all who pass of their most notorious sons. Rather, you should go to the cemetery on a rise on the outskirts of the village. Look closely at one of the larger tombstones, in polished black marble, with one of those gilded copies of Michelangelo's *Pietà* so beloved of monumental masons. Carved into the cold stone are the names MASO Antonio, born 12.12.35 died 17.4.91 and TESSARI Maria Rosa, born 21.2.43 died 17.4.91. Some gaudy tulips in silk – so much easier than the real ones: they do not need changing – had been been placed in a vase, as well as some white lilies. They were a gift of their only son, Pietro.

Pietro Maso was born at San Bonifacio, a suburb of Verona, on 15 May 1972. That made him a month short of his nineteenth birthday when he beat the life out of those who had given life to him. His testimony in his police interrogation, and to the psychiatrist called to assess whether he was mentally fit either to stand trial or to face the charges later proffered against him, and his answers in his subsequent trial, make chilling reading.

For together they paint a portrait of unalloyed greed, of an obsession with fast cars and designer clothes, of discos and gambling, hand in hand with a total absence of those moral values considered basic to traditional societies. But the testimony did not deal solely with Maso. It analysed too the society that had produced this teenage parricide. What the evidence revealed was a society in transition, a society that had undergone rapid change in appearance and on the surface but that had failed to adapt fundamentally to changing circumstances.

The first the authorities knew about any crime was in the early hours of 18 April 1991. It was Pietro Maso himself who reported to the carabinieri of San Bonifacio that, on his return from a discotheque in Verona that night, he had come across the bodies of his parents. Maso told them that he had been out with three friends: Giorgio Carbognin and Paolo Cavazza, both eighteen; and a third, Damiano Burato, who because he was under eighteen was to be tried in the court for minors.

It did not take long for Maso to confess that he himself had perpetrated the crime. Which raised the question: was Maso mad? He certainly seemed to lack any human feeling, any sense of remorse, any awareness of the heinousness of the crime he had committed. For example, the transcript of the first interview he gave to the local TV station the day after the murder of his parents, before he was arrested for the crime, shows that he managed to reply calmly and coolly to the questions. It was as though he were playing a part.

'What time did you return home last night?'

'Around two o'clock.'

'What did you find?'

'Nothing. Everything was normal. I found the doors open, and lights on, but I was frightened at first, I went to have a look, and when I was going upstairs I found legs poking out. Then I went to see that lot up above [indicating the carabinieri].'

'Are we talking about something wild, ghastly?'

'Yeah, I suppose we are.'

The next day he made a rather different statement to the carabinieri.

'In November 1990, I had the idea of leading a more glamorous life, for which I needed a lot of money. The only way to have this money was to lay my hands immediately on the inheritance due to me when my parents died. I also wanted everything they had, so I would also have to kill my sisters. A couple of weeks later, I explained my idea to my friends, including Giorgio Carbognin, who is also from Montecchia. We were driving to Verona in my car. I told him I knew a way to make a lot of money but it meant getting rid of people. He was a bit surprised, but then welcomed the idea. Then I told him the people to suppress were my parents, so that after they died I would have my share of the inheritance.

'I also told a third friend about this, Paolo Cavazza, because two weren't enough to do the job properly.

'We decided to carry out our plan on the Wednesday night

when my parents came back from the meeting [a religious meeting at the convent of San Daniele at Lonigo] where they went every Wednesday and Saturday evening. So when they went out, I went to the square in Montecchia to the bar John where I met up with my friends. We stayed there until about 9.30 p.m., then went over to Damiano's place where we had left two bags containing overalls, a metal tube, about 5 centimetres (2 inches) in diameter and 50 centimetres (20 inches) long, a carnival mask, and a steel anti-theft crooklock, the type you clamp on the car steering wheel. When we got home, we put on the overalls and waited behind the door. In the meantime we put out the light.

'Around ten past eleven, my parents parked the car in the garage underneath the house, and we heard them coming up the steps. As soon as my father got into the kitchen, and so on my side, I hit him with the metal tube on the head one or two times and Damiano did the same with a saucepan and I remember that the saucepan handle broke, and my father fell to the ground near the window. In the meantime my mother arrived and she was set upon by Giorgio and Paolo who hit her about the head. I remember that my mother put up a certain amount of resistance dragging herself towards the kitchen so Giorgio covered her with a sheet from the divan and held it down with his foot and over her head and suffocated her.'

According to this account, they cleared up as best they could and put all their stuff in the car. They made the house look as though there had been a burglary. Then they drove off to Verona, with Maso at the wheel, and went to Berri's disco to try and establish an alibi. But that night the establishment was holding a private party by invitation only, so they could not get in. They drove around a little, then they headed back. Maso arrived home around two o'clock, then rushed out to alert his neighbours that something had happened. They rang the carabinieri.

Giorgio Carbognin bore out Pietro's statement. Among other things he stated:

'Some time before, perhaps at the end of 1990, Pietro Maso had proposed that I take part in killing his parents and later also his sisters, so that he could be sole inheritor. He promised that he would give me part of the inheritance . . . I saw the woman fall on the ground near the kitchen. I ran after her and I cannot say if the woman was sobbing on the ground and so to make her shut up I covered her mouth with a plastic bag and called Pietro to tell him she was still alive. Pietro hit her hard with the metal tube. After a while, the woman no longer gave signs of life. First Pietro had hit his father again with the same tube to finish him off.

'At this point one of us took the white sheet to cover the faces of the two and in the meantime we took off our overalls and masks, which we put in the plastic bags. We washed our hands in the bathroom and dried them with a towel, which we put in one of the bags. Before leaving we went into the main bedroom and turned out some drawers to make it look as though there had been a break-in.'

The bald prose of the pathologist's reports is a model of scientific analysis. But, put flesh on the bare bones of the account, and you have a picture of what must have been a frenzied battering to have caused such carnage. The faces of the victims were reduced to bloody masks. Maso's mother had sustained at least twenty blows, and was covered with bruises and welts across her head and body. Both victims had traces of blood in their lungs, signs that they had been some time dying. Both were fully clothed. They had resisted and proved difficult to finish off. They did not go down easily, with one strike, like in the movies. It was messy. It was hard physical work.

The killers made a couple of mistakes. They left behind one of the carnival masks they wore during their savagery as in the film *A Clockwork Orange*. And they left traces of blood in the bathroom when they cleaned up. But these clues were never needed by the investigators. For Maso confessed all.

There was never any question that the crime was premeditated. Not only was it planned beforehand, but there had been several other attempts or projects to do away with the Maso parents. Nor was it in question that the originator, the mastermind of the crime, was Pietro Maso. One plan had been to blow Maso's parents up with leaking gas cylinders installed in the basement of the house. The explosion would be set off when the entire family – his parents, his two sisters, and the husband of one sister – were at home for a family lunch. Maso rigged it up with strobe lights to act as the timer-cum-trigger device. But the attempt did not work, either because one of Maso's sisters did not show up, or because his mother heard a strange ticking sound, went to investigate, and discovered the gas canisters. His father made them safe, and waited for his son to explain. When Maso came back that night he told his father that the cylinders were to heat up a room for a party. If the attempt had worked, and part of the house had been destroyed, this would have reduced the value of the property and therefore of the inheritance. But Maso had taken this into account. He knew he would not lose out. He was aware the house was covered by insurance.

The second murder attempt took place on a Saturday. Maso's mother had been going through her son's trouser pockets and found a large wad of notes: 800,000 lire (£350) in some versions, 2 million lire (£900) in others. She confronted her son, and asked him how he had managed to get hold of such an amount when he was out of work at the time. He concocted some story that he was still working part-time at the car showroom he had been at before, and selling cars on commission by some special arrangement. His mother was not convinced. She told him she wanted to check out the story the following Saturday with his former boss. Maso agreed to go with her, together with Giorgio Carbognin.

Carbognin went prepared, armed with a meat cleaver. Their plan was that at a given moment he would hit her from behind. They had the other details worked out too. They would dispose of her body by bundling it into the boot of the car. They would then go home, call Maso's father to the garage, kill him, and put his body in the boot as well. They would then set the car alight and tip it over a ravine.

On the appointed day, they set off. Maso drove, his mother sat in the front passenger seat and Carbognin sat behind. But Carbognin never carried out the plan. Maso had to think quickly to get out of a confrontation which would reveal his dishonesty. When they arrived at Maso's former workplace, he suddenly announced he was not feeling well and they decided to go home.

The *locus delicti* of the third attempt was to have been the garage. Maso and Carbognin were to drive in. Maso would call up to his mother to come and inspect a scratch on the bodywork. As she came down the stairs, Carbognin would hit her over the head from behind. Then Maso would call his father, for whom a similar fate was reserved. Again, the bodies would be put in the car boot, then driven off to a remote spot and set alight.

Everything went according to plan. They parked the car in the garage, and called up to Maso's mother. She started down the stairs. But at the last minute, Carbognin chickened out.

Maso was not to be thwarted. He was determined to do away with his parents. He devised yet another plan. They would hire a professional killer. The going contract price was several million lire. They even went as far as to contact Verona's Third World underworld. But that is as far as that particular option was pursued.

There could be no doubt therefore. All these fiendish plots amply demonstrated that Maso and Carbognin had for some time been entertaining the idea of committing murder. Many times they must have played through in their minds how and where they would commit this crime, and the whole *modus operandi* of the killing.

Then in mid-April 1991 their hands were forced. Suddenly they no longer had the luxury of choosing their own time. Their spendthrift habits caught up with them, and they had to find a way out. By that stage, they knew of no solution other than the one which for months they had been living with, planning for.

Some time before, Carbognin had made up his mind to buy a new car. He went down to the local showroom for a look. There in the window was a dream car. As soon as he set his eyes on the brand-new four-wheel-drive Lancia Delta Integrale, his heart followed. It cost 23 million lire (£10,400). He ordered one exactly the same as the display model. He agreed to pay cash. Financing was simply arranged. He went to a bank to ask for a loan. The manager had no problem agreeing, after he had received a letter of recommendation from Carbognin's boss. The problems began when he went home. His family raised all sorts of objections. How could he squander so much money on a car? He caved in to the pressure, and pulled out of the purchase. But instead of returning the cheque to the bank, he cashed it and went on a wild spending spree with Maso.

Afterwards the two of them were to recall that these were the happiest days of their lives. They went to discos and bought rounds of drinks, impressed the girls, how they impressed the girls! Maso seemed totally in charge. Carbognin worshipped him. A witness told the carabinieri that on one evening in February he recalled Carbognin paying for all the drinks for a group in a discotheque where the bill came to about 200,000 lire (£90). They drank champagne, beer, Ferrari — one of Italy's top sparkling wines — and various spirits. Another time, Carbognin and Maso pulled out great wads of 100,000 and 50,000 lire banknotes to pay their bar bill. Italy may be a cash society, but few teenagers have such amounts at their fingertips. In a month and a half of high spending, the entire sum, all 23 million lire, was gone, frittered away.

The day approached, however, when Carbognin's loan repayment fell due. But Maso had a plan. He would see them through. He stole his mother's chequebook, forged her signature on a cheque made out for 25 million lire — that is, the loan plus interest charges — and gave it to Carbognin. He took it to the bank to pay off his debt. It was the morning of Tuesday, 16 April 1991.

That evening, Maso realized that the forged cheque was now being processed, and that sooner rather than later his mother would find out. There was no time to waste. The group decided to carry out the final and definitive part of the plan.

They had calculated precisely the value of what he was due to inherit. There was the house, at number 43 Via San Pietro, the kind of property known in Italy as a villa and in England a detached house. Maso's father Antonio had a job building roads. But like most manual labourers who had come from the countryside, he had not given up his land. So he had a second income from his vineyards, plus the capital value of the land. The family vineyards, 3.2 hectares, were made up of eleven *campi*, each *campo* of 3,000 square metres, whose market price was about 70 million lire (£32,000). There were other savings too, and the whole lot came to more than a billion lire — some half a million pounds sterling. Not bad for a road builder. The amount is staggering testimony to the economic boom that had rapidly transformed rural Italy in the postwar years — in the North at least. Such riches had been amassed by people who a generation before were often peasant farmers making a subsistence living.

Maso *figlio* had already determined how the proceeds would be split. Paolo Cavazza and Damiano Burato would get 200 million each (about £90,000). The rest would be split equally between Giorgio Carbognin and him.

What Maso's friends and partners in crime did not realize at the time – how could they have done? – was that he had no intention of honouring his commitments. As he revealed later under cross-examination, and as he had told Carbognin, it was his intention to do away with Paolo Cavazza and Damiano Burato after they had killed his parents.

The whole Maso case was extraordinary. Or was it? Was Maso simply the product of his society, his age, his upbringing, his environment? Or was he an aberration, an exception in a world which was still fundamentally decent? The trial verdict is in, but the jury composed of 57 million Italians is still out on the broader questions raised in the case. What kind of people could have committed such a ghastly crime? And what could have made them do it?

This was the main area of inquiry of Professor Vittorino Andreoli, the consultant psychiatrist brought in by the prosecution to test the mental responsibility and sanity of the accused. His conclusions were a savage indictment not only of the mental make-up of the teenage murderers but also of the sickness of the society that threw them up.

Professor Andreoli looks the part. With his bushy eyebrows, and long, unkempt, wavy hair shooting off in all directions from the sides of his head, he is central casting's archetypal professorial shrink. But his qualifications and professional experience are irreproachable. He won a British Council scholarship to study biochemistry at Cambridge in the 1960s. There he encountered the English academic system at its worst and best. At first, his colleagues and hosts were aloof, closed. Then halfway through his period of stay, he was suddenly invited to join a small research team that was among the world's leaders, in a city which at the time boasted in its own understated way eight Nobel prizewinners. It was a tremendous experience for a man coming from a country which, though now one of the richest in the world, only thirty years ago was still underdeveloped in many areas.

He then spent a few years at Harvard, before returning to head psychiatric services in Verona. Psychiatry was going through a turbulent period in Italy in the late 1970s. Professor Andreoli was one of those at the forefront of the wave of so-called social psychiatry, of seeking an explanation for human behaviour in society. The result of this intellectual mood was Law 180 of 1978 (the so-called Basaglia Law), which closed the psychiatric hospitals and sent patients wherever possible back to the community. The controversial move was the fruit of an ideological struggle between the different schools of psychiatry in the country, and was a triumph for Franco Basaglia whose aim was to restore human dignity to the mentally ill. Since that time, the law has been bitterly criticized by those who argue that patients suffering from a recognized mental illness such as severe schizophrenia need specialized treatment in specialized hospitals.

After the psychiatric hospitals were closed down, Professor Andreoli was given a choice of where he would like to go. He decided on becoming the resident consultant psychiatrist with his office (more than a surgery) at the hospital at Soave, 16 kilometres east of Verona. Since then he has acted as expert witness in a number of celebrated cases, including that of the bomb explosion in the Piazza della Loggia, the main square in Brescia, which killed eight people during an anti-Fascist demonstration on 28 May 1974. He has also written a book on famous murders.

For the Maso case, the professor carried out a series of standard psychiatric tests on the accused. They included the test devised by J. Richard Wittenborn, the Minnesota Multiphasic Personality Inventory, the Wechsler Adult Intelligence Scale, the Kock, Machover, and Rorschach tests (the last consisting of ten inkblots, the responses to which were once used for the diagnosis of brain damage or schizophrenia). Maso refused to undergo the Rorschach test.

In his report, the psychiatrist stated that Maso showed a highly developed narcissistic complex. This manifested itself in several ways. He was obsessed with how he looked. He would spend millions of lire on designer clothes. In court he made a special effort always to appear dapper. When in custody awaiting trial, he took the best-paid job in the prison. This earned him about

950,000 lire (£450) a month. He did it so that he could buy the clothes he wanted for his court appearances. He never wore the same clothes twice. If there were sessions in the morning and the afternoon, he would change during the lunch break. He told the psychiatrist that he had a collection of aftershaves and men's toiletries at home. These he applied in an elaborate ritual: some behind his ears, some around his sexual organs, depending on his mood and where he was going.

But his personality disorder went beyond appearances. It extended to how he projected an image of himself to the world. He wanted to be considered assertive, in charge. In fact he found it difficult to show emotion. He was of below average intelligence (he had an IQ of 79), possibly as a result of the meningitis he suffered shortly after birth. He had left school at fourteen after completing his compulsory period of education. And he was given to emotional outbursts.

Most of all he had lived much of the time in a world of fantasy, unable to distinguish between fiction and reality. His fantasies were many: about unlimited success, power, charm, beauty, true love. And he showed envy towards those who seemed more successful than himself. In short, he was immature, green and insipid like the Soave wines his father produced.

Maso had had a number of reverses in his life. After his undistinguished school career, he tried to enter a seminary to study for the priesthood, but was rejected as unsuitable. Shortly after his eighteenth birthday, he was duly called up to do his military service. During 1992, the government was to take a number of measures to reduce the compulsory military service for men, and introduce a professional volunteer force as in Britain or the United States. But these changes were too late for Maso. Within days of being drafted, he was in trouble. He spent a week, from 24 to 31 May 1990, at Verona military hospital. The military doctors pronounced that he had a personality disorder. He was discharged.

These setbacks were a blow to his self-esteem. He needed somehow to find compensation. He found it in the fantasy world he created for his group. Within it, he was acknowledged leader. From them, he commanded great devotion.

What was all the more galling about his final rejection by the military doctors was the fact that his two closest friends, Cavazza and Carbognin, had left to do their military service. What hurt his psyche even more was that they were volunteering for careers in the armed forces, one in the carabinieri, the other in the air force. Worse was to come. In December 1990 Maso was sacked from the supermarket where he worked. But he had a reprieve. In February 1991 he was taken on by a car showroom. But he was often absent from work. It was about this time he began talking more openly about doing away with his parents. He felt a need to appear someone of importance. Another jolt to his self-esteem was to follow. At the end of March he heard he was being sacked by the car showroom.

'I had always lived a lie,' Maso said in one of his interviews with the psychiatrist. 'I gave the impression to the outside world that I was strong, and contented, with my designer clothes. Maso was two people. I wanted to be believed in even more, and so I needed a larger car; I was no longer happy and satisfied with the one I had and wanted another one. I needed more money, and this was the way to get it. I like to be able to buy people drinks.'

Maso's chosen friends were all young, immature, impressionable, not very bright scholastically, and above all malleable. By contrast with Maso, Giorgio Carbognin was a dependent character, though not in the psychiatrist's assessment mentally sick. Maso became like a mother to him. Not only did he tell him what to wear. He also took him around with girls, with whom he was said to have had extraordinary success.

For Carbognin, the most important structure was the family, the key moral reference point for his actions. The others were the church and work. Maso took him away from all this. When he was with Maso he seemed to be taken over. They went together, as the Italians say, like a key in a lock.

Cavazza was also a typical product of Montecchia di Crosara. He went to church and school, and then at fourteen went out to work. He did various jobs, the last in a photographic studio in Verona where models were chosen for clothes catalogues. He left just before April for his military service. And he had a career mapped out in his mind: he wanted to stay in the armed services. Cavazza had a steady girlfriend. He would go home to her parents' house, and knew her father and mother. It was all very respectable, all very normal.

According to Professor Andreoli, the crime took place among people who showed no outward signs of having anything wrong with them. The psychiatrist performed the tests for schizophrenia and obtained no result. He found in his tests that Maso and his friends had no 'pathological deficit'. In other words, they might have had personality disorders, but were not mentally sick. Yet they had committed a terrible homicide.

So how is it that a young man, suffering from what is, after all, a fairly common condition of teenage fantasy, of attention-seeking, should have broken every taboo of society, committing not just murder, but killing his parents? Or, put another way, if he was in fact normal, why do not sons (or daughters) kill their parents all the time? Or why have there not been copy-cat parricides?

In a sense, Maso's role was the most comprehensible. But what can have induced three other apparently normal young men, with to date respectable lives, who up to then had jobs with steady salaries and career prospects, one in the carabinieri and the other in a branch of the air force, to have embarked on a scheme so harebrained, so absurd, it would have been laughable if it had not been so tragic, and to have carried it out with such monstrous ferocity and cruelty?

The simplest explanation is that they were simply living out a teenage fantasy. Professor Andreoli said they lived in a world of unreality. They never considered that their crime would be anything but perfect. They never contemplated that it could fail, and that they would end up in prison. The whole episode suggested they were all out of touch with the real world, and were operating outside the ethical canons of the community.

'This was not normal behaviour done by normal people. The old story that criminal behaviour is a symptom of some pathology does not apply here. Today society has to face a situation of a terrible criminal act which could not be a symptom of pathology. In any family it could happen. You have to ask yourself: what do you mean by normal?'

Professor Andreoli blamed Maso's upbringing for in part creating the monster. At one level he was an obedient and respectable son. At Christmas he went to church and made the sign of peace with his parents after the mass. Yet his family never criticized what he did. He had an indulgent and doting mother who spoiled him. He always wanted to be different. He had several heroes. He wanted a red jacket like James Dean. His mother bought the material for him, had it made up for him at a tailor, and then sewed on the buttons herself. It was a caprice, but she satisfied him. His father, too, spoilt his son. Just before Maso's eighteenth birthday, his father bought a new Alfa Romeo. Maso still had a provisional licence, but his father let him take the car out by himself, illegally.

It was in their attitude to money that Maso and his friends showed their split personalities. At one level they were highly traditional. Cavazza and Carbognin would each month earn about 1.5 to 1.6 million lire (about £700) take-home pay. They would give this to one or other parent. This was not for housekeeping. The parents would give them perhaps 15 or 20 per cent for spending at the weekend. They would invest the remainder for them either in a savings account or in BOT government bonds.

This money was sacred, untouchable. Peasant culture dictates putting something aside for a rainy day and as we have seen Italians are some of the biggest savers in the world. They followed these dictates. Cavazza, for example, had some 30 to 35 million lire (£15,000) in his bank account (enough to buy a car). But according to Andreoli that was not the point. They needed money, but they also needed a certain amount to be gained in some way that was not normal.

Andreoli in one of his sessions with Maso asked why if he needed money so badly he did not deal in drugs. During the trial it emerged that Maso had at one time smoked a few joints. And the defence suggested that he had an appetite for Ecstasy. But Andreoli said he was against drugs. For when he posed his question to him, Maso recoiled in shock. His hero was Don Johnson of *Miami Vice*, the archetypal American designer-TV police series. He was easily seduced by the antics of the small-screen law enforcers. There the bloody and violent struggle against the Latin American drug barons was waged by agents clad in elegant Armani suits and directed from the car phone of the hero's irresistible white BMW sports coupé.

What Professor Andreoli attempted to show was that the accused were at all times in control, that they were fully responsible for their actions, but that the social context in which they grew up was in large part to blame for their behaviour.

The area around Montecchia where they were raised was a cultural desert. There were no high schools in the valley, not even technical schools for children to go to after the end of compulsory schooling. There was nothing for the young bloods of the village to do but buy bike magazines and dream about cars.

And they had money, lots of it. And love of money is the greatest curse. 'Money without cultural context is terrible. It is not evil in itself, but it's like giving a knife to a young person: it could be dangerous,' Professor Andreoli said.

His final judgement on the society in which these boys grew up was as damning an indictment of a whole way of life as could be found.

'We are talking about a society which on the surface has the appearance of being solid, but is incapable of facing contemporary problems. Society instead tends only to deny or hide them. It is a society where people go to church without any real religious feeling and above all without this representing any source of morality or model for ethical behaviour. A society that seems peaceful and acquiescent but in fact is aggressive and, what is worse, self-pitying. This sense of victimization has provoked self-pity and a feeling of being abandoned and badly treated. This is a society which seems to be based on the family where, instead, the dominant culture is that of open conflicts, or what is worse, hidden ones, which generate ever greater hatred. Where loyalty is a big lie because everyone has at least one story of betrayal to relate. It is the same society where the husband is still the father figure and, if he is not impotent with alcohol, possesses his wife with or without her consent. She is, in the best of cases, a useful slave, and in the worst, an object into which to discharge one's rage and drunkenness. A society dominated by a political class which thinks it has obtained lesser or greater power by innate genius or through God-given gifts, which gives it the right to do what it chooses. It is a society where a pig or a pair of oxen are worth more than a wife. It is a society that has been filled to bursting with money because of the agricultural boom and where the banknotes are as likely hidden under the bedroom floor as in the bank.

'The only real god in these places is money, and it is hidden under the mattress. It is money accumulated stupidly without thinking, but people are prepared to do anything to get it. No one must know, least of all the taxman. In this society school is considered a waste of time. The sons go to lessons in the morning. In the afternoon they must work and there is always something to do. In this society of *furbi*, there are people who are still convinced that ignorance is the best way to survive. In this society there is no place for anything new. The only cultural revolution has been the old taverns with names like Angelo's or Mario's becoming bars called John, where the only drinks sold are wine, grappa and whisky.

'There is not a single bookshop in the area. The newsagent survives only because it sells cigarettes and the *carte bollate* [the paper embossed with a government duty stamp for official correspondence] used for making false claims: false disability pensions for the sound of body; falsifying one's income to entitle one to free health care; seeking exemption from military service on the pretext of some made-up illness of the father and main wage earner, so as not to lose a year's earnings. In this society no one listens to the children and a girl of twelve can give birth in a bathroom at home without her parents knowing anything.

'The only hope for young people if they have any sense is to get away first to the bigger towns, then to the city. In these places, the only preoccupation of families is to avoid spending money. The question of responsibility does not strictly enter into the domain of psychiatry. But it is impossible to ignore the responsibilities of society. It is no more possible to separate an individual from the group than a newborn baby from its mother's arms.

'We must look at the personalities of Pietro Maso, Giorgio Carbognin and Paolo Cavazza and link them to the social environment in which they lived.'

The trial was held in the court of assizes in Verona in February

1992. There were eight judges: six people's judges, a judge proper and the president of the court, Mario Sannite. They handed down their sentence on 29 February 1992 but the 117-page-long reasoning for their ruling was not made public until 15 May.

The prosecution had asked for a life sentence for Maso, and twenty-eight years each for Carbognin and Cavazza. In the end Maso got thirty years, and Carbognin and Cavazza twenty-six years each. In other words, the court rejected Professor Andreoli's argument. The accused received reduced sentences on the grounds of diminished responsibility. It was not possible for sane people to murder their parents. Maso, their judgement declared, could not be totally bad. He must be slightly insane.

Against Professor Andreoli's argument must be set the record of history. Murder and greed are as old as mankind. Society has changed, in the sense that a poor peasant community now enjoys the fruits of enormous riches. But human motivations have not changed much. The professor did expose a change in society's values. How else can one explain the fact that each day the court was thronged by young people who wanted a glimpse of Maso, that he receives dozens of fan letters in his jail cell? Yet by the same token, if these young criminals were merely the by-products of a fundamentally flawed society, then we would be seeing more such cases. Which, at the time of writing, we were not.

NINE

The Church

In an old Carmelite convent in Rome, among the fish restaurants in Trastevere, where Romans come to eat outside on balmy summer evenings, can be found the headquarters of a remarkable institution, the Community of Sant Egidio. It is unusual in that it is a smallish community rather than a mass movement. Its spiritual home, its place of common worship, is round the corner at the magnificent church of Santa Maria di Trastevere, which is widely accepted as the oldest church in the city.

I went there one February to attend the special service of thanksgiving the community has each year. It was refreshingly free of the smug complacency that can surround such occasions. There was a real sense of participating in a common act of worship. The church was packed. The usual crowd of Sunday Christians and fur-coated Roman matrons was nowhere to be seen. In their place were modest nuns in knee-length skirts, young men in beards, middle-aged men in beards, beards everywhere, the uniform of the socially committed. Priests of many nations, from Ireland, from the United States, some of them in priestly robes, many of them in simple clerical collars, were there as supporters, to bear witness.

At the end of the celebratory mass, the congregation erupted in sustained clapping. It was electrifying, and sent a tingle down my back. One understood the power of prayer, of common endeavour. As the service ended, African ambassadors clambered into chauffeur-driven black Mercedes with diplomatic plates waiting in the piazza. A reception followed at the former convent. Banana plants in a quiet courtyard seemed transported from some tropical Eden. Inside the painted reception room, whose vaulted ceilings once gazed down on the refectory, dignitaries from all over the world swirled around in their exotic costumes. In one corner stood the turbaned figure of the ambassador to the Holy See of the Islamic Republic of Iran. A man approached, suave and elegant in blue blazer, with sleek grey hair. He introduced himself. He was General Luigi Ramponi. 'I am the head of the Italian secret service,' he announced in American-accented English to the Mullah.

It was an extraordinary gambit. But then Sant Egidio is an extraordinary institution. It is a curious mixture of high diplomacy and humble service among the down and outs. Its members are driven by the same motive force: living out the word of God. (And the good secret service chief was not using the place as neutral territory to meet people interesting to his organization; he had been contributing food to the community's soup kitchen from before his time with the secret service, when he was with the guardia di finanza.) In Rome itself, the community ran homes for those without shelter; operated schools for Gypsy children who otherwise as nomads could not fulfil the bureaucratic requirements of residence and would fall through the educational net. Volunteers took evening meals round to old folk, others helped Somali refugees find lodgings and learn Italian.

Sant Egidio's remarkable pursuit of international diplomacy has taken many paths. In October 1991, it hosted a Middle East peace conference in Malta. Politicians and men of religion from every faith came from all over the Mediterranean: Jews, Catholics and Muslims. For this link between politics and religion lies at the heart of the mission of the community. The community also led an approach to the government of Albania. The Albanians may have been Muslims, but neither the Vatican nor the Italian government was prepared to initiate direct contacts. The result of this démarche was the eventual establishment of full relations by the Vatican.

Perhaps the most exceptional exercise in what was tantamout to freelance diplomacy was the hosting of direct talks between the Frelimo government in Mozambique and the Renamo rebels, who had earned a well-deserved notoriety as some of the most brutal and intransigent fighters in a bloody continent. The sponsorship of Sant Egidio was all the more astounding given its small size. It had none of the prestige or influence of the Vatican. Or the resources of a foreign ministry. This was part of its attraction to the two warring sides. For it was seen as an honest broker.

Andrea Riccardi, one of Sant Egidio's founding members, was lay professor of the contemporary history of Christianity at Rome's Sapienza University. The walls of his flat next to the church of Santa Maria di Trastevere were covered with seventeenth-century engravings of Rome. He explained how the community grew out of the general student movement of the late 1960s, and was nourished by the reforms of the Second Vatican Council of 1962–5. But how did the community transform itself from a 1960s student movement with a religious bent to a major diplomatic player? 'Rome is a port, a crossroads. Everyone passes through. We believe in international co-operation, and peace. Our Christian mission is to work for peace. There is no point in merely demonstrating for Third World causes with placards in Piazza Venezia. In the seventies, we were all about neighbourhood politics. Now the problems are about peace, and that is how the Church and Christian folk have got into international politics.'

Sant Egidio has grown up inspired by the teachings of the Church, but operates independently of the Church establishment. It would be a mistake to suggest that the Pope does not still have a great draw. Tens of thousands of Italians, many of them young people, descend on the Vatican's headquarters in St Peter's Square every Easter. But the place of the Church in society continues to shrink.

The changes wrought by the Second Vatican Council inaugurated by Pope John XXIII in October 1962 redefined the relationship between Catholic communities and the Church not just in Italy but throughout the world. It consecrated the shift for the lay members of the Church from passive participants into active ones. The central act of worship, however, the sacrament of mass, remained closed to all but the ordained clergy. All that the lay members could do was perform the readings during the mass. So on a liturgical level there was no space for the new laity. They had to try to find channels elsewhere. Some did so in administration, of the churches, of parishes, as counsellors. Many others in voluntary work. The lay movements were not only given a fillip by the Second Vatican Council. Many of the key positions were filled by more liberal-minded people. This reflected not only the personal bent of Pope Paul VI, but also the mood of the times. Since the election of Karol Wojtyla as Pope John Paul II in 1978, the pendulum has swung back. Many liberal clerics have been edged out of positions of influence. For example, the Jesuit Father Bartolomeo Sorge was removed from the editorship of the influential paper *Civiltà Cattolica*.

The history of the Italian Church is the history of the shifting balances within that curious ménage à trois: the Vatican, the Church in Italy, and the state. Only in recent years has a distinction properly been made between the Vatican and the Italian Church, although the latter has always owed allegiance to the authority invested in the Holy Father. For most of the previous 450 years, the histories of the Vatican and the Church in Italy have been so intertwined that they have been scarcely distinguishable. An Italian always occupied the papal throne, from 1522 until the election of the present pope. The entire administration of the Vatican through the Curia was overwhelmingly, often exclusively, Italian. It was only after the reforms initiated by Pope John XXIII that the Italians lost their majority in the College of Cardinals.

The old era in Italy came to an end on 20 September 1870, when Italian troops, taking advantage of the absence of the Pope's usual French protectors, breached the defences of the papal state at Porta Pia, the graceful arch in the city walls designed by Michelangelo. The seizure of Rome spelt the end of the Pope's temporal authority. Pius IX hid himself away in self-imposed incarceration. In pique the Church then refused to recognize the new state of Italy, excommunicated the sovereign, and issued an edict banning the faithful from holding office or from voting in national elections. It even refused to accept an annual tribute that the new Italian state offered, lest this would prejudice the final resolution of the status of the new arrangement.

Such a reaction to lost power and privilege failed to take account of the changing tide of history. The Vatican's reaction served also to speed the changes. As a result, many good Catholics felt constrained from serving in the new administration. This exacerbated divisions between the Catholic community and anti-clerical forces, which dominated the early governments.

The status of the Church in Italy went some way to being resolved by the Lateran Accords signed with Mussolini in 1929. The Italian state paid compensation to the Vatican for the loss of its papal possessions, and also recognized the creation of the Vatican as an independent city state. The Vatican was to lose all its lands but have control of a number of churches in Rome, as well as basilicas outside Rome at Padua, Loreto and Assisi.

The new constitution drawn up after the end of the war, which came into effect on 1 January 1948, incorporated the Lateran Accords as they were, without revision. Thus began a new era in relations between the state and the Church.

The most important single development for the reincorporation of the Church in the body politic of the country was the founding of the Christian Democratic Party in 1943. The party emerged from a grouping of pre-Fascist organizations including the Catholic Partito Popolare, trades unions and Catholic professional associations. The new party served as the tool of the Vatican both as a bulwark against the establishment of a Communist state – a very real fear in the 1940s and 1950s – and as an instrument for the creation of a civil society based on the teachings of the Church.

But the move only delayed the inevitable diminution of the influence of the Italian Church and the Vatican in the daily lives of Italians. For, over the past century and more, the formal influence of both the Italian Church and the Vatican has been seriously eroded. A hundred years after the physical breaching of the Pope's authority in Italy at Porta Pia came the single event that symbolized the undermining of the Church's authority on moral and civil affairs. In 1970 the Italian parliament passed a law legalizing divorce. The Vatican protested. It argued that the law violated the Lateran Accords as they related to personal status. The Vatican appealed to the constitutional court of the Italian state. In 1974 a vote by the people in a referendum confirmed the provision. Worse was to follow. In 1981 another referendum was held, this time over the legalization of abortion. The referendum was approved by an overwhelming majority.

Since the legalization of divorce had undermined a main plank of the 1929 concordat, a revision, or addendum, was inevitable. It was not an easy process. For twelve years of intense activity, a mixed Italian-Vatican joint commission met producing over this period six draft treaties. Always the same issues proved insurmountable. These were the three major concessions Mussolini had made to the Church in the civil life of Italy. They were: compulsory religious instruction in state-run schools; recognition by the state of an annulment by the Church of a marriage; and tax breaks for ecclesiastical institutions.

It took a non-Christian Democrat prime minister to iron out most of the outstanding issues from the first Lateran Accords. In February 1984 Bettino Craxi, leader of the Socialist Party (which opposed the incorporation of the Lateran Accords during the debate in 1947 on the constitution), signed an agreement with the Vatican secretary of state Cardinal Agostino Casaroli on a revised concordat.

Presented merely as an appendage of the original concordat, the 1984 treaty radically changed the whole relationship between the Vatican, the Church and the state. These changes reflected the waning influence of the Church in an increasingly secular society. No longer was religious instruction compulsory in Italian schools (although crucifixes still had to be hung in classrooms and many other public places such as law courts). And the great sacramental event of adult life, marriage in church, was further downgraded in the eyes of the state. Henceforward, a church service was not in itself sufficient to ensure validity in civil law. It had to incorporate wording consistent with the legal requirements of the state.

The third main area redefined to the detriment of the Church was that of clergy stipends. Until then, the clergy had been paid by the state and were, in effect, public employees, even receiving index-linked cost-of-living allowances. In 1989 the system cost 388 billion lire (£150 million). Some 26,000 priests obtained an average stipend of 800,000 lire a month (£390).

From 1990 the Church was now set to be self-financing, relying on voluntary contributions. These included tax-deductible gifts of up to 2 million lire (£800). More importantly, taxpayers could stipulate that eight parts in a thousand, nearly 1 per cent, of their taxes paid could be directed to one of four named potential beneficiaries. These were the Roman Catholic Church, for religious or charitable ends; two small sects, the Seventh Day Adventists and the Assembly of God; and the state.

Communities have to pay for their parish priests, with the dioceses only topping up stipends where necessary. This meant nearly everywhere. In 1989, the year before the new system came into effect, only fifty parishes in Rome were entirely self-support-ing. The Church went to the marketplace to help enlighten the faithful in how to make the most of that which was not rendered unto Caesar. The Italian Bishops' Conference hired the advertising agency Saatchi and Saatchi to run the campaign. Saatchis devised a clever poster and TV commercial depicting a basket of fish and a basket of bread with the slogan: 'Without your help, we cannot work miracles.'

That the Church in Italy in effect had to seek charity through the state taxation system, from the people, signified the level to which it had sunk in society. This sorry pass, however, at no point blunted the enthusiasm of bishops and prelates for exploiting the pulpit to speak out on political and social issues. The lead came from the top. Recent popes have variously intervened in the major debates of the day. That great spiritual figure, John XXIII, had always maintained a certain distance from politics. Paul VI after him emphasized the spiritual nature of the lay movement Azione Cattolica (Catholic Action). Pope John Paul II never felt so circumspect, or circumscribed. Wojtyla, as he was known – Italians always refer to their popes by their surnames – did not appear to consider that being Polish disqualified him from taking a direct interest in the political life and moral welfare of the Italians. He was after all Bishop of Rome. He has spoken out throughout his papacy not only in general terms about spiritual revival and moral rectitude. He has addressed issues specific to Italy, singling out, as we have seen, what he has castigated as the heady consumerism of Bologna and the other cities of the Emilia-Romagna plain.

The Pope's pronouncements on international diplomacy, his leading role in bringing down the Iron Curtain, cannot be underestimated. But on occasion he has been out of kilter with the political establishment in Italy, even though this has been dominated by the Christian Democrats. During the Gulf crisis of 1990–1, Pope John Paul II repeatedly appealed for a peaceful solution, expressing a horror of war. On the eve of the unleashing of American forces against Iraq, the Pope spoke to over a hundred ambassadors accredited to the Holy See. He criticized Iraq for seizing Kuwait: 'The law of the strongest cannot be imposed on the weakest.'

Yet he expressed great reservation about the justice of taking up arms to right that wrong. 'Recourse to force on behalf of a just cause is only allowable if it is proportional to the result that one wishes to obtain, and if one weighs the consequences that military action, made ever more devastating by modern technology, can have for the survival of populations and of the planet itself. The needs of humanity today require us to proceed resolutely towards the absolute banning of war and the cultivation of peace as a supreme good to which all programmes and strategies must be subordinated.'

Italy, despite its long anti-militaristic and pacifistic tradition, and a political establishment dominated by the Christian Democrats, came out in favour of a just solution based on international legitimacy. That is, Italy joined the US-led coalition ranged against Iraq. In large part this was due to the more rigorous approach to international affairs of the then foreign minister Gianni De Michelis, a Socialist and non-Catholic.

The central role in politics arrogated to itself by the hierarchy of the Italian Church, centred on the Italian Bishops' Conference, might have been understandable, when moral leadership was called for in the first elections after the defeat of Fascism in the war, and the threat of Communism was real. But the Italian Church persisted in what became an increasingly anachronistic attitude to the democratic process. Before the general elections of April 1992, the Italian Bishops' Conference launched its strongest appeal ever to an electorate for a united vote. It would have been against a centuries-long tradition of obscurantism to have stated clearly 'Vote Christian Democrat', but the intention was obvious enough. The appeal, however, failed. The Christian Democrats obtained their lowest vote ever since being founded half a century before, less than 30 per cent. In the North, the main body of deserters went over to the Northern League. In Sicily, many voted for Leoluca Orlando's La Rete. A later survey showed that a third of those Catholic voters defined as observant had ignored the bishops' instructions and voted for parties of their own choice.

The affair led to serious rethinking by many Catholic groups. In Caserta the diocese organized a conference of Catholic associations to discuss the theme under the title 'God sold to Caesar'. It was a fitting venue. The city is controlled by the Camorra. It is virtually impossible to obtain any service except through political patronage. And it is here that, in the past, the Church sided with the dignitaries and men of power.

The invocation of religion by the temporal powers is not new. Nor is the blessing by the Church of political forces. But the appeal of the Catholic hierarchy was all the more extraordinary given the disappearance of the old enemy, the Communism of godlessness and anti-family values. The Church therefore had to invent a new anathema. It devised one in the shape of secularization. But this was an old battle. The drift away from the practice of Christian values had long been apparent. The referendums on divorce and abortion in the 1970s and early 1980s showed how few of the population heeded the appeal of the Church.

The second justification given was that the unity of Catholics within one party, the Christian Democrats, would serve to counter the electoral fragmentation which threatened the proper functioning of Italian democracy. It was a specious argument. For it was clear that electoral fragmentation was a consequence of Italy's system of proportional representation that gave virtually every party, however small, a voice in parliament.

The bishops' appeal was a singular failure. By keeping quiet, the bishops would probably not have much lowered the vote for the party they favoured. By exposing themselves, and so ineffectually, they tainted themselves with the practices of a party that though still the largest in the land was discredited for its corruption and sordid pursuit of power. The Church has never exactly run the party. But it had direct links with its members at all levels.

Indeed, for all the good works done by individual priests and nuns, for all the orphanages and drug rehabilitation centres, the summer camps and educational programmes, the schools and hospitals, the publishing houses and voluntary workers in Catholic charitable organizations, for all the social services which for years the Church and churchpeople provided in the absence of the state to complement the family, the Church has a major responsibility for perpetuating in power the party which has been most identified with the corruption of the political system, the Christian Democrats. The Church continuously turned a blind eye to the party's moral turpitude. It pardoned or forgave the party leadership's ambiguous links with organized crime. It promoted a general support for the party, without examining too closely the personal and public records of individual candidates. And by identifying its own interests so closely with one party, it was unable to take an irreproachable moral stance on social issues.

What then was the role of the Church in modern Italian society? If the Church expressed an opinion on social affairs, which in these times increasingly impinged on the political sphere, it risked being accused of transgressing the confines of its competence. The leader of the Northern League, Umberto Bossi, had come out in highly critical terms about the pronouncements of Cardinal Carlo Maria Martini for doing just that. The Archbishop of Milan, even so, was a man widely regarded as one of the most committed churchmen on social issues. If the Church did not speak out, it was accused of failing to take a moral lead. As elsewhere, it was damned if it did, and damned if it did not.

Serious Catholic thinkers, especially of the liberal tradition, felt that the time had long since arrived for the Church to play a more constructive role. The first step, however, would be through a disestablishment, a separation from the ties with the Christian Democrats. Pietro Scoppola, who teaches contemporary history at the faculty of political science of Rome's Sapienza University, has actively campaigned for such reform. He stands in the best tradition of academics who descend from their ivory towers to the turmoil of political activism. Professor Scoppola was author of the Referendum Pact, and guarantor of the movement led by the Christian Democrat deputy Mario Segni for a cleaning up of the political culture of the country.

He has argued cogently that the Church must provide spiritual and moral leadership not for one party, but the whole of society, particularly in the search for a new grouping of the left. This quest for a new enemy risked compromising or ignoring the most important duty of the Church: 'to feed and reinforce each day the ethical fabric of civil society, to reconstitute those reserves of the living world, without which democracy becomes simply a clash of interests. This is the prime duty of religion in public life, not playing party politics. At this deeper level, religious experience can condition and inspire different political trends, be they moderate or progressive. It is hard to understand why the Church in Italy should give up trying to influence the process of building a new left alliance no longer linked exclusively to one ideology but open henceforward to different cultural and ethical values of the Christian tradition.

'It is hard to understand why John Paul II considers that the Catholic faith should provide the moral foundation to underpin the new world being born in Europe, while at the same time the Italian Church should be so tied to the past. We are the only country in Europe in which the Bishops' Conference called on Catholics to vote together in general elections.

'I would not wish the Italian Church to be less present or gagged within the political arena. Rather, it should be present, in many ways. What is under discussion is not the political role of the Christian Democrats in Italian life, but its privileged links with the Church.'

For Professor Scoppola the key to understanding the institutional decline and paralysis of the Italian system was the Roman question. In other words, the Pope's decision in 1870 not to collaborate with the newborn Italian state, indeed to forbid the faithful from co-operating with it, laid the foundations for the division between a backward-looking church and the progressive forces seeking to create a new state. Historians could argue that such divisions between supporters and opponents of the Pope had antecedents in the medieval battles between the Guelphs and Ghibellines.

'It is difficult to understand the role of the Catholic Church in Italy. Because it is a role always very tied to politics. We had always on our backs the Roman question. The Roman question deeply marked the history of our country. This break between the state and the Church, the national conscience, the Catholic conscience, left a deep scar. Which meant that the Catholic Church did not play a spontaneous role like religion did in the early United States, where the ethical fabric of democracy was formed by Christian experience. In Britain, the Labour Party and the

Tories spring from Christian roots. They didn't come from Marxism.

'This break in Italy meant that the Church remained apart. The problem now is how to get out of this situation in a definitive way. The Communist threat was what had once more brought the Church back into the political arena, the years of confrontation, of the Cold War, when one could counterpose a church which had become a political movement and a Communist party which resembled a church, with its rites, with its liturgy, with its myths, with its Stalin, its almost anthropological issues, the way the masses were mobilized.

'Resistance to this is in the party headquarters. Public opinion is evolving in this direction. Today there is a Catholic religious life which is much closer to, or should we say less far away from, the tradition of the reformed Church. Leave aside the theological aspects, or the question of papal authority. The way people think of living out their lives in a religious way, the way people pray, the way people form part of a religious community, is much more similar today in the Catholic Church to the reformed Church than it was in the past. There are today the conditions in Italy for relations between the Church and society and politics which are new, constructive, for civil society.

'Within the Catholic Church hierarchy there is a great difference in opinion. You must not believe that the opinions of Cardinal Ruini reported in the newspapers are the only ones among the Italian bishops. I know many bishops who invite me to express these ideas to their dioceses. The Bishop of Caserta, for example, an area which is struggling against the Camorra. There is a tremendous difference in opinion. And also in lay society. Because there are many people who engage in voluntary work, who are close to the environmentalists, the Greens. The old blocs that we had before don't exist any more. The wall has come tumbling down. There is a rich fabric now. There is collaboration between believers and non-believers. Types of Christian solidarity have always existed. But today they are more spontaneous. There is no longer a single, monolithic Catholic bloc. It is much more diffuse and varied.

'I see a very narrow link between institutional change and this evolution of the culture of the country. There is a relationship between the cultural problems, the anthropological relationship between the Church and the state, and the institutional question, if we manage to achieve a democracy along the lines of western ones, the democracy of alternating governments, or a system where there are distinct differences between the government and opposition and their respective responsibilities, and there is a possibility of change.

'Italy can only be understood through Catholicism. Catholic intellectuals have not always had an easy time. They were caught in a vice, so to speak, between a Church hierarchy hostile to freethinking and a secular environment which only valued Marxist-inspired or left-wing thinking. Italy cannot do without Catholics. The new left cannot be born without this moral sense of the Catholic world.'

One of the commonplaces of Italian society, a paradox that has been frequently observed and commented on, is that, despite having the headquarters of the Catholic world and being by tradition one of the most Catholic countries in Europe, Italians should in recent years be more divorced from the institutional church than ever. By 1991 nearly a third of children in Rome were not baptized; over a quarter of marriages were celebrated in register offices only. Church attendances were down. According to one survey commissioned by the Church, only a quarter of Romans regularly take communion, a quarter infrequently, and half never. The figures were even lower in the industrialized North. The areas where the Church – and by extension, the Christian Democrat Party – had been traditionally strong were the Veneto in north-eastern Italy and the South, especially Sicily. Italy is an overwhelmingly Catholic country in that 98 per cent or more of the population are nominally Catholic. This provides for greater homogeneity than many Italians, obsessed with nitpicking over regional differences, will give credit for. It also means that the whole moral base for society, the common ethical underpinning as Professor Scoppola stated, is essentially derived from the fundamentals of the teaching of the Church.

Some lay movements predated the Second Vatican Council.

The longest-established was Azione Cattolica, to which many of the leading Christian Democrat politicians have at some time belonged. Another, Comunione e Liberazione, was a mass right-wing, anti-libertarian youth movement founded by Monsignor Luigi Giussani in 1956. Often equated with Opus Dei, it is popular on student campuses, where its adherents are known as *ciellini* (C-L-ini). It controls two important Catholic newspapers, the daily *L'Avvenire* and the weekly *Il Sabato*.

If the CL is the new army of conservative Catholicism, its vanguard is the Movimento Popolare. But conservative Catholic militancy is very different from of old. It is mainly pacifist. Its head, the hyper-energetic Euro MP Roberto Formigoni, led a couple of ill-fated peace missions to Iraq in the diplomatic period of the phoney war between the Iraqi invasion of Kuwait in August 1990 and the US-led assault the following January. He founded Movimento Popolare together with Rocco Buttiglione, the Catholic theologian, and brother of one of the best-known faces in Italy, the television newsreader Angela Buttiglione.

The rejection of the Catholic Church during the twentieth century, for both political and social reasons, did not, however, signify a loss of the spiritual dimension in Italian life. Indeed, that vacuum was often filled outside the context of the Catholic Church. Many of the searchers for The Truth rejected the Church's teaching and sought the way through other, mostly newer, religious movements. These varied from established religious alternatives or sects such as Protestantism, Buddhism, and Jehovah's Witnesses to fads in the realm of folklore, such as satanic sects.

As for the priesthood, it was afflicted by falling vocations. By 1992 numbers had shrunk to a little over 36,000. This was not their only plight. The vocation itself in certain areas posed dangers never envisaged when many of its priests first started their studies in a seminary. The existential risks were physical not metaphysical.

In the spring of 1992, Monsignor De Zen was stabbed seriously about his person in the precincts of his church in Padua. His assailant was a madman screaming that he was the true Messiah. In north-east Italy, around Trento, parish priests in outlying districts have given new meaning to the expression canon law. For they have been packing pistols and shotguns to protect themselves against a spate of robberies of church plate. Police said that most of the robbers were itinerants or drug addicts, many of them in their teens or early twenties. The clerics' initiative coincided with the extraordinary admission by the minister for justice and deputy prime minister Claudio Martelli that the state was unable to guarantee the personal safety of citizens. He suggested instead they adopt self-defence methods.

A picture later emerged, half comical, half tragic, of ancient prelates sleeping with firearms at night. Some of these gun-toting clerics explained their apparent preparedness to breach the most basic commandment of all, Thou Shalt Not Kill. Window bars were not enough, they lamented. In Veneto, the flat plain of the Po Valley that makes up the hinterland of Venice, parishes outnumber local councils. But for several years the priests have been feeling victimized by bandits. They have been threatened, attacked, insulted, robbed, and sprayed with foam from fire extinguishers. No place is sacred. The Trevignano priesthood which took up arms against this pestilence was scarcely young. And during the service, between the lesson and a prayer, in the place of the usual parish notices, the priest would add another announcement: 'Dear worshippers, I am armed.'

A photograph of one of these exponents of the Church Militant was circulated around the world. I went to see Don Olivo Visentin at the imposing presbytery where he lives beside the parish church of Sernaglia della Battaglia. His housekeeper opened the door. A rich smell of country cooking pervaded the hall. We went into his study, where he talked about his parish, with its 2,800 souls, and the changes he had seen during his long ministry.

Like most villages in the area, it had one single tall building: the free-standing belfry, built of brick with a stone base, and topped with a spire. All around was rich farming land, with vineyards which produce the light white wines of Treviso. Large new houses dotted the dull featureless countryside, overshadowed by the Dolomites rising up to the North. Many local people had emigrated to Africa, New Zealand or Australia, then come back with their fortunes, and the knowledge of different ways of doing things, to invest their money in small productive ventures.

A little to the east, at the village of Tezze, a circus troupe was decamping beside the British war cemetery, one of those oases of calm to commemorate the fallen of the world wars. The remains of 355 officers and men who fell in this region during the First World War had been buried there. Most of the gravestones were marked with the same date: 27 October 1918. The previous December, the British XI and XIV Corps had arrived to take up position in the Montello sector. The main defensive area was the right bank of the River Piave. The last battle, only days before the bloody conflict came to an end (the armistice was signed on the Italian front a week earlier than elsewhere, on 4 November), began on 24 October. On 27 October, the British troops passed through the Piave. As silent witness to that terrible day were the lines of gravestones, in spanking new marble, of men from the Yorkshire Dales and the hills of Northumbria, who had lost their lives somewhere in northern Italy.

It was hard to imagine the terrible suffering endured in these parts that now were so tranquil. Or, rather, that had been so. Things had begun to turn nasty, the priest confided. He said that in the past seven or eight years he had had eight burglaries or break-ins. The latest was a few months before, on the Feast of the Epiphany. The burglars had forced a door on the first floor, trashed a room looking for gold or money, and left empty-handed.

On only one occasion had he actually seen the robbers. They were real criminal types, he said, *zingari* Slavs or Gypsies. They rang his doorbell. When he opened up to them, they set about him with a billiard cue, striking him on the head and arms. 'Two of them carried pistols. They wanted money. They took the Sunday collection, sitting on a plate in the hall, and my wallet. They were real delinquents. They were picked up later. They had the same 7.65 calibre pistol I saw.'

Don Olivo identified two types of housebreakers. There were criminal elements from the South. And drug addicts who needed money for a fix. There were more drug addicts than ever. 'It's a by-product of the wealth of these young people. There is too much good living, which has brought disadvantages too. There's been a fall in moral values. There's no unemployment in this area.

Far from it. There are even now immigrant labourers from Morocco, Algeria and Senegal. But things aren't what they were.'

And for this reason he had taken up his rifle, an old hunting gun that had belonged to his late father. He had fired it once, 'to scare them off. I fired in the air. It certainly did the trick. They scarpered smartish. But I would never shoot to kill. I could not do that. It was only to frighten them. There are many wonderful things in life.'

The language of Rome has always needed an intermediary to render it intelligible. For the educated classes of Europe, it was, of course, at various times a *lingua franca*. Why else, how else could one explain the hold the Roman Catholic priesthood exercised for centuries over the non-Latin-speaking peasantry? The Second Vatican Council, by prescribing the departure from Latin rites and promoting the use of the vernacular, to some extent demystified one area of potency of the priest as man of learning, as intercessor and indispensable dispenser of blessings. But, in Palermo, I found that the Roman way of speaking could still be an obstacle to universal understanding. I had asked the taxi driver to take me to the church of Magione. He looked uncomprehending. 'Magione,' I repeated, in what I thought was passable Roman. 'Magione.' He again looked blank. And then he slowly began to smile. The scales were lifted from his eyes. 'MaSHONe. MaSHONe. That's what we say in Sicily. When you say in Italian MaGIONe, we don't understand.'

Maccione, Magione, what you will, the fine old church rose strong and virile over the waste ground all around. Fifty years before, Allied bombs and shells had pummelled this ancient part of Palermo into ruin. Little had been done since to reconstruct the shattered remains of the quarter. Palermo was the only city in Italy whose historic centre had not had its war damage extensively repaired. The once magnificent gothic and baroque palazzi of the aristocratic families were in variously advanced stages of dilapidation and ruin. The denizens of the centre had become a curious mixture, a sprinkling of noble families in a vast sea of the poor, many of them immigrants from North and West Africa.

No new monument had been erected in the flattened Piazza

Magione, except a huge metal water tank. Only the church had been completely rebuilt. On the wall outside was fixed one of those familiar yellow plaques declaring that this was a historic monument. It announced to the very few tourists who picked their way over the rubble that the church was in the Arab-Norman style.

The church itself was restrained and sparse, almost completely without adornment, in contrast to the overblown masterpieces of the baroque. A long, low building like the side of a cloister ran along the drive up to the church entrance. This was where parish business was conducted. For, in parallel to the faithful reconstruction of the church building, the parish priest had been working on the moral and spiritual resurrection of the community in the urban wilderness.

'Have you seen round this part of town? Well, jump in then,' Padre Giacomo Ribaudo pointed to an early-model Fiat Uno, its doors almost off their hinges. He looked the part, a short man in black beret and ill-fitting trousers. And he drove with all the fatalism of the southern Mediterranean, that abandon of those who put their lives in the hands of a higher authority.

'This was one of the most beautiful parts of Palermo,' he said, lifting both hands worryingly off the wheel, as he scooted the wrong way up a one-way street. 'That palazzo you see on the right used to be a hospital. It closed down tens of years ago.'

Norman Lewis portrayed Palermo as an essentially oriental city. Not just in the Arab architecture, but in the customs and habits of the people. 'A baroque façade of dimpled statuary has been built over the wall-eyed Saracenic town with its pink-domed *kubbas* and its stumps of minarets, but the relaxation of Palermo remains oriental in style ... the public display of leisure inherited from turban-wearing ancestors.'

There was little leisure, publicly displayed or otherwise, in this part of town. A Vespa raced past on the flagstones. 'Here a few new houses have been built,' the priest said, indicating a drab block of working-men's homes. 'See how the fine old houses alternate with the squalid slums.'

'That, in fact, is like what we are trying to do here. To bring the good in among the bad. This church is like a twin. We are eight parishes in this area known as the Tribune Castel del Mar waging a common struggle for the benefit of these poor people. They have ancient traditions. When we had a Procession of the Bambino, the Infant Jesus, people flocked around. When the sea came right up here, eight hundred years ago, the Bambino blessed the sea to show the links between the island and the sea, between the island and the world beyond.'

His metaphysical musings were constantly interrupted by the rather more prosaic sounds of the street around. Ignoring the increasingly raucous horns of the oncoming motorists going the correct way up the one-way street, he carefully manoeuvred his tiny car on to the pavement as if it were one of those four-wheel-drive jeeps beloved of yuppie Italian city dwellers.

'What we are trying to achieve is greater integration between the cultural and intellectual life of the city and these poor people. Palermo is a city with some of the best artists and poets and writers and university people. There is a rich tradition. Now the poor are poor in the sense of economic deprivation and low level of educational achievement. But they have something they can offer others. My vocation is to be a bridge between the two, between the Palermo *perbene*, of decent people, and the others, those who have been abandoned by society, but who can give something of that sense of family, of solidarity between each other. The two can gain from each other, but only if there is a point of contact between them. A number of people from the university, and businessmen, and doctors, have accepted this idea. We have formed an association of all the parishes. We called it the Servants of the Trinity to help provide medicines and legal advice, not free but at prices people can afford. You've seen the film *The Godfather*? Well, that's what they are. But they've chosen a new way, as a witness for young people, to create a real link or association. This is not charity, reaching into pockets, but a real bridge of friendship, of care to develop human relationships.

'The parish also runs a school. The Cardinal wanted it here, not in the smarter end of town, to be nearer to the real problems. Many young people specialize in services like Caritas, voluntary work and social services as well as the fight against the Mafia. Now these thirty godfathers. So much of Palermo is under the control of the Mafia and organized crime. We want to make it easier to say no so that they won't feel they have sold out to the Mafia. The Mafia is in the heart of the state. The problem is not political. We need a moral rearmament. The Church can do a lot if there is hope. Cardinal Pappalardo wrote a very fine speech addressed to the local-government officials. What the political movement needs is a moral base.'

But was not Giulio Andreotti, then prime minister, a deeply observant Catholic? Father Ribaudo sniffed scornfully. 'Hernando Cortez, who murdered hundreds of thousands of men, every morning went to mass, recited his rosary, and gave alms. But Catholicism entails real obligations. The first is to practise justice with regard to the poor and humble, to protect widows, to give shelter to orphans, to take in strangers.'

In Sicily and parts of the South, in Calabria and Campania, many priests and bishops were carrying on the ancient tradition of warriors of Christ in the front line against the ever-present enemy, the Mafia.

The hierarchy had not always been so evidently ranged with the forces operating against the Mafia. Past bishops of Palermo and princes of the Church frequented the salons of the local nobility and the palazzi of the Christian Democrat leadership, which was closely tied in with the Mafia.

The Church has had its own shadowy history not just as passive condoner of the Mafia but as active protagonist within organized crime. The most celebrated case was that of the Franciscans of Mazzarino, brought to trial in 1962. Then the court in Messina heard how Padre Carmelo, the venerable prior of the convent, headed an extortion racket run by the monks. Any victim who refused to pay up risked early fulfilment of the Church's own teaching on mortality. The richest man in Mazzarino, Angelo Cannada, stood up to the monks, and was gunned down by four men.

Investigations showed that though the monks had only a modest declared income from charity and an orchard, they were all millionaires. Furthermore, women were frequent visitors to their hallowed precincts. The trial in Messina failed to obtain any convictions. The absolution of the defendants' sins demonstrated the power these men of religion still commanded over the Sicilian psyche. In the words of Norman Lewis, 'the fact that the monks were immoral would be unimportant. What was important was that they were the human vehicles of magic power. The supernatural offices they performed were in no way lessened in their efficacy by the monks' own extreme human fallibility. The monks were not good men, but they were powerful men, and it was their power to which the Sicilian subconscious automatically responded.'

The acquittals provoked an outcry. A retrial was ordered. All were convicted and sentenced to long terms. Since then, no scandal of such an organized nature has afflicted the Church. However, individual clerics have continued to perform rites of passage for known mafiosi, baptizing their children into the Church, marrying their sons and daughters, and granting them a Christian burial despite the blood on their hands.

The current archbishop, Cardinal Salvatore Pappalardo, has undertaken a number of initiatives to head the official Catholic crusade against the Mafia. But his position is at times delicate. In March 1992, Salvo Lima, exponent extraordinary of that old cosy relationship between the Mafia families and the Christian Democrat Party establishment, was murdered. Motorcycle gunmen shot him down on the streets of his native Palermo, where he had been born sixty-five years before. He had been mayor during the whole period of the reconstruction of the city when the Mafia moved in on the building contracts. Re-elected four times, he was then elected deputy in Rome. Finally, when judicial investigations were closing in, he was sent off as a Euro MP to Strasbourg. But the odour of his Mafia association was always around him. In the 1976 report of the parliamentary anti-Mafia commission, his name cropped up no fewer than 149 times. Yet somehow the evidence never managed to stick. It was widely assumed that he had protection at the highest level, which ensured that investigations never ran their course. He was, after all, proconsul on the island – an island that throughout most of its history had been ruled from the mainland – to Giulio Andreotti. Lima it was who delivered the votes for Andreotti's faction within the Christian Democrat Party at national elections. In return Andreotti might not have asked too closely how those votes were secured.

It was Cardinal Pappalardo's duty to conduct the funeral of this dubious man. That the most senior clergyman in the city should have taken the service, and delivered the eulogy, seemed to many to symbolize the whole ambiguous support of the Church for the Christian Democrat establishment and their shady connections with the Mafia. Most politicians of other parties were happy to stay away from the funeral. All Cardinal Pappalardo could hope to do was to distinguish between Lima as a human being, whose death merited the send-off appropriate to a city dignitary killed in such violent circumstances, and Lima's record.

Other men of the cloth, who are not arrayed in crimson or purple, were more outspoken against the men of honour. One of the best-known was Father Ennio Pintacuda. He ran the Pedro Arrupe study centre in one of the newer areas of Palermo to train young aspirants in the moral bases of political and business leadership. Outside the premises armed police guarded the gates and screened visitors. The window of the porter's lodge was made of bulletproof glass. Man of God or not, Father Pintacuda's outspoken attacks on the Mafia make him a target.

Like so many troublesome priests, Father Pintacuda was a Jesuit. And almost more important than his own pronouncements was his work in training others. His most prominent protégé was the former mayor of Palermo, Leoluca Orlando, leader and founder of La Rete, the movement for democracy. Father Pintacuda was Professor Orlando's mentor, spiritual guide, and political confessor. And Father Pintacuda urged Orlando to broaden his scope first from town to regional politics on the island, and then on to the national level to Rome. Why had he done this when Cosa Nostra, the Sicilian Mafia, was most concentrated in Palermo itself? 'My work has always been to insist that true liberation from the Mafia comes through political change, through new ways of politics.'

This was shorthand for saying that the Mafia survived because it was protected in some way by political forces in Rome. Rome needed a spiritual and moral purge of the political establishment before any serious new campaign could be launched against the Mafia without being thwarted by interested political elements. The electorate seemed to agree with this diagnosis of the ills of society, and the prescription for recovery. In the April 1992 general elections, the charismatic Leoluca Orlando received more personal preference votes in Palermo than any other candidate in the entire country.

Father Pintacuda is not alone. Nor is Father Ribaudo. Many bishops have used the pulpit to speak out against the brutality of the Mafia. Bishops in Lecce and Locri, in Campania and Calabria, have not shrunk from castigating the men of honour. And in his pontificate, Pope John Paul II has excoriated them as never before. But it is actions, not statements, that matter. The Church and individual clergy have continued to grant succour to known mafiosi. Even Cardinal Pappalardo, widely respected for waging a crusade against Cosa Nostra, could not bring himself to mention the Mafia by name during the eulogy for the fallen judge Giovanni Falcone, talking instead of the men of violence.

TEN

Not such cosy nostrums about Cosa Nostra

There were no markings on the executive jet which landed at Palermo's Punta Raisi airport at 4.43 on the afternoon of Saturday 23 May 1992. The Falcon 500 was one of several run by a discreet agency called CAI and at the disposition of the Italian security services, SISDE and SISMI, for use by VIPs (in the original meaning of important people). As it taxied to a halt, a motorcade of bulletproof cars drew up. Judge Giovanni Falcone, the country's leading campaigner against the Mafia, was coming home to Palermo for what was left of the weekend.

He never made it. A huge explosion blasted his motorcade as it raced along the A29 motorway from the airport to Palermo. Subsequent inquiries focused on the supposed mole within the ministry of justice where Falcone worked, or the secret services, or the élite police-escort service, or indeed workers at either the military or civilian part of Ciampino airport; any of these could have phoned through to Palermo to tip off their colleagues that Falcone was on his way. Much was made in the Italian press about the search for a hidden informant. A member of parliament was investigated for allegedly using his portable phone to warn Mafia contacts. All that was in part an answer to that Italian obsession with plots and conspiracies. How was it, people asked, that a man like Falcone, with a security section of 60 permanently assigned to him, and whose movements were closely guarded secrets, could have been so easily despatched? How was it that the helicopter look-outs used to track his drive from the airport had been scrapped only just days before, ostensibly for reasons of cost?

Yet no such mole need have burrowed into his entourage. It was widely known that Falcone had, since his transfer to Rome, returned to Palermo most weekends to join his wife, Francesca

Morvillo. She was also a magistrate, the daughter of a councillor at the Palermo Tribunal. She had applied for a job in Rome to be nearer her husband, but had been turned down. He more than anyone knew of the security hazards of venturing into Palermo. He would stagger his departure times, sometimes leaving on Friday afternoon, sometimes on Saturday morning. Forensic evidence suggests that the assassins did not have any prior knowledge of Falcone's exact departure time from Rome. Investigators eventually discovered the spot on the hillside from where the assassins set off the bomb by remote control. They found the area among the olive orchards covered with footprints and cigarette butts, evidence of a long wait. Evidence too of the absence of the most simple precautions, in an age when the saliva traces on a cigarette end can be accurately identified through DNA testing.

Initially the assassination was described as highly professional. It was certainly effective. A crater 7 metres (20 feet) deep was gouged out of the embankment that carried the road. However, closer examination showed that the technique was not flawless. The bomb was packed into a drainage channel running beneath the road. The assassins had set off the bomb just before Falcone's car – the second in the convoy – went over the culvert. It was as if they were shooting game – aiming ahead to allow time for the shot to reach the prey. But with remote-control devices, the detonation occurs instantaneously. There was no need to compensate for a time lag. So it was that the lead car containing the bodyguards was catapulted across the other side of the dual carriageway and into an orchard. I saw it a few hours later where it had landed, a mangled heap, on the sea side. Falcone's spanking new white Fiat Croma, the latest model bulletproof car which cost 200 million lire (£90,000), was stopped in its tracks. The road surface had buckled like thin tin foil, curling up in front of its wheels. The vehicle had lost its entire front section. The engine had disintegrated. Massive chunks of tarmac and rubble had landed on the roof. The windscreen, 4 centimetres (1.5 inches) thick of supertoughened laminated glass, had been blasted out of its frame. It lay on the ground, shattered but in one piece. Falcone should have survived. But he had chosen, as he often did, to drive himself, with his wife beside him. He took the full force of the explosion.

His driver, relegated to the back seat, lived. He was later to explain that he realized as they were bowling along the motorway that *his* keys were in the ignition, but Falcone was going to drive him home first. So Falcone whipped the keys out of the ignition, handed them to his terrified driver, and inserted his own keys in their place, all while they doing something over 140 kilometres an hour.

Besides Falcone and his wife, three bodyguards were killed in the explosion. They had worked with Falcone loyally for years. Any suggestion that the Mafia seeks to spare innocent civilian casualties was dashed by the nature of the attack. A couple of Austrian tourists who were travelling by hire car in the opposing carriageway were injured in the blast. It was a miracle they were not killed.

Two days later, thousands of Palermo people thronged the basilica of San Domenico for the funeral service of the five victims. The coffins were placed on the ground before the altar. Grouped round them, facing the congregation, were Falcone's colleagues from the Tribunal at Palermo, wearing their black robes of office. Leading the magistrates was Paolo Borsellino, Falcone's childhood friend and closest colleague, who now inherited the dead man's mantle as the leading campaigner against the Mafia.

The two men had grown up together and worked together. Borsellino was born in the heart of the old city of Palermo, in Piazza Magione. He grew up with Falcone in the popular Alberghería quarter. Their lives followed similar though not identical courses. Both studied law and became magistrates. Both married the daughters of their respective judicial mentors at the Palermo Tribunal. Falcone was twice married. Where they differed was over politics. Falcone never actively engaged in politics. Borsellino by contrast as a university student was a member of Fuan, the students' association affiliated with the neo-Fascist MSI party. But he was scrupulous in not allowing his political sympathies to colour his judgements. The first time I met him, I was taken by a left-wing Italian journalist, himself a Sicilian, who described him as a tough old nut, but straight up and down.

We saw him in the specially adapted wing of the Tribunal, after passing through several sets of solid steel doors, guarded by young plain-clothes bodyguards – as much as the casual trousers and fashionably cut jackets could ever be construed as plain clothes and their machine pistols ordinary fashion accessories. Inside his office, Borsellino could monitor comings and goings in the corridor outside on a TV screen high in one corner.

Borsellino never believed he had the talent of the charismatic Falcone. But after Falcone, he among those on the side of the law knew the Sicilian Mafia Cosa Nostra better than anyone alive. Less than two months after Falcone was buried, on 19 July 1992, Borsellino was struck down in his turn. He was a victim of a car bomb. It was a Sunday afternoon. He had gone to visit his mother. Once again, Mafia killers using a remote-control device set off a small Fiat packed with explosives outside the apartment block. Five escort officers including a policewoman were also killed.

Borsellino knew after the death of Falcone that he was next in line. So why did he do it? When I asked Borsellino why he ran the daily risk of being killed by continuing his fight against the Mafia, his stern face cracked into what passed for a smile. He did not believe the Sicilian leopard could not change its spots. 'Because I am not a *gattopardista*. I don't believe that things cannot change. And for Sicilians there is a choice. Either they can leave the island, or they can stay behind and try to improve the situation.'

Gattopardista. It was one of the key words for understanding Sicily. It meant subscribing to the thesis of *Il Gattopardo* (*The Leopard*), Giuseppe Tomasi di Lampedusa's novel, and the book's pessimistic, fatalistic view of the unchanging nature of Sicily. For di Lampedusa, the succession of rulers over the centuries had not altered the enduring reality of Sicily where the one constant was the indomitable sun. 'The sun was showing itself the true ruler of Sicily; the crude brash sun, the drugging sun, which annulled every will, kept all things in servile immobility, cradled in violence and arbitrary dreams.'

Why did Falcone do it? What made men like this give up their lives to fight against the Mafia and organized crime? This question, how ordinary people confront the Mafia, often performing extra-ordinary acts of courage, has as much bearing on the future of secret criminal organizations as their own internal ability to survive.

For Falcone and Borsellino, it was not a question of *whether* they would be victims of the criminal organization they were hunting, but *when*. And in their cases, the answer was some time in the summer of 1992. One could argue that, as Sicilians, they had that sure sense of the inevitability of death. The culture of death is, as Falcone himself wrote, so much part of Sicilian life and literature, from the rock-hard cakes at funerals to the ironic fatalism in the works of Pirandello and Sciascia. Yet they also took all precautions possible to ensure a stay of execution. More persuasively, they had a sense of mission. Just as Cosa Nostra is a Mafia organization made up of Sicilians, the majority of those who have devoted and in many cases sacrificed their lives to the fight against organized crime are Sicilian too. Judges, policemen, campaigning journalists – all brave men and women who have carried on this thankless task.

As an adolescent Falcone would quote the somewhat trite aphorism of Giuseppe Mazzini (1805–72), the driving force for Italian reunification, 'Life is a mission and duty its supreme law.' After the first attempt on his life, in 1989 when fifty sticks of dynamite were found in a holdall on the beach beneath his holiday house, Falcone declared, 'Sure, they haven't killed me yet. But the show's not over yet. My account with Cosa Nostra is still open. And I know that I will close it only with my death, natural or otherwise.'

When the supergrass Tommaso Buscetta began his confession, he warned Falcone, 'First they'll try to kill *me*, then it will be *your* turn. And they won't give up until they succeed.'

Falcone was to write: 'I know the risks that I run doing the job I do, and I do not believe I should give a gift to the Mafia by offering myself as an easy target. In Sicily the Mafia kills the servants of the State that the State has not been able to protect. I am simply a servant of the State in *terra infidelium*.'

What set Falcone apart was that he was more than just the country's leading campaigner against the Mafia. He had become a symbol of the battle waged by the State, and of good men and true, against Cosa Nostra. He was widely credited with devising the system of the pool of magistrates in Palermo to deal with Mafia crimes. In fact, it was set up after the murder in 1983 of the chief examining magistrate in Palermo, Rocco Chinnici. It was the then chief investigating magistrate Judge Antonino Caponnetto who founded the system. Falcone perfected and developed it. The aim was two-fold. It was to pool resources, so that magistrates working on different but related cases could more readily compare notes and tap into the central computer brain. And it was for their greater collective security. Individual magistrates would be less easily intimidated if those who would threaten them knew that the investigations would continue without them. The system imposed a great cost on the magistrates themselves. They immediately became potential targets, and had to give up any pretence of leading normal lives. They lived under constant protection. Armour-plated cars took them to work. Bodyguards hovered round them wherever they moved. And they were obliged to work inside offices of reinforced steel and concrete, with armour-plated doors. No more could they go to restaurants or the cinema. They in effect lived underground.

Despite the precautions, they remained at risk. Judge Chinnici was killed by a Mafia bomb under a car parked in front of his house set off by remote control. Falcone was to cite this as an example of the inevitability of his death, given the balance of forces at the time. 'Rocco Chinnici had not underestimated anything. Competent and courageous, he was rigorous in his attention to self-protection, and made great personal sacrifices to achieve it, with bodyguards and an armour-plated car. Yet Rocco Chinnici's death was the most natural, most normal in the world, the exception which proved the rule: that in the war that he was waging against the Mafia, even though he could not improve on his tactics, he fell into a trap and lost his battle. The Mafia proved itself stronger and more able than he was.'

Chinnici's death was also foreseen. A Lebanese playing a double game as arms smuggler and police informer had telephoned the Palermo flying squad to warn of an impending car-bomb attack.

Falcone's great success was in all cases dealing with Cosa Nostra both in Italy and on the other side of the Atlantic. It was the anti-Mafia pool that traced the hundreds of millions of dollars made from the international heroin trade that were laundered through financial institutions in the United States and Switzerland. The pinnacle of the pool's achievements came in the so-called maxi-trial in the mid-1980s. The trial reached its conclusion in December 1987. It handed down nineteen life sentences and a further 2,655 years in prison to 338 defendants. Another 127 were acquitted. More significantly, twelve out of the thirteen members of the Commission, the ruling body of Cosa Nostra, were convicted and sentenced – albeit some *in absentia*. They included the man widely believed at one time to have been the Boss of Bosses, Michele 'the Pope' Greco, although he may never have been such a dominant figure in practice. He was charged with 78 murders.

The maxi-trial was a major coup in several respects. Not only did it bring so many Mafia bosses to court. More importantly, the prosecution had sought to establish for the first time the existence of Cosa Nostra as a rigidly organized hierarchical structure, rather than merely a loose collection of rival families or clans. The prosecution case was set out in a massive 8,067-page indictment. This opened with the words: 'This is the trial against the Mafia-type organization called Cosa Nostra, a very dangerous criminal organization that, through violence and intimidation, has sowed and still sows death and terror.'

But success in Italy is short-lived. Italians love a winner – but not for long. The work of the pool was questioned at several levels: organizational, political, personal and, most damaging of all, judicial. A whispering campaign started against Falcone. He was said to be abusing his powers. His phone was tapped. The anti-Mafia pool was disbanded. Falcone was passed over for the job of top anti-Mafia investigator in Palermo. He continued as an anti-Mafia investigator, but was also assigned more mundane cases, such as investigating break-ins. Eventually he took a job in Rome, as director of penal affairs at the justice ministry. It was a very senior post, and was a springboard for international co-operation on inquiries. He had the job when he died, but he was poised to take the top job of all, that of the newly created *super-procuratore* or investigating magistrate for the entire country, to co-ordinate the activities of all the regions.

Falcone and his colleagues had to fight not only against the Mafia. They had to overcome the feuding jealousies of the magistrates' own self-ruling body, the suspicions of colleagues, and the interference of malign politicians. There were some notorious obstacles. Barely a month after Falcone was killed, the head of the Italian supreme court, Judge Corrado Carnevale, cancelled the sentences against four leaders of the *cupola*. Judge Carnevale had already earned a reputation for overturning convictions of mafiosi, especially when they relied too heavily on the testimony of *pentiti* or supergrasses. And once again Judge Carnevale denied the existence of a *cupola*, of a hierarchical structure within the Mafia. Instead, he insisted that organized crime was run by a collection of families.

Falcone neither underestimated nor romanticized the Mafia. He saw them as a brutal organization whose obsession was power. Cosa Nostra was a secret society, whose men of honour may not have numbered more than 5,000 according to Falcone, or 1,500 in the estimate of the *pentito* Antonio Calderone. But Cosa Nostra can only be understood within the context of Sicilian society and its set of cultural values and historical experiences so alien to the outside world that they seem incomprehensible. The concept of honour on which the Mafia was based was broadly shared by most Sicilians. It was not fear of retribution alone that made witnesses to Mafia killings reluctant to come forward. It was the more general suspicion and distrust of the authorities, and the feeling that society alone should deal with its management. Investigators would arrive at the scene of a murder, often a crowded street, and be unable to find anyone who would acknowledge having seen anything at all. This cultural hostility to the agents of the outside world may be changing, but the result was that by the 1990s Cosa Nostra had achieved a *de facto* sovereignty over the lives of many Sicilians. It was to the men of honour that ordinary Sicilians would turn if they wanted a favour done, a new flat, a job for their son or brother, a place at university, or to nobble a competitor for a contract. In that sense the Mafia applied the rules of exchanging favours that characterized the rest of Italian society. What set it apart was the brutality with which it was prepared to secure its aims, and the pervasiveness of its influence throughout the island.

The economic consequences were dire. As the sociologist Pino Arlacchi explained in his book *Mafia Business*, in large parts of the

South, Cosa Nostra and its criminal counterparts dictated who employed whom, at what salary, to make what product, and to sell to whom at what price. The economic distortions this has wrought make it the major obstacle to successful economic development. The *pentito* Leonardo Messina told a court in Rome how the Mafia carved up government contracts – and anyone who stood in its way. Only contractors whose companies were linked to the Mafia or were prepared to do the Mafia's bidding were allowed to tender. The Mafia set the price and the rake-offs. It stipulated who would be employed, often former convicts. Resistance would bring dire consequences. Business premises would be blown up or businessmen murdered.

A great deal of romantic guff has been written about the Sicilian Mafia, about its respect for women and children, about its code of values, about its dislike of the international trade in heroin. Films and books like Mario Puzo's *The Godfather*, in its many parts, have stressed the code of honour of the Mafia at the expense of the reality, the way that the Mafia operates as a state within the state, what sociologists call a parallel state. The Mafia has its own territory and population and laws. On the plus side is, of course, the enforcement of a certain amount of law and order. There is, for example, less bag-snatching and petty crime in Palermo than in Naples. Yet the Mafia has changed, so as to take advantage of the rapid shifts in society.

The Mafia's origins are, often like its victims, shrouded in myth. In the nineteenth century its main function was to act as a mediator between the feudal landowners and the peasant farm labourers on the great estates. It also acted as a cartel, forcing prices up or down for its own ends through violent disruption of any attempt to form labour unions on the one hand, and by threatening landlords with destruction of their property on the other.

What is not contested is that the modern Mafia was resurrected from its near-terminal suppression under Mussolini's harsh crackdown by the US forces of liberation in the Second World War. Co-operation had begun even before the Allied landings, as intelligence was gleaned from Mafia mobsters released from US prisons to assist the war effort. In the wonderful opening pages of *The Honoured Society*, Norman Lewis describes how that came about. Four days after American and Allied forces landed on the island in July 1943, a lone fighter plane flew over the village of Villalba, in the centre. It circled, then dropped a package near the church. The next day another package was dropped. It was addressed to Calogero Vizzini, 'Don Calo', head of all the Mafia in Sicily. It was a message seeking his help in fighting against the common enemy, Mussolini. Thus began the co-operation between the American forces and the Sicilian Mafia that led to its rehabilitation and reinsertion into the social, economic and political life of the country for which we are paying the price today.

In the 1950s, Palermo no less than the rest of the country engaged in rapid urban development and industrialization. Agricultural workers left the land to work in the towns. There was an immediate need for cheap and quickly built housing. The Mafia saw that gains could be made in taking a major stake in the control of the construction industry. Mafia families bought up plots of land. They tore down existing buildings. They started building afresh. This kind of work, however, required the services of different skills from those required in the past. The Mafia no longer had to mediate between the peasantry and the landowners on the big estates. It still had a mediating role of sorts. But it had to mesh its common interests with local politicians and administrators and all those who were responsible for giving out permits and licences, including surveyors and civil engineers.

The spoils increased. Sicily enjoyed its own regional autonomy. It became the beneficiary of huge development funds from Rome, · and later from Brussels. It was at this time that a new generation of local politicians grew up, most of them Christian Democrats. Giovanni Gioia, Salvo Lima, and Vito Ciancimino all saw the way forward through modernization and industrialization. They created a whole army of bureaucrats and civil servants – and thus the opportunities for patronage.

For years that head of the pyramid had eluded capture. So when, on 15 January 1993, TV programmes were interrupted for a newsflash, the ensuing announcement was a sensation. Salvatore 'Totò' Riina, the Mafia's *capo dei capi*, boss of bosses, Italy's most wanted man, who had been on the run from justice for more than twenty years, had been apprehended by the carabinieri in Palermo.

'*La belva*' ('The Beast'), as he was known, or '*Totò u curtu*' ('Totò the short') had been run to ground. The forces of law and order could not hide their delight, especially after such a miserable previous twelve months. Interior minister Nicola Mancino advised caution. 'It is an extraordinary coup. But we have not beaten the Mafia. We have only arrested a most dangerous criminal.'

The manner of Riina's arrest was the height of bathos. He was travelling unarmed, and without escort, through the morning rush-hour traffic in Palermo in a Citroën driven by a friend, Salvatore Biondolillo. The car was stopped by the members of the Ros, the carabinieri's élite force *Raggrupamento operativo speciale*. Riina initially pleaded innocence, and that he was the victim of mistaken identity. But they knew they had their man.

At first it appeared the police had caught him by a mixture of good fortune and systematic sleuthing. After all, the army had been deployed in force on the island since the assassination of Judge Borsellino. Scores of mafiosi had been picked up by security sweeps in November 1992 and thereafter. The tongues of the new *pentiti* had been wagging. Surely it was only a matter of time before the dragnet pulled in the biggest fish of all. But when it did, it emerged the authorities had been acting on a tip-off. Riina's long-term driver, Baldassarre Di Maggio, known as Balduccio, the son of a shepherd from the village of San Giuseppe Jato, had shopped his employer and protector. He had fallen out with his master over a woman: he had left his wife and was sleeping with the wife of another man of honour.

Di Maggio was not the first mafioso to betray his comrades. For, time and again, the mafiosi found reason to break their oaths of *omertà*, of silence. Di Maggio had been picked up by the police in northern Italy on another charge, and then decided to co-operate with them on what he knew about Cosa Nostra. He revealed not only the secret hideaway of Riina, but also the names of dozens of people of all levels of society in Palermo with whom Riina had had regular contact over the previous quarter of a century while he was a fugitive from justice.

To say Riina was on the run would make a mockery of the expression. He had lived in a large villa among other substantial houses in the heart of the Uditore quarter of Palermo. Here he passed his life of seclusion, locked away with his family and thousands of papers. He was not alone. Other men of honour hid with him.

The capture of Riina raised all manner of questions. First and foremost, why had it taken over twenty years to track him down? Who, Italians asked, were the politicians and leading members of the establishment who had protected him and prevented his capture earlier? When he was finally caught, it was not somewhere obscure and remote on the Italian mainland, but in Sicily, in the heart of Palermo itself, less than half a kilometre from where his chief pursuer Giovanni Falcone had lived.

There were other seemingly scandalous circumstances. He managed to marry while a fugitive from justice, and fathered and raised four children. Each child was registered with the authorities, although none had an identity card. Their vaccinations were up to date, in their own names. Time and again people reported sightings of him on the streets of Palermo. But he was never picked up. Subsequently, the priest who solemnized his marriage was arrested and charged with criminal association.

For years it had been widely put about that Riina had undergone plastic surgery to remodel his face. How else would he have been able to escape capture for so long? And pundits had been pontificating about the new Mafia, how they were different from the old peasant mafiosi, exchanging their old farm boots and corduroy jackets for business suits and smart white collars, how they had evolved in short from rural intermediaries into multi-billion-dollar brokers and financial players in the world's markets.

When the police pictures of the just captured sixty-two-year-old were shown on television screens, viewers had a shock. Even allowing for his own attempt to portray himself as an ignorant victim of mistaken identity, it was clear that Totò Riina typified the old-style Mafia boss. He was short – only 1.60 metres (5 feet 3 inches) – and squat, with thick features and heavy jowls. His hands were the hands of a labourer – or a strangler. When he was put on trial he again protested his innocence. But there was a steeliness about him. When he was being questioned he would fix his interrogator with unwavering eyes, and ask politely but insistently, 'I'm sorry, I didn't catch your name.' It was enough to unnerve the most resolute policeman or magistrate.

So where was the evidence of a new streamlined Mafia, the stuff of American movies or the highly successful TV drama *La Piovra* ('The Octopus') – the popular term for the spreading tentacles of the Mafia organization? The public had tended to disbelieve the testimony of its own experts. Yes, the Mafia had moved into ever more sophisticated activities, and had developed complex money-laundering transactions. But as Falcone and Borsellino were at pains to emphasize, there was no old Mafia and new Mafia: just the Mafia. The Mafia might no longer operate in the *latifondia*, the big farming estates of Sicily, but its operational structure, its hierarchy of members, was as rigid, secretive and brutal as it had always been. Riina was barely literate or pretended to be so. It was hard to imagine that this man, brought up among shepherds, came to control an international empire which engaged in complex traffic of drugs, investments, shares, currencies, and stock-exchange speculation.

Yet the life of Totò Riina was the history of the modern Mafia. He was very much in the mould of previous supreme bosses, peasant types who had grown up in the hilltowns and villages of the Sicilian interior. Yet another question was then raised. Who would succeed him? Who would preside over Cosa Nostra's worldwide interests in heroin and cocaine, its traffic in arms and its financial empire that spanned the globe? Would it be one of his two lieutenants, Bernardo Provenzano and Leonardo Bagarella? Bagarella was also the brother of Riina's wife, Antonietta, the elegant young schoolmistress he had married in secret in 1974 and who had been at his side since. Or would Riina continue to run his nefarious affairs from jail?

Salvatore Riina, known as Totò, was born in the town of Corleone, in the rugged hills inland from Palermo, in 1930. Corleone gave the most famous fictional Don his surname, in *The Godfather*. In real life it bred the family which came to dominate the Mafia and became a byword for terror. Riina came from a poor peasant family and was the second of five children. Like most such boys, he left school when he was ten. Later he was to say that he could not read, although it was said he had learnt to read in prison. His apprenticeship began early, when he joined a group of young hoodlums headed by Lucciano Liggio. Liggio, like Riina, was a simple man, without education. But he had amassed considerable power and influence, moving from banditry into a whole series of more lucrative enterprises. Yet he aspired above all to power. Standing in the way was the formidable figure of Dr Michele Navarro. The doctor had not only sworn the Hippocratic oath. He had taken the vow of *omertà*. For the good physician doubled as the local Mafia boss in Corleone.

The rivalry between the doctor and Liggio led in 1958 to the first major battle of Riina's life. In the end, Navarro sent a nine-man hit team to get rid of Liggio. But he managed to escape. The following week, Liggio sent six men to do away with his rival. As the doctor was driving into town with a young medical student, he was gunned down by men with machine-guns. Liggio became undisputed boss of the Corleone Mafia. He was to become the bridge between the rural and the urban Mafia after the change in 1958. In the early 1960s, factional feuds between the families helped the Corleonesi extend their influence and power into Palermo itself. It was during this period that the state was prompted to its first serious attempt to take control, following the killing of seven carabinieri bomb-disposal experts by a booby-trapped car packed with explosives.

Liggio spent the next period encroaching more and more on Palermo, the regional capital of Sicily and centre of the Mafia as a worldwide network. Until that time the *cupola* or *commissione* had operated more as a confederation of the families. The Corleonesi formed an alliance with the Greco and Calò families, in confrontation with the opposition of the Inzerillo, Spatola, Bontate and Badalamenti families. Luciano Liggio and his Corleonesi were the main victors of the Mafia wars of 1981–3.

Riina had become Liggio's right-hand man, carrying out his orders to despatch rivals and opponents. Riina was wanted by the authorities for his part in at least 150 murders, of which he was said to have perpetrated forty himself. But Riina was more than just a killer. He was also a strategist. Although his lawyer, Nino Feleccia, was to declare that his client had never once left his native Sicily to inspect his global empire, he was regarded by the authorities as responsible for cementing the links with Mafia families in North and South America.

The ascendancy of the Corleonesi-Greco group was maintained through brutal repression of dissent. But that brutality had its costs. In the months before Totò Riina's arrest, *pentiti* had been coming forward, bemoaning how he had turned it from a form of collective democracy into a dictatorship. One supergrass also revealed the emergence of a new threat to the dominance of the Corleonesi. These were the *stidde*, which is Sicilian dialect for stars. In effect, these were like janissaries, small-time criminals, used as soldiers by the bosses, who had then joined ranks with mafiosi opposed to the Corleonesi. Or they were men of honour humbled because of an infringement of one of their strictly enforced codes, such as having too public an affair. They are believed to have been behind one of those periodic bouts of murder that afflicted a number of Sicilian towns, although the importance of such peripheral groupings is open to question.

The authorities were happy to take the credit for picking up Riina. It is too early to say that Riina's arrest means the end of the Corleonesi control of Cosa Nostra and of the subjection of the families of Palermo to the rule of the men from the hills. But it certainly represents a shifting of the pendulum. For with Riina's brutal leadership now either ended or circumscribed by prison walls, the primacy of the Corleonesi could at last be challenged. After Falcone's death, Riina's lawyer announced that he had had frequent and regular contacts with the *capo dei capi*. That the lawyer should be able to do so with impunity was a direct challenge to the authority of the state.

But there were other signs of open defiance by groups or individuals of the ascendancy of the Corleonesi. The period of relative calm between competing gangs in a sort of Pax Mafiosa that had held for most of the previous years appeared to be coming to an end. The first sign was the emergence of a new generation in territory controlled by the Madonia clan. These were said to resent Riina's harsh and dictatorial methods. The murders of both judges were carried out on Madonia territory. In the past such killings of senior representatives of the state could only have been carried out by common consent of the entire Mafia commission. But Riina dominated the commission. He faced no opposition to his bloody will.

Some commentators saw in the killings the acts of a desperate organization. The Mafia only killed in such a way, it was argued, when it felt it was losing. Whatever the reasons, the effect was the same. The killings spelt the beginning of the end for Riina. For they stirred the state into action. The Direzione Investigativa Anti-Mafia (DIA), modelled on the FBI, was finally given teeth to investigate Mafia activities nationwide. For it was a legacy of Italy's past that the jurisdiction of judicial investigators is confined to specific areas: they cannot pursue their inquiries in towns or regions outside their designated areas. Henceforward, the work of the different branches of the police and the carabinieri as well as the state security apparatus was to be co-ordinated to combat organized crime.

The most detailed descriptions of the inner workings of the Sicilian Mafia came from the *pentiti* Tommaso Buscetta and Antonio Calderone. Buscetta's story is well known but worth repeating, because his is a model which others followed, in increasing numbers.

Buscetta had been at the centre of the Mafia during its years of enrichment from the production and distribution of heroin. He had always denied being active in the heroin trade, although his denials were greeted with scepticism. But he had become caught up in the bloodletting of the Mafia wars of the 1980s. At one point there was an average of one murder a day in Palermo. Most of Buscetta's immediate family were killed between 1981 and 1984 as the Greco-Corleonesi seized control of Cosa Nostra. Among the victims were his sons Antonio and Benedetto. Since they were not members of Cosa Nostra they were not by rights legitimate targets of the gunmen. Buscetta was arrested in Brazil in October 1983 and extradited to Italy the following year. In a last effort to preserve what remained of his family, he decided to collaborate with the Italian authorities.

In the course of his debriefing by Judge Falcone during 1984, Buscetta described the Cosa Nostra as having a highly structured organization with a command system that resembled a pyramid. At the base of the pyramid were the *soldati*, the foot soldiers, or simple men of honour. Each one was affiliated or owed allegiance to a clan or *famiglia*. The ties were not necessarily of blood, though often they were. On average each *famiglia* had fifty or so members. Each *famiglia* was presided over by a *capo*, who was elected, and who had a *vice-capo* and one or more *consiglieri* or advisers. The *capi* in turn sent representatives to the *commissione*, which took decisions collectively. Outside Cosa Nostra, the *commissione* was often known as the *cupola*. In turn the head of the *commissione* sat on a regional *supercommissione*. And at the pinnacle was the *capo dei capi*, the boss of bosses.

Among the most authoritative accounts of how the Mafia functioned, drawing on the debriefing of Buscetta and other *pentiti*, is the book by Giovanni Falcone written in collaboration with Marcelle Padovani, *Cose di Cosa Nostra*. The series of long interviews, which Falcone had with the journalist for the French magazine *Nouvel Observateur*, make a fascinating study of the Sicilian Mafia's methods, and an equally absorbing account of how Falcone went about trying to understand the enemy he was up against. He saw that the key to confronting Cosa Nostra lay in knowing as much as possible about the organization. Some criticized him and others for relying too much on the testimony of the *pentiti*. But like any intelligence agency, he needed human agents inside the organization, or ones who had once been inside, to confirm what he had garnered through other means. So he came to know the members of the honoured society, some of whom he had grown up with. He knew their language and their hidden meanings and the warnings concealed in the inflection of their voices. 'The interpretation of signs, of gestures, of messages and silences, is one of the principal activities of the man of honour,' he said. 'And consequently of the magistrate who investigates him.'

Much has been made of the methods Mafia killers chose to despatch their victims, as though the means chosen were always intended to give some message: the singer Pino Marchese with his genitals shoved in his mouth for having an affair with the wife of a Mafia boss man, the journalist shot in the mouth for talking too much. The most celebrated was the *lupara bianca*. A *lupara* is a sawn-off shot gun. *Lupara bianca*, a bloodless killing, meant the way a person disappeared without his body being discovered to leave those tiresome incriminating forensic traces. But Falcone said the method chosen was dictated solely by one principle: 'the shortest and least dangerous path. It has no fetishistic preference for one method over another.' There was *incaprettamento* or goat strangling, for instance, where the wrists and ankles are tied behind the back and at the same time around the neck of the victim so that in attempting to break free he strangles himself. Falcone dismissed speculation that this was a punishment reserved for the most cowardly of traitors. 'The reason for using this method is, in fact, much more banal: it is that the neatly packaged corpse can be transported more easily in the boot of a car.'

There was another principle, he said. In the organization violence and cruelty were never gratuitous. Rather they were the last resort when all other attempts of persuasion or intimidation had failed, or when the seriousness of the error was such that it merited only death. Cruelty was not an end in itself. Indeed, men who committed gratuitous acts of violence provoked disgust within the organization. As, for instance, Pino Greco, 'Scarpazzedda' (his father was known as 'Scarpazza'), who – according to Buscetta and others – cut off Inzerillo's son's right arm for having expressed the intention to avenge his father. He was sixteen years old. Pino Greco then finished him off with a shot in the temple.

'Cosa Nostra is a society, an organization which to all intents and purposes has its own legal system. Its regulations, in order to be respected and adhered to, require effective means of sanction. Given that within the Mafia structure there are no courts and no police force either, it is essential that each of its "citizens" knows that punishment will be carried out immediately. Whoever breaks the rules knows he will pay with his life.'

Falcone paid tribute to the *pentiti*: Buscetta, Antonio Calderone, Marino Mannoia, Contorno. Their information, each with a different slant or angle, ended up giving the investigators a complete picture of Cosa Nostra. Buscetta had been very close to the world of political power, yet he did not reveal a great deal of information in this area. He was, however, the most broad-ranging. Contorno, on the other hand, simply executed orders and therefore had limited knowledge, but he gave an accurate portrait of a perfect 'soldier'. Antonio Calderone, arrested in Nice in 1987, provided incriminating evidence on the political contacts of Cosa Nostra. Calderone mentioned the name of Salvo Lima, ex-mayor of Palermo, who had been given the concession – something that seems scarcely believable in a modern European state at the end of the twentieth century – to collect taxes on behalf of the regional government. This he did until 1984. Calderone reported that the thirty families in Palermo could between them deliver some 180,000 votes. No politician elected in Palermo could have been unaware of where his votes came from. For in the manner in which the Mafia worked, favours had to be repaid, at some time or another. It would have been pointless to have delivered votes to a politician without some reciprocal favour. Marino Mannoia was best on the most recent evolution of Cosa Nostra.

The *pentiti* justified their betrayal of their oaths of *omertà* in different ways. There were many reasons why mafiosi decided to collaborate with the authorities. Few did so because they had had enough of the killing. Buscetta, for example, felt that others had betrayed the values of the organization he had joined. During the first official meeting Falcone had with Buscetta, the man of honour declared, 'I am not an informer. I am not a supergrass. I was a mafioso and I am responsible for crimes for which I am ready to pay my debt to justice.'

Mannoia evoked more Catholic terminology: 'I am a repentant in the simplest sense of the word, given that I have understood the great mistake I made in choosing a life of crime.'

Contorno stated simply: 'I have decided to collaborate because Cosa Nostra is a band of cowards and assassins.'

Falcone liked to compare the Mafia with the Church. Becoming part of the Mafia is the equivalent of a religious conversion, Falcone wrote.

One cannot retire from the priesthood, or from the Mafia. At the moment of initiation, the candidate or candidates are taken to a room, in a secluded house, in the presence of the representative of the 'family' and of ordinary men of honour. Often, the latter stand at one end while the initiates line up at the other. Sometimes the candidates are locked into a room for several hours before being taken out one at a time. At this point the representative of the 'family' explains to the future men of honour the rules that regulate the organization, stating first of all that what is commonly known as the Mafia is actually called Cosa Nostra. He then warns the candidates that they still have time to renounce their affiliation and reminds them of the obligations entailed in belonging to the organization among which are: not to desire the woman of another man of honour, not to profit from prostitution, not to kill other men of honour, except in cases of absolute necessity, not to talk to the police, not to seek conflict with other men of honour, always to behave responsibly and correctly, to keep absolutely silent about Cosa Nostra to all those who are not part of it, never to introduce oneself to another man of honour. [A member should never himself reveal that he belongs to Cosa Nostra. He should always be introduced by a fellow member.]

Having explained the commandment, and confirmed the candidate's desire to join the organization, the representative invites the candidate to choose a godfather from among the men of honour who are present. Then the swearing-in ceremony takes place: each man is asked which hand he shoots with, the index finger of that hand is pricked and a drop of blood taken and spread on to a sacred image: often a Virgin Mary at the Annunciation, whose feast is celebrated on 25 March and who is considered the patron saint of Cosa Nostra. The image is then set alight and the candidate passes it from hand to hand, trying not to let it go out, and solemnly swears never to betray the code of Cosa Nostra and if he does so to burn like the image.

The idea is that an initiate will enter the Cosa Nostra with blood, and he will leave it only with blood.

Falcone cites the example of the supergrass Antonino Calderone, who grew up in the bosom of Cosa Nostra.

It was a family calling. In 1960, his uncle, who was a big Mafia boss in Catania, was admitted to hospital with a tumour. At the time, Antonino had not yet formally become a man of honour. He went to see his uncle in hospital. Their relationship was very close. At the end of the conversation, the uncle seemed to want to give Antonino a message. He took the usual precautions, because a member of the organization must never mention Cosa Nostra to one who is not a member. He sighed, and after a long silence, knowing very well that his nephew was more than likely to join the Mafia, he said, 'You see that rose on the windowsill? It's very beautiful, very beautiful, but if you pick it up, it will prick you.'

Another silence, then the uncle who felt himself growing weak whispered, 'If only you knew how beautiful it is to fall asleep without the fear of being brutally woken in the middle of the night. And to walk the streets without constantly having to look back for fear of being attacked from behind.' He wanted to say, 'Think carefully, nephew, before becoming a soldier of Cosa Nostra, of this exquisite rose. Think before you make the leap. Because you will enter a culture of death and anguish, and infinite sadness.' Antonino Calderone still remembered this long-past and veiled conversation when he repeated it to me in 1987, concluding, 'I agree with what my uncle said.'

Initiation into the Mafia was more like acceptance within a masonic lodge. Both after all are secret brotherhoods. It was therefore not surprising that links have emerged over the years between Freemasons and Cosa Nostra. Some saw this as the key to understanding the supposed link between the Mafia and the political establishment. The *pentito* Calderone talked of a project to create a special lodge for Cosa Nostra members. In 1981, the year that the scandal about the P2 Masonic Lodge broke, five lodges were founded in Trapani, on the coast near Palermo, under the collective name Circolo Scontrino. Present at the founding ceremony as guest of honour was the Venerable Master of P2 himself, Licio Gelli. Another guest was an East European ambassador. The Circolo's power and influence grew, until most economic activity in the area was controlled by it.

Then, in 1985, the head of the flying squad in Trapani ordered a search of the premises. The police officer was immediately taken off the case, on orders from Rome, and without explanation transferred to a less-sensitive area in Palermo. His transfer only gave ammunition to the conspiracy theorists who held that political figures were either controlling the Mafia or being controlled by it. What the Circolo Scontrino did reveal was that there were important points of contact between two major secret societies, one avowedly criminal in intent, the other more political. Further evidence of the East European connection had been uncovered by deputy prosecutor Carlo Palermo. He had been working on a link between arms for a drugs-smuggling run by an East European intelligence service and the Mafia up in North-eastern Italy. He asked for a transfer to Trapani to pursue what he felt was the source of the operation. Within days, the Mafia tried to kill him. A car bomb exploded but blew up the car behind his, killing a young woman and her two children. Four weeks later a heroin refinery was discovered at Alcamo, in the province of Trapani. Also found were clippings from newspapers describing Palermo's activities, as well as East European-made equipment and jute sacks marked with Cyrillic script, which had once contained morphine base.

Cosa Nostra, the Sicilian Mafia, is the best-known and most powerful criminal organization with roots in Italy. Each of the four main groups based in Sicily and Southern Italy has its own methods, its organizational structure, its own preferred business enterprises, and its own ways of seeking accommodation with the state and corrupt politicians. The others are the Neapolitan Camorra; the 'ndrangheta of Calabria, Italy's toe; and the latest addition to this unholy grouping, the New Holy United Crown of Puglia, in Italy's heel. Cosa Nostra is the most impenetrable of all those entities generally called Mafia organizations. The Camorra of Naples and the Campania hinterland is different in that it is a collection of 'families' which are known to their local communities. A 'family' or clan is known as a *cosca*, the word for the leaf of an artichoke, which illustrates the relationship between them. The modern Camorra originally controlled the black markets in and around a starving Naples at the end of the Second World War. But no longer are its activities confined to controlling the smuggling of cigarettes into Naples harbour on fast motor launches. Like Cosa Nostra, the Camorra has a truly international operation.

Once Cosa Nostra dealt mainly with heroin, while the Camorra in effect were the European distributors of cocaine for the Medellin drug barons of Colombia. Now all three organizations deal with both drugs. The Camorra has hub operations in the Netherlands and in Germany. And it is the Camorra under its best-known boss, Michele Zaza, which moved into the casinos and property market of the French Riviera. Like Cosa Nostra it has found that much greater gains can be made from the huge construction projects and development plans for the region funded by the central government. As rapidly as vast sums were appropriated by the state for the reconstruction of Irpinia after it was devastated by an earthquake in 1980, they were misappropriated by the Camorra. Hardly any of the planned housing was completed, but many grew rich on the diversion of funds. The diverted money did not remain idle, however. It was used to buy into legitimate businesses, particularly in construction and cement production.

The 'ndrangheta of Calabria was mainly confined to its own harsh and rugged territory around the Aspromonte mountains, with occasional forays north to kidnap wealthy businessmen or professionals or their children for ransom. The word 'ndrangheta is believed to be derived from a Greek word, *andragathia*, which means manliness. And it is this cult of manliness that has led to the highest murder rate in Europe, if not the world, and bloody feuds and family vendettas, which can go from one generation unto the next. Like the other crime groups, the 'ndrangheta obtained its initial huge sums of disposable money through protection rackets and the sale of drugs, in its case in the distribution of heroin which came through Turkey. These illegal earnings put it in a position to buy into legitimate business enterprises. Many of the unspoilt beaches of the Calabrian coast have been ravaged by developers acting on behalf of the local bosses of crime.

The New Holy United Crown of Puglia is the least organized and potent of the criminal organizations but it is growing fast. Hitherto the main entrepôt for smuggled goods into the country was the Bay of Naples. But with the collapse of the former Eastern Europe, particularly the demise of the old regime in Albania, Puglia and its long eastern coastline suddenly looked far more attractive to importers keen to avoid the eyes of the guardia di finanza. It became what Venice once was in its heyday, a gateway to the east.

But the Holy Crown was behind more than the depressing list of smuggling and heroin distribution on its home turf. More than any other organization it has engaged in direct challenge to the authority of the state. Bombs have been planted in the outskirts of Bari, at the law court in Lecce, and in the town of San Vito, whose mayor was leading a citizens' revolt against paying the *pizzo* protection money. And in its most notorious act of all a bomb was planted on the railway line for the main Ancona express, no less an act of terrorism for the fact that the bomb did not explode.

A common thread in these organizations is the connivance they have enjoyed from local politicians at all levels: town hall, regional government, and the national parliament in Rome (at least for Cosa Nostra and the Camorra). One European Commission crime report estimated that as many as 15 per cent of local government administrators in Sicily and the three southern regions, Calabria, Puglia and Campania, were under investigation for association with organized crime. Many would put the figure higher. Recent history provides sufficient examples of that cosy relationship between the political establishment and the Mafia, between the *onorevoli* and the *uomini d'onore*. This has led many to assume that certain politicians actually pull the strings of the Mafia. It is a hypothesis firmly rejected by Falcone. 'It is clear that the Mafia imposes its conditions on the politicians and not vice versa. In fact, it has no interest whatsoever in any kind of political activity which is for the general good. What matters to Cosa Nostra is its own survival and nothing else. It has never thought of taking or controlling power. That is not its job.'

That does not mean that Cosa Nostra does not interfere in politics if it feels constrained to do so. The long list of political figures who have ended up statistics in the annual tables of murders demonstrates this. *Cadaveri eccellenti*, illustrious corpses, include Piersanti Mattarella, president of the Sicilian region, a Christian Democrat, killed in 1980. He had put himself in the forefront of the struggle against the Mafia by trying to ensure that government funds were kept out of Mafia hands. Pio La Torre, the Communist member of parliament, and author of the law which bears his name on combating the Mafia, was killed in 1982. Judges Falcone and Borsellino were only the latest. The most senior servant of the state killed by the Mafia was the former deputy commandant of the carabinieri, General Carlo Alberto Dalla Chiesa, who, after his success at beating the Red Brigades, was despatched to Palermo as the prefect or representative of the state. He lasted only weeks. On 3 September 1982 he and his wife were riddled with bullets as they were driving to a restaurant. There were others. Besides Judge Chinnici there was the newly appointed chief examining magistrate for Palermo, Cesare Terranova, killed in 1979, and the following year Gaetano Costa, public prosecutor for Palermo.

The fact that no one was ever brought to book for these crimes led the conspiracy theorists to speculate that there must be some 'third level', a network over and above the hierarchy of Cosa Nostra, a sort of P2-type shadowy fraternity of politicians, business leaders, captains of state industries and bankers that commissioned the Commission to carry out these murders on their behalf. It was a thesis propagated with great vigour by the movement for democracy, La Rete. Falcone was totally dismissive.

> This hypothesis, which sees a structure such as Cosa Nostra under orders from a body which it does not control, is altogether unreal and reveals the profound ignorance of the relationship between the Mafia and political power. There is no shadow of proof or of evidence that supports the hypothesis of secret power which uses the Mafia, transformed into an armed extension of political power. The reality is far simpler and more complex at the same time. If we were dealing with such inventions, with a sort of Italian Spectre, we would all have already defeated them: after all, all it takes is James Bond.

It is widely believed that the Mafia has enjoyed support and succour in high places. For example, in recent years a senior police officer was arrested and accused of colluding with the Mafia dons, after having been named in confessions by four *pentiti* which when transcribed ran into hundreds of pages. They accused him of tipping off the Mafia bosses in advance of any impending round-up or police action. This thesis could provide an explanation of how it was that top Mafia bosses consistently managed to elude arrest, and how those entrusted with smashing organized crime were themselves often left unprotected.

This arrest raised other questions. Not for the first time, the validity of the evidence provided by supergrasses was questioned. In other words, were the supergrasses telling the truth, or were they merely settling scores with an assiduous former policeman who had had them locked up? In Italy although by law convictions can be secured on the basis of testimony from *pentiti*, in practice they never are without further corroboratory evidence.

Other evidence of corrupt or sympathetic officials came to light. It emerged that the clerk in the Supreme Court responsible for apportioning top Mafia cases had routinely deliberately misfiled them or held them up so that convictions could not stick. In 1984, the police had failed to raid a hotel where a Mafia boss was celebrating his wedding even though 150 police and carabinieri were surrounding the place. Thus was lost an opportunity to pick up other leading mafiosi among the guests. No explanation was ever given.

What had largely eluded the courts – inquiries had been made, but convictions not secured – was a true assessment of the nature of the links between politicians and Cosa Nostra, especially at national level. Often there is merely a coincidence of interest between them. So politicians at local, regional and national levels would be happy to accept the offer of votes from Mafia bosses. As mentioned, according to the evidence of at least one *pentito*, Mafia clans controlled at least 180,000 votes in Palermo alone. I gained some idea of how the system operated on my visit to Palermo for the April 1992 general elections. A bar in the working-class Zen district was operating like a bookmaker's. Men came in with scraps of paper, which they handed to the *galoppini*, the fixers who are a necessary part of any interaction in official Italian life. The *galoppini* would run their eyes and fingers down their checklists, guarding as best they could their activity from the gaze of any interested onlooker. The *galoppini* in this case were also the party workers, canvassers-cum-official-scrutineers. They had offered voters some bribe – either a bag of flour, petrol coupons, a small sum of money, say 50,000 lire (£23), or in some cases a job of work or the promise of a pension. These were offered in exchange for voting for a certain candidate. The *galoppini*, however, had to check that the voters had voted in accordance with their commitments. Details of some of the techniques deployed to check up on this electoral chicanery were published in a semi-satirical booklet put out by La Rete called *Manuale del Perfetto Brogliatore* ('Manual for the perfect vote-broker').

The commonest way was to give a form of stencil issued to illiterates which could be rubbed to reveal the candidates' names underneath. To express preference for a specific candidate, voters had to write in the candidate's name. It was not enough simply to mark a party list with a cross. It was not any old stencil. Rather, the stencil would have the candidate's name written in a slightly unusual way: there would be no dot on an 'i', for example, or a stroke would be missing from an 'e'. Scrutineers who saw a voting slip similarly marked would check it against voting records. Voting, of course, was meant to be secret. But voters would follow strict instructions to enter booths in a certain order. Then the corrupt scrutineers would simply examine ballots for the tell-tale marks. Naturally, such practice was not confined to the Mafia. Party chiefs in Naples would use their own machinery to ensure that they would buy votes. But the Mafia bosses could promise the delivery of block votes. It was merely a refinement of that system of doing business in Italy through the exchange of favours.

The most prominent exponent of this delicate relationship between political power and the Mafia was Giulio Andreotti's friend Salvo Lima. Andreotti stood by his friend when he was being vilified after his death. Lima was never a mafioso, he would say. And anyone who said he was was seeking to tarnish the party they both belonged to for political gain. Andreotti's assertion was borne out by the *pentito* Leonardo Messina, who declared that Lima was 'not a man of honour himself but very close to men of Cosa Nostra and acted as their intermediary with Andreotti'.

Lima himself was at pains to question why the Mafia was portrayed in such a poor light. At a conference in 1987 of the Christian Democrat Party in Sicily, Lima declared, 'I know that I am seen as a force of evil as opposed to a force for good. But I serve my constituents. I am perhaps part of the evil here, but at least I get things done.' Seldom has a senior politician so openly recognized his co-operation with organized crime. Lima, however, paid the ultimate price for his association with the men of honour. He was gunned down in a leafy suburb of Palermo by two hitmen with machine pistols on a powerful motorcycle. A subsequent judicial inquiry asserted that he had been killed because he was not able to deliver on promises made to use his political influence to ensure that the long sentences handed down in the maxi-trial of the 1980s would be overturned on appeal.

Both in life and death Lima was a constant reminder of the impotence of the state and its institutions. In life, because he always managed to avoid being brought to book. And in death, because, despite his shady associations, he was an elected member of the European parliament and was entitled to expect the minimum of protection. His killing was both a Mafia murder and a political assassination. The Mafia was settling an account with one of its own, and sending a political message to Lima's patron in Rome, Giulio Andreotti.

The reluctance of the political establishment to challenge the growing encroachment of organized crime into everyday life in large part provoked the popular revolt against it. The anger, the sense of frustration felt by many at the failure of the state to confront the Mafia led many to take their fate into their own hands. But not all believe that the point has come when society at large has the collective will to resist the Mafia.

Every Mafia killer has, of course, a mother, a wife, a mistress. A few, a very small number, have come forward to denounce the organization. One such was seventeen-year-old Rita Atria. Her father had been killed in a Mafia vendetta in 1985. When her brother was cut down one summer's night as he was clearing up the small pizzeria he had started in a village near Agrigento, she decided she had had enough. The police had made some half-hearted efforts to track down her brother's killer. But the village was in the heart of Mafia country. People respecting the rule of *omertà* did not talk, least of all to strangers. It was an area where the worst insult was to call someone a *sbirro* – police informer.

Rita knew who the killers were. She went to the police with her secret. She was brought to the attention of Judge Borsellino, who personally took charge of the case. She told him everything she knew about the Mafia wars in her village where thirty people had been killed. She named names, including those who had killed her father and brother.

Borsellino knew that she was in danger, and moved her to a safe house in Rome. It was on the seventh floor of an apartment block. No one knew she was there. But when she heard the news that Borsellino had been blown up, she felt her lifeline was gone. A week later she wrote a suicide note, then threw herself to her death from a balcony.

Her body was taken back to her village in Sicily for burial. At the funeral, leaders of women's groups from the mainland and anti-Mafia organizations outnumbered locals. Her family stayed away. For by going to the police she had betrayed the fundamental rule: that disputes were to be settled by the local people themselves. Subsequently her grave was profaned.

Rita Atria was not the first to break the law of *omertà*. But few have done so with impunity. And the only way that the authorities are going to encourage more women to betray everything their upbringing and culture has taught them is to offer the same kind of protection from retribution that they offer the *pentiti*. More often, however, the women are either passively complicit or in some cases actively implicated in Mafia business. When the Camorra boss Raffaele Cutolo was arrested, his sister Rosetta took his place.

Others, too, doubt whether society has really changed enough to throw up the mafiosi in their midst. Davide Grassi for one had his doubts. The two policemen were not written into the will his father Libero wrote. But Davide inherited them when his father was gunned down outside his home in Palermo on 29 August 1991. It is not just with the benefit of hindsight that people have since stated that the old man signed his own death warrant. Libero Grassi had become a talking point on the mainland as well as on the island when he openly defied the Mafia in an article printed in the newspaper of the Sicilian establishment, *Il Giornale di Sicilia*. He denounced the payment of the *pizzo*, the protection money demanded with threats by the Mafia gangs which for years have intimidated the business community in the regional capital of Sicily. After he publicly declared that he was refusing to pay the *pizzo*, many said the result was inevitable. For the *pizzo* was not collected primarily for the revenue it yielded. It was too small for that. It was instead a constant reminder to local businessmen of where real power resided in their neighbourhood.

His killing was the culmination of a long campaign to suborn him to the rule of the Honoured Society. The first demand for payment came in 1981. He refused to pay. Then came threatening phone calls from a man calling himself *zio* (uncle) Stefano. There followed the most gruesome warning of all, like a scene from *The Godfather*. One morning when he arrived at his factory, he found the body of the guard dog at the gates, beaten to a pulp. There was no mistaking the message. It was the traditional way in which the Mafia warned a reluctant subject that its intentions were for real.

Then, in 1984, there was a robbery. Three masked men forced their way into the factory and stole 130 million lire (£60,000).

Libero Grassi decided to go public with his experience shortly after the contents of a secret book came to light. This was known as the Libro Mastro. It gave detailed accounts of every payment made by some 500 manufacturers and businessmen in Palermo to the Mafia. It was discovered in the hideaway of Nino, son of the Mafia don Francesco Madonia, in December 1989. Its discovery and the publication of its contents were a major embarrassment to the Mafia. For it broke the fundamental contractual relationship of the Mafia in its business dealings: that of the mutual respect for silence and secrecy. Not only were those making the payments not to breathe a word, on pain of death. But the Mafia, too, respected the importance of not allowing any evidence to come to light, to preserve the good reputation of their business 'partner'.

Within the clans and families who make up Cosa Nostra, the publication of the ledger was yet another factor which led to the loss of control of the Salvezza quarter by the Madonia clan. And the struggle for control of the rackets was to lead to considerably more bloodshed.

Examining the book, Falcone noticed a reduction in the number of requests for large sums of protection money. He took little heart from this. He saw it as further evidence of what he already knew: that the mafioso himself was becoming a businessman, and investing his illegal profits from the drugs trade in legitimate business enterprises. Falcone warned against false illusions. The mafioso who had grown rich from illegal earnings and now engaged in legitimate business activities was not a sign that Mafia Inc. had turned honest.

After his public stand, Libero Grassi was offered a police escort. He refused it, saying it was too great an encumbrance and restriction on his freedom. 'It's a paradox,' his son explained. 'If he had been told that if he went public he would have had to have an escort, he might not have done so.'

In death, Libero Grassi became a national hero. The ministers of justice and the interior pounded their fists on the table and promised tough action against the racket. Libero Grassi was named 'man of the year' by Giampaolo Pansa, editor of the liberal weekly news magazine L'Espresso.

But in Palermo his death met with knowing nods. 'You have to choose between life and money,' one small businessman confided. 'Grassi chose money. He lost life.'

'He wanted to be a hero,' said another. 'Look where it got him. You can't beat the Mafia.'

Some months after the killing I went down to Palermo to see what if anything had changed, whether Grassi had had any posthumous influence on the popular will to resist the Mafia. I met his son Davide, who dismissed the posturing of the politicians and spoke bitterly about the society he grew up in. 'There was no such solidarity at the level of the man on the street. The response of the banks, of the business community was a great disappointment.'

At his father's funeral he was photographed bearing the coffin and giving a V for Victory sign. It was a gesture many of his friends thought inappropriate at his father's obsequies. But it was a way in which he could say, We will continue the struggle.

He met little response from the business community. And Davide Grassi, who turned thirty-five in the November after his father's death, spoke about leaving Palermo, to give it all up. To get away from the daily pressures, to go somewhere where he could lead a more normal, unrestricted private life. Somewhere he could indulge his great love, sailing. Trophies, mainly for second and third place, adorned his plain office. Few places offer such good all-year sailing weather as Palermo. But he was looking around. Sydney, the United States, but also Spain: 'It's got a young king, and a young prime minister. It is a country that has avoided the mistakes of others in development.'

He was an unprepossessing-looking young man wearing cheap shoes and thick glasses. At the time he was still working in the pyjama factory his father had founded in the 1970s. With 100 employees ('sometimes 99, sometimes 101') and an annual turnover of 7 billion lire (£3.27 million), Sigma was the third largest industrial enterprise in Palermo.

Davide was not always destined for the family business. 'At school I did a lot of politics like everybody else. Of the extreme left, like everybody else.'

By the time he reached university, educational reforms had been enacted which in effect removed the target for most student protests. He left after a year and joined his father. He was not politically active any longer but saw himself close to the Radical Party, the most libertarian of all the political parties.

He started off in exports and sales. 'In 1978 our main clients were in the Arab world, above all Lebanon. Unlike everybody else, we found the Lebanese very good to do business with. Then our product went up in quality, and our prices rose accordingly. Now we export to the Corte Inglés in Spain and the Galeries Lafayette in Paris. We've tried England but the market is very tough: you have a lot of producers.'

The firm had also just sent off a small shipment to a store in Dallas, its first ever export to the United States. But although the business appeared to be going well, Davide Grassi was not happy. Sicily's special circumstances posed particular difficulties for businessmen, quite apart from the exceptional demands of the Mafia for protection money. 'Interest rates are higher in Italy than in the rest of Europe, and higher in Sicily than in the rest of Italy. Then we have a problem of absenteeism. Almost all the workers here are women. Absenteeism rates in Italy are 2 to 3 per cent for men and 5 to 6 per cent for women. Ours are 15 to 16 per cent. Still, that's better than the two other big companies in Palermo.

'I'd like to leave Italy. I don't like the daily life here. But I'm very tied to my work. I've discussed it with my *compagna* [his partner, Francesca, who had two children from an earlier marriage] and she is happy to go. I'd like to sail, but I don't go to sea any more. It needs a lot of concentration, but I can't concentrate any more.

'I've never liked daily life in Italy. The relations between people. Here we are more extrovert than the rest of Europe, more cordial, but we rely too much on violence. And the general political system is bad too. Last spring my father said, "By November we will be broke." I think he was right, because this state is so degenerate. You've heard about this idea to launch a party of honest people? It's very easy to be honest when there is nothing left to steal.'

Elsewhere in Italy, including Sicily, people have been inspired by Libero Grassi's example to resist racketeers, and stop paying the *pizzo* which according to surveys is paid by half Italy's shopkeepers. The most celebrated case is at Capo d'Orlando, some 150 kilometres to the east of Palermo on the Northern coast of Sicily. There businessmen clubbed together to denounce the racketeers. A number have been tried and convicted.

Davide Grassi was dismissive. Palermo was different. 'There the extortionists were outsiders. The people closed ranks as if the Turks had arrived. Here in Palermo business and the Mafia are so completely intertwined. There have probably been other people killed for not paying the *pizzo* but no one did it publicly.'

In the previous ten years, eight businessmen had been killed by organized crime in Palermo.

He recognized that leaving would be seen as a victory for the Mafia. But he had to think about the future. 'It is running away but one has a certain responsibility to one's life. Is it more just to stay and suffer or to lead my own life if I've got to live another forty years? You've got to understand, there is more suffering when there is an alternative. If I go, it is because of the people, not the Mafia. At first I thought I'd go to Lombardy where the life is calmer, and the two children can go to school by bus . . . But I've lost faith in Italy.'

His mother, Pina, by contrast, successfully stood for parliament as a Green in April 1992 and took her seat in the senate.

Davide Grassi was, for all his radical politics, more essentially Sicilian in his pessimistic and fatalistic outlook than others. Green shoots of hope can be seen. Falcone had observed that the Mafia was losing the tacit complicity of the people. Once the Church, both as a conservative institution bent on preserving the established order, and through the nefarious activities of some of its priests, had appeared actually to support the Mafia. In recent years, the Church hierarchy and individual brave clerics have taken a strong line against the men of honour. Some priests have publicly stated that they will not welcome the mafiosi within the hallowed precincts of their churches, even for marriages and christenings.

In Capo d'Orlando, in Gela, in Calabria, shopkeepers have marched in protest against the racketeers. Extortionists have been denounced and jailed. More importantly, the men of honour no longer represent a role model for the young of today – at least, not in Sicily.

Perhaps the greatest manifestation of this popular revolt against the old political order, against the hold of the Mafia, has been the support for the political career of a very remarkable politician from Palermo, Leoluca Orlando, founder of the party La Rete. Orlando's following is unevenly distributed outside Palermo. There he had fallen out with his own party, the Christian Democrats, because they did not want him as mayor. He had been trying to break the deceitful and cynical relationship between the political establishment and the men of honour. Yet his crusade against the Mafia in Palermo and what he sees as the root of the problem in Rome has garnered tremendous support. 'The Mafia is not just against the state,' he was fond of declaiming. 'It is inside the state. It is not just in Sicily. It is in Milan. Organized crime is a national problem.'

In Palermo, people who daily lived with the Mafia, especially the young, responded to his call. Elsewhere in Italy, voters demonstrated their sympathy for his appeal for a moral renewal in

Italian political life. Like many at risk, Orlando always travelled around by bulletproof car, with escort cars in front and behind. It almost became a journalistic cliché to interview him in the back seat of his car, racing at 140 kilometres an hour through the traffic, the figure of a man in a trilby and dark glasses cradling a pump-action shotgun in the escort car ahead. Orlando's critics say that he has no specific programmes, that as mayor of Palermo he was long on blarney and short on practical measures to fight the Mafia. That he received more votes than any other candidate in the country – and ones not bought by him or for him by the Mafia – suggests that he struck a responsive chord, that the mood among the populace of Palermo, the Mafia capital of the world, was indeed changing.

It is not merely in Palermo that ordinary people have to make moral choices about whether or not to deal with the Mafia, or how to confront it. But elsewhere the risks of not bowing to the pressures of organized crime are less great. In 1989 the distinguished Milan-based architect Gae Aulenti was approached about restoring the historic centre of Palma di Montechiaro. This was one of the homes of the di Lampedusa family. She was already internationally famous and had created the spectacular Musée D'Orsay out of the old railway terminus in Paris. She had worked in Berlin and Barcelona and brought to glory the Palazzo Grassi in Venice. She was unsure, however, of the first telephone calls from the authorities down in Sicily and decided to go and have a look for herself. 'I discovered one of the most beautiful places in the world. The orange orchards all around. The blue blue sea of the Mediterranean. The baroque centre all destroyed. Then the city covered with signs of *abusivo* construction, built without proper permits. Electricity lines along and across the streets which were blatantly illegal, but also, so to speak, protected. Ah, the beauty of this place. So I said to myself, first I must see what is possible. Then I must see who are the people I am dealing with.'

She quickly discovered that those who were seeking her participation did not really have any technical know-how. They lacked any sense of urban planning. This was disturbing for an architect who required specific plans. She sought the assistance of urban planners at Palermo University. They began work on the initial study. One thing still troubled her. How would the study be financed? She asked around. The Sicilian region, she was told. She contacted the region directly. They told her that they knew nothing about the financing of the project. She stopped work immediately. 'I wanted to be very clear,' she told me in her studio in central Milan. 'I don't work for nothing.' Did she not feel almost a national duty to help restore one of the country's great architectural treasures? 'That's not my problem. That is the responsibility of the state, the region, the public domain. It already cost me, for the work I did on the study, which I was not paid for.'

There was another problem. Any work down there in the building and construction industry is controlled by the Mafia. She would be unable to avoid collaborating, in some form or another, with organized crime. While stressing that her main objections to continuing the project were technical rather than ethical, she declared, 'The Mafia exists. But I cannot recognize it. The suspicions always exist about the financing.'

It was a prudence that has characterized her career. She is one of only a tiny number of architects not tainted in the Milan political bribery scandal for the simple reason she never undertook public-works contracts in Italy, preferring instead to work for private clients such as the Agnellis or to enter competitions for work abroad.

Can the Mafia be beaten? It has become popular to argue that the Mafia is a mentality as much as a criminal organization. To beat Cosa Nostra, one has first to transform the mentality of a people. Once again we must turn to Falcone for a firm rebuttal of this argument. To confuse the Mafia and the Mafia mentality, the Mafia as an illegal organization, and the Mafia as a simple way of existing was, he said, a great error. 'One can easily have the mentality of a mafioso without being a criminal.'

'The Mafia is not a social service that operates for the benefit of all, but rather an exclusive association which acts against society as a whole for the sole benefit of its members.'

The so-called popular revolt against the men of honour, the shopkeepers who are a sign of the deep revulsion and disgust that so many in Sicily feel against the Mafia, these are major social trends. But Cosa Nostra is not an organization that relies on popular support or consensus. Of course, it has benefited from the complicity of a population which has not spoken out, either because it is cowed and afraid of retribution or because it is genuinely opposed to any co-operation with a state which it regards as an alien presence. Rather, as we have seen, it is a secret organization, with strict membership criteria, harsh rules, and brutal treatment of any who get in its way.

A greater willingness of members of the public to come forward with information about organized crime will help. But the most important way to combat the Mafia is to improve the weapons in the hands of the authorities, and to loosen some of the political restraints on their use. The Mafia prefers order to chaos. In the absence of order offered by the state, the Mafia had to provide it. The greatest successes of the early 1990s in combating Cosa Nostra came not as a result of a sea change in public opinion but rather from improved legislation enacted in 1991 offering *pentiti* protection if they co-operated with the authorities. Spurred by the killings of Falcone and Borsellino, parliament passed a package of legislation designed to give the police special powers to combat the Mafia. Police were given greater powers to tap telephones. The courts were allowed to take control of the assets of Mafia suspects. In the first year, billions of lire worth of assets were seized. Magistrates also noticed that where once their inquiries were blocked by some political interference, now they could pursue them with comparative freedom to act.

More recently fourteen convicted top mafiosi were transferred to the prison islands of Asinara and Pianosa, a measure of questionable constitutionality for those merely remanded in custody, but of great effectiveness in punishing convicted ones.

The results came quickly. The authorities were soon able to announce that 250 *pentiti* were collaborating with them. This kind of bragging by politicians might have undermined some of the investigations then going on. But it was also designed to tempt other men of honour to hand themselves over before they too were gunned down by their fellows. For Totò Riina's brutal methods eventually proved his undoing. He made too many enemies. And as soon as the state was able to offer an alternative to the Mafia, the *pentiti* came forward.

The Italian state had no room for complacency. On the eve of the arrest of Totò Riina the senior state prosecutor in Rome gave his annual review of criminal activity throughout the country. His report made depressing reading. In every sphere there was evidence that organized crime was spreading. Murders were up over 10 per cent. Robbery with violence was up. Drugs abuse was up. Throughout Italy, the police and judicial authorities noted an increase in Mafia activity and penetration. In Florence, for example, and the Tuscan region, the chief prosecutor, Luciano Tonni, noted in one annual report that there had been an increase in crime both in quantity and quality. The authorities had uncovered various attempts by the Sicilian Mafia to buy up textile factories in Prato, outside Florence, and found that they had moved into the nightspots of the Tuscan coastal resorts. The Mafia presence was a result of the ill-judged decision some years previously to move convicted Sicilian Mafia bosses off the island. This stemmed from the controversial *soggiorno obbligato*, a kind of internal exile introduced in 1956. This enforced exile from Sicily merely spread their influence across the country. But the authorities in Florence took heart from the fact that ordinary businessmen were more willing than others elsewhere to come forward and denounce attempts by organized crime to extort money in protection rackets.

The spread of the Mafia's tentacles has implications not only for the rest of Italy, but also for the rest of Europe and the world. It would be easy to dismiss the murder of a few hundred drug pushers and gang members killed in Mafia wars each year as self-inflicted misery imposed by socially undesirable elements. (Of the 1,697 murders committed in Italy in 1992, half were Mafia killings, either in Sicily or in Southern Italy.) But it is more than that.

One could cite notions of sovereignty and authority, and say that the operation of any criminal organization beyond the writ of the state is undesirable in the new Europe. Or one could express humanitarian concern for the loss of life, however tainted the victim. But there are very real practical reasons why other Europeans should be worried. Cosa Nostra does not limit itself to the Western half of an island in the Mediterranean. Rather, it engages in activities which directly threaten everyone. The advent of the single European market, the relaxation of border controls, and the absence of effective policing in the newly emerged states of Eastern Europe, all create a more hospitable environment in which the Mafia can operate.

The dangers are obvious. The Mafia pushes drugs that have become one of the scourges of modern civilization. It rips off European Community funds paid by taxpayers in the United Kingdom, the Netherlands and Germany and other rich Community members. It pressures legitimate businesses throughout Southern Italy into paying protection money. It takes a rake-off from many construction projects in Sicily and the South paid for by the state and so ultimately by the Italian people. So much so that state funds are its largest source of income, even larger than drugs trafficking or protection rackets. According to Pino Arlacchi, 'Italy's are the only criminal organizations in the world to be largely financed by the government.' Figures for the annual turnover of organized crime in Italy rise to $US 20 billion in the estimate of the research institute Censis – putting it on a par with the country's biggest industrial concern, Fiat. Others put the figure even higher, at $US 32 billion. It is not known how much of the Mafia's profits are reinvested in legitimate businesses. One senior guardia di finanza expert reckoned 60 per cent went into the financial sector. The easiest way to launder money, to acquire a legitimate provenance, is to buy treasury bonds. This makes the Mafia a significant lender to the government. The huge resources it has, and its ability to move vast sums around the stock exchanges and money markets of the world, make such a criminal organization capable of influencing the monetary policy of one member state of the EC, and therefore of all of them. Whether or not it does is not the issue. It has a potentially destabilizing effect.

Different Mafias may be linked only by alliances between drugs traffickers and arms dealers that shift as often as Lebanese political groups. Yet those shifting alliances pose threats for individual countries, whether it be the takeover of the gambling casinos of the South of France by the Camorra, the spread of protection rackets run by the Sicilians in Southern Germany, or the tie-ups with local organized crime networks in Russia and the states of the former Soviet Union. Cosa Nostra went some way to buying up two islands in the Caribbean, Aruba and St Martin. In the early 1990s, it made moves to buy up pizza parlours in what was East Berlin. This expansion had several objectives: to launder money by buying into legitimate business enterprises, to create a distribution network for the selling of hard drugs, and to move into a new market. How soon will it be before Berlin is divided again, carved up between the Sicilian Mafia and the Russian Chechens?

For the European drugs market is more vibrant than ever. By the 1990s, Sicily itself was no longer a net producer and exporter of drugs. Indeed, there was evidence that drugs were actually imported into the island for local use. In the early 1980s, some 30 per cent of all heroin going to the United States was estimated to have passed through Cosa Nostra hands. Ten years on, only 3 to 5 per cent was said to be doing so. One researcher established that by the end of the 1980s, 50 per cent of heroin found in Europe, and almost all the heroin found in Italy, came along the Balkan corridor. It was produced in south-west Asia (the Golden Crescent) or south-east Asia (the Golden Triangle), passing through Turkey and landing at ports in Italy such as Trieste, Brindisi and Bari. International police and drugs co-operation to stop the trade has had limited successes.

The trade in Italy itself was still largely controlled from Sicily. Outside Italy, the Sicilians were facing competition for both markets and product. The Colombians had moved in to many of the markets, and many users preferred cocaine and its derivatives to heroin, whose administration through intravenous injection was the cause of the high incidence of AIDS in Italy.

One key to defeating the Mafia is better co-operation between national police forces and security agencies. Co-ordinated police operations have had a number of spectacular coups. The Green Ice operation, which bore fruit in 1992, linked police forces in Colombia, the United States, Italy, Britain, Venezuela, Canada, Spain and Switzerland to smash an international network to launder the profits from the distribution of Colombian cocaine by investing them in legitimate business enterprises. A rogues' gallery of leading criminal organizations was implicated: all the Italian Mafias, the Medellin, Cali and Pereira cocaine cartels from Latin America, and a Dutch money-laundering expert, arrested in Rome on the point of meeting a contact. Most of the business had been conducted through the Cuntrera brothers, who had left Sicily for Venezuela in the 1970s to establish the transatlantic trade. A subordinate of the Cuntrera brothers moved to London at the same time and set himself up as the biggest importer of heroin into the UK.

In the 1980s, it was co-operation between the US authorities and Falcone that broke the Pizza connection. As important was the relationship he struck up with the Swiss, both the chief prosecutor of Lugano, Paolo Bernasconi, and his successor Carla Del Ponte. For between them they established how Swiss banks had been the key to laundering dirty money from Italy, not only of the Mafia but also of the political parties. Hundreds of millions of pounds were known to have passed by this route. Swiss banks are still among the most secretive, but measures have been taken to make it more difficult to recycle profits from drugs and other illegal sources. In Italy itself, legislation has been passed enabling the authorities to examine bank accounts. The assets of known mafiosi may be seized. By legislating against recycling cash, through better monitoring of computerized bank transactions, and by closing tax havens, anti-drugs agencies can hit the drugs traffickers where it hurts, the banking of the profits. Cutting the link between the traffickers and their profits is seen as the first step towards combating the drugs trade.

Yet the Mafia seems always one step ahead. There have been ominous warnings by Italian magistrates against the dangers of organized crime using its networks to buy or obtain chemical or other non-conventional weapons from the former Soviet republics. The fear is these could then fall into the hands of terrorist or other undesirable groups. The Mafia therefore is a worldwide problem.

The key to the current phase of the struggle against the Mafia has been the cracking of the link with Sicilian politics. Cosa Nostra may have been severely weakened by this onslaught. Yet it is likely to adapt and assume new forms, profiting, for example, from the country's growing economic problems and rising unemployment to insert itself firmly once more within society.

There may well be historical and social reasons for the Mafia's continuing insidious presence within Sicilian society. The final word of hope comes from Falcone. As he said, the Mafia, being a creation of men, even men of honour, is necessarily fatally flawed. 'The Mafia is a human phenomenon and like all such human phenomena it has a beginning, an evolution and will also therefore have an end.'

ELEVEN

Immigration and the united colors of Italy

The number 280 bus in Rome runs only on Fridays. For an hour or so either side of midday according to the sun it describes a short loop from Parioli to the latest addition to the myriad places of worship in the city, the new mosque. The mosque is somewhat out of the centre, overlooking a green field occupied by another interloper on the Italian national scene, the local rugby club. Yet the mosque's architecture does for the Islamic presence what the baroque, the style of which the city is the supreme expression, did for the Counter Reformation. Its Islamic domes and arches share the same religious inspiration – a triumphant assertion of a faith under assault from reformist ideas and modern thinking about man's place in the world.

When plans were first drawn up in the 1970s, the Rome mosque was set to be the largest in Europe. Since its inception, the building has been dogged by controversy. The art critic Bruno Zevi castigated it as 'monumental kitsch'. The Green lobby (of the environmental, not Islamic hue) protested at its siting. But the real row has been over whether the Eternal City, where St Peter fled from Palestine two millennia ago, should have allowed a house of prayer for Muslims at all. Most of the money for its construction came from the government of Saudi Arabia, a country whose proud guardianship of the Holy Places of Mecca and Medina is cited as justification for its own rigid intolerance of any form of religious expression other than officially sanctioned Islam.

At times, the mosque looks like an oriental bazaar. On one Eid il-Fitr, the feast day ending the month-long fast of Ramadan, Egyptians were selling video cassettes of Muslim preachers. Pakistanis were offering books on the Koran. One stallholder was selling frozen chickens, slaughtered in the hallal fashion, and imported from France, a country not widely considered to be on the path of Islamic righteousness. The Rome mosque might have been built in part for political reasons – the city after all has diplomatic representatives from the Islamic world accredited to the Italian republic, to the Holy See, and to the United Nations Food and Agriculture Organization. But the majority of the faithful who traipsed to the mosque on Friday during its construction were humble folk, only partly conversant with broader geo-political considerations.

Other Italian cities and towns have their Islamic centres too. In the forecourt of a car park tucked away off Milan's Via Jenner, scrubbed white marble tiles lead to the entrance of the Islamic Cultural Centre. It is run as much as a community centre. Egyptian cooks prepare vegetables and hallal chicken for some of the Egyptian and North African workers who come in at lunch time. You can hear the sounds of children learning their lessons by rote upstairs. At the centre they estimate that there are some 120,000 foreigners in Milan, of whom about 80,000 are Muslims. The deputy head of the centre, Yousry El-Harmil, from Egypt, also runs a co-operative society for the community.

The building of the mosque in Rome, and the proliferation of others around the country, are just some of the more visible manifestations of the rising presence of immigrants from outside the European Community, and their growing desire to find a less temporary accommodation within the Italian state. Unlike elsewhere in Europe, immigrants have shown little inclination to settle. Alitalia, the national airline, counted all the Algerians coming into Italy, and counted them all back. A rule of thumb is that only one-third of immigrants regard themselves as definitively resident in Italy, one-third are temporarily resident, and a third are there for the season or in transit, to make enough money to send home to their families. Official figures are misleading. The highest are given for Umbria, in large part because of the university for foreigners in Perugia, whose law-abiding students have all registered with the *questura*. Few actually applied for citizenship in a country which grants it with great reluctance. Only 25,717 foreigners obtained Italian citizenship between 1983 and 1991, according to the interior ministry.

Non-Catholics remain a small minority in Italy. Over 98 per cent of the population is nominally Catholic. There are an estimated 350,000 Protestants, 200,000 Jehovah's Witnesses and 36,000 Jews. Adherents to Islam form the largest non-Catholic religious or confessional minority. Few of Islam's practitioners are Italian citizens. Most of the non-EC immigrants in Italy, from North Africa and Senegal, from Albania and Bangladesh, are Muslim, and most of them in turn are Sunni. The colour of Italy is changing.

Historically, immigration to Italy is nothing new. Successive waves of invaders have left their imprints, racial, linguistic, cultural and administrative. Not all have been beneficent presences. The Vandals and more recently the Allied forces during the Second World War did their share of destroying Italy's cultural patrimony. At one point during the Roman Empire, a third of the population of Rome – the domestic servants, the menial workers – came from overseas. Many of the later Roman emperors were from the imperial possessions. Their African physiognomies, captured in marble, adorn the façades of the palazzi on the Campidoglio, including the city hall designed by Michelangelo where Roman politicians to this day convene to discuss the situation of immigrants.

Rome has long housed places of worship of religions, sects and denominations which do not owe their allegiance to the Vatican. The basilica of San Clemente has an underground chapel dedicated to the Rumanian Orthodox. The imposing dome of the main Jewish synagogue on the edge of the Tiber, a huge landmark in the old Jewish quarter, was given a fresh coat of paint in 1990 to assert the self-confidence of this minority. The Waldensian Protestant sect have their church on Via IV Novembre. Jehovah's Witnesses go knocking on doors in search of converts. Lutherans, Seventh Day Adventists, Bahais, Pentecostalists, the Salvation Army, Methodists, Baptists and Greek Orthodox, all have their houses of prayer. At the church of San Calisto, just off the square with the oldest church in Rome, Santa Maria in Trastevere, the Egyptian Coptic Orthodox Church has been lent the premises on Sunday and Monday evenings to promote the Monophysite heresy of belief in a single divine nature of Christ.

What is new is the extent and the origin of the immigration.

For two hundred years or more Italy has been a source of migrants, not a destination for them. There is hardly a town or city in the developed world where there is not a settled Italian community, gone in search of the American dream or to run a sandwich bar in London's Soho. Now the *belpaese* has been attracting foreigners in its own right. The largest numbers have come from North Africa, the Southern Mediterranean seaboard, and from Eastern Europe.

Compared with other countries in Western Europe in 1992, Italy had a low proportion of immigrants from outside the European Community. The 1991 census put the number at 900,000 but most unofficial estimates put the number of non-Italians resident in the country, legally or illegally, at around 1.2 million, or about 2 per cent of the total population. This compares with an immigrant population of over 6 per cent in France, 8 per cent in Germany, 4 per cent in the Netherlands and 6 per cent in Great Britain.

Italy's experience differs in several ways from that of other European countries. France and Britain have for years had large communities of immigrants, mainly from their respective former colonies. France also had sizeable numbers from Spain and Portugal. These are now more or less integrated, and are into their second or third generation. Belgium, Luxembourg and the Netherlands have similar experiences.

The influx of immigrants to Italy, however, happened in a very short time. Immigration only really became a feature in the 1980s. The country has no imperial burden. Few from the ex-colonies · came seeking absorption, except for a small number of Somalis, Ethiopians and Eritreans from the Horn of Africa, some of whom were given political asylum. But now immigration to Italy is fragmented and diverse, with immigrants from a great number of countries of origin. In 1992, for example, there were 1,073 foreign pupils of 77 different nationalities enrolled in Rome schools. Immigrants did not go only to big urban centres. They spread throughout the country. Even the smallest village now has its one or two Moroccans or Malians.

In Christopher Columbus's Genoa, a port city more used to bidding farewell to departing Italians, whole areas of the medieval centre have been taken over by immigrants. Its narrow alleys resemble a North African casbah. Blue-black Senegalese and Malians, lanky and Francophone, labour as journeymen in the tomato fields in the South or hawk their imitation Louis Vuitton shoulder bags in the tourist hill towns of Tuscany. Black Nigerian and Ghanaian prostitutes work the red-light districts of Rimini and Rome and Bologna. They have so undercut native prostitutes' rates that these have in some cases offered free sex to clients as a novel form of industrial action. Girls from the former Soviet Union and Hungary and Eastern Europe populate the massage parlours. In the Trastevere restaurant district of Rome many of the typical local dishes such as *carciofi* (artichokes) *alla Romana* are prepared by cooks from Cairo and Alexandria, with a hint more chilli pepper than usual. At traffic lights, scuffles have broken out between Poles and Moroccans over the privilege of washing drivers' windscreens. None of this was there fifteen years ago. And the flow is growing every day. In Sicily, new quarters of Tunisian tuna fishermen and stevedores have grown up. Around Umbrian hill towns like Cortona, most of the seasonal agricultural work is performed by non-EC farm hands.

How is Italy, a traditionally tolerant country, reacting to the changing faces of its inhabitants? It was in Florence that I found examples both of racial intolerance, and also of a possible paradigm for racial and cultural integration. Florence has its own long history of attracting generations of foreigners, albeit from different backgrounds. A plaque in Piazza Santa Maria Novella, dedicated to the poet Henry Wadsworth Longfellow (1807–82), is testament to past migrations:

> *tra le fiorentine dimore*
> *ebbe questa*
> *nella piazza che fu detta*
> *La Mecca degli Stranieri.*

[Among Florentine dwellings he had this one in the piazza which was called the Mecca of the Foreigners]

The unnamed writer of this accolade can have scarcely foreseen how his words were later to become more literally appropriate. For on the grass in front of the great Dominican basilica huddles of black faces and brown faces, of Filipinos and Africans from North and West, have made this a regular spot to foregather in their own Mecca of the Foreigners.

Florence, however, has been less receptive to this influx of people from the Third World than it was to the literary and artistic souls from Northern Europe in former years. In the spring of 1990, a succession of incidents occurred by which Florence traduced its legacy as the birthplace of humanism and the Renaissance ideas of the universality of man. There was a series of outbursts, some violent, against foreigners. North Africans particularly were blamed for what was seen as an increase in petty crime, especially bag snatching, pickpocketing, and drugs dealing. The street vendors of San Lorenzo market marched through the streets of the city demanding greater protection from the authorities. One of the organizers of the demonstration was Marino 'Groovy' Orlandi, the straight-talking owner of a string of shops selling American-style jeans and clothes. 'Get this clear. We're not racists. But we think in Italy we must only allow in those who have guaranteed work. The problem is they come without work. The worst are the Moroccans and the Yugoslavs. Look, I'll show you. See there, in that alley. What do you see? Syringes. People shoot themselves up. It's no longer safe for young girls to walk around at night. We need more police. We haven't got enough of them.'

In 1991, in a hamlet outside Florence, an early portent of possible future strains of a racial hue appeared. The setting was the otherwise unremarkable village of San Donnino, a ward within the *comune* of Campi Bisenzio a couple of miles south-west of Florence airport. The village like so many of those all around has a couple of attractive churches with Renaissance loggias. Low houses line the main road. A few generations ago, San Donnino had had its own mini industrial revolution when the local population realized that there was more to be made making bags and leather goods for direct sale to the boutiques of Florence than from the land. Dozens of small family businesses were set up in this way.

By the early 1990s, however, the village had been transformed. For it had become a beacon for hundreds of Chinese immigrants.

They came first in a trickle that from 1988 onwards swelled to a rush. By 1992 they numbered between 1,000 and 1,300 against the local population of between 2,200 and 2,500. In some parts, notably the main street, they became a majority.

Visible signs of their presence were few. No Chinese lanterns announced they had established their own restaurants and entertainment parlours. Florence, by contrast, had by then an estimated sixty Chinese restaurants, including countless Great Walls of China and Pekings. Besides a few Chinese faces on street corners waiting for a lift into town, most were inside the workshops cutting and sewing and packing the cheap and nasty bags of imitation leather for sale throughout the country. These were not even the fake designer bags you see being sold everywhere by street hawkers.

Off one of the side streets, the Rosa dei Venti had all the appearance of one of the more respectable, up-market, established local bagmakers. On either side of the building, Italian workmen were using super-quiet state-of-the-art cutting machines to work the leather. The old two-storey building had been recently restored, its soft pink brick carefully repointed. Outside, the brass plaque, of elegant understated modern design, announced that the company made leather travel bags. Upstairs it was all quite different. A dozen Chinese, men, women and children, were crammed into the room. Ancient sewing machines whirred at the touch of the footpedal. As I entered with a colleague, the men got up and everyone stopped what they were doing. We said we were journalists. They looked uncertain, suspicious of the intrusion. As well they might. There were three young children on the floor, tools in hand, in breach of Italy's child-labour laws. The school term had just ended, and they were brought in to help out. The older ones relied on their children for more than an extra pair of hands. For it was the children alone who appeared to speak any Italian, picked up at the local school. We found the spokesperson was a moon-faced girl, who could not have been more than eight, the enamel on her front teeth already beginning to go. When we came in, she had been wielding a large pair of scissors, cutting up material.

In one of the largest workshops on the main street, it was a highly self-confident young boy, who said he was fifteen, who appeared in charge. He had been in Italy four years and spoke fluent Italian. He seemed more integrated into his surroundings than his older relatives. He was preparing to go off on holiday for a week to Sardinia with a group of friends, all of whom were Chinese living in Italy. As we left, an Italian trader was loading bags into his van, and with a nod and wink telling his new partner to make out two sets of invoices, one for the taxman, one for himself.

The Chinese presence had provoked a measure of hostility which, until then, had not spilled out into serious aggression. In the local bars men muttered darkly about their alien ways. They had nothing against the Chinese as such, they said, only that anyone who comes to Italy must be subject to the same rules and regulations as Italians. There could not be one law for the Chinese and another for Italians. Italians had to observe labour laws, and rules on working hours and practices. So then should the Chinese.

The arguments would have been more persuasive if Italians were themselves more law-abiding. The fact is that the Chinese came in, worked hard, were prepared to put up with long gruelling hours for minimal wages to undercut the established competition, and were becoming too successful. A little like the Italian migrant communities abroad in the great waves of emigration of the past. The Chinese of San Donnino were otherwise unobtrusive. They were industrious and kept to themselves. Other than their non-observance of labour regulations, they had not, up to that time, been implicated in any known major criminal activity.

Elsewhere, police have come across rings running illegal immigration rackets, where passports of dead Chinese or Chinese already in Italy were used to spirit new blood into the country – the Italian authorities find it difficult to distinguish between these unfamiliar names and faces. And the Triads started to move into Rome and Milan to extort protection money from Chinese restaurants. The best Chinese restaurant in Rome, in Via Nomentana, was forced to close by men demanding protection money; they said they were from the Triads. It was not clear if this was true, or if they were merely opportunist criminals. The restaurant closed anyway.

San Donnino is the most extreme example of a community which has had to come to terms with a large influx of immigrants from outside the European Community. It is an interesting microcosm of intercommunal tensions and strife in an increasingly multiracial and multicultural society. The largest Chinese community in Italy is tucked into this tiny pocket of territory. Nowhere else is such a number concentrated in so small a space. Their presence has provoked many of the social and demographic problems you find in areas of high immigrant concentrations throughout Europe, where the dividing line between racial prejudice and real social grievance is often blurred. In June 1992 the local population reacted. They staged a march through the city streets, protesting against the Chinese. They accused them of being dirty, of cooking fish and leaving it on windowsills to pollute the atmosphere, and of creating disturbances by working their sewing machines well into the night.

One of the first people to recognize that the community of San Donnino was a proving ground for future interracial relations in the country was the Bishop of Florence, Cardinal Silvano Piovanelli. He decided to send a new priest to report on the situation. The man he chose for this extremely delicate and sensitive task was Don Giovanni Momigli. He could not have picked a better qualified man. The priest, himself a Tuscan, arrived in the village in October 1991. He was barely out of the seminary. But he was not wet behind the ears. Before taking holy orders he had spent ten years as a trades union official with CISL, the Catholic trades union confederation, for which he had been regional secretary for the construction sector. He was well used to standing up during often tempestuous labour disputes and he quickly identified the difficulties. The problem, he said, rapidly became insurmountable when the institutions were lacking and the law was not applied. He said he would like to see the law properly enforced.

Don Momigli was forty-two when he came to the community. I caught up with him one evening as he was dashing between taking mass in one church – the incumbent was sick – and hearing confessions and preparing for a confirmation class in another. In his office in the presbytery he had all the equipment of a modern labour organizer: a fax machine, photocopier and personal computer.

In a few short sentences he described the situation. 'The problem is not so much immigration, as that it is so fast and so uncontrolled, and that so many are coming to one place.'

When he arrived, he said, he found the two communities were not talking. Tension was very high. The community was divided into two factions: the pro- and the anti-Chinese. The antis wanted to kick them out. The more supportive faction reckoned that the social and economic problems of the village were not of their making, though the Chinese may have profited from them. Rather, they were a result of Italy's spiralling labour costs which made their products uncompetitive.

At New Year, during the mass, Don Momigli announced his challenge. Either the situation would change, or he would close the church. It was a remarkable piece of brinkmanship. But the gesture had the desired effect. It made the local community stop and think.

At the same time, he had to speak to the Chinese community. It was difficult. When he first went to speak to them in their workshops, he encountered a great wall of silence. The Chinese hid behind what the Italians call their 'almond eyes'. But his public stands had an influence. He made clear that the Chinese should obey the law. That was the stick. At the same time he opened a help centre. That was the carrot.

One day a Chinese came to the sacristy. Chang Shao Wu was the grand old man of the Chinese community. He had arrived there twenty years before. And he revealed that not only were there problems between the Chinese and the Italians but among the Chinese themselves, between those who were well established and the new arrivals. He explained to the priest that they had begun to live with greater peace of mind after the police had raided a number of the sweatshops working illegal hours.

The priest learnt a considerable amount about how the Chinese community operated. Zhejiang, where they came from, was poor and remote but had a tradition of entrepreneurial activity. The first who came in the 1970s quickly discovered they could make more money manufacturing bags than as waiters in restaurants in Florence. To find a job outside Zhejiang, a prospective emigrant had to pay several thousand dollars in bribes to local officials, another few thousand dollars for his passage, and then even more to the family abroad who would find him work and a work permit, and to whom he was in effect indentured for the first years. The danger was that he was so massively in debt on arrival that he might be tempted by less legal ways of earning money. Even if in the Florence area – including Pistoia, Prato – criminal activity by Chinese was so far low the risks of an increase were there.

The new arrivals were open to exploitation not only by those who had come before. Such was the desperation of the Chinese to find a place to work that the Italian landlords of the workshops found they could charge up to three times the going rate for renting space. Property prices soared, bucking the usual market trends where newly arrived immigrants would often force prices to tumble as the indigenous residents rushed to sell up and move out.

The priest learnt that the older established Chinese families were at times worried that the new arrivals would in turn undercut them, with their greater willingness to work longer hours for less money. Evidence of the abuses were everywhere. In the backs of some of the workshops, dirty plates were stacked up. Cardboard boxes divided off areas where workers slept, despite attempts by the mayor and health inspectors to get them to live in more hygienic surroundings.

After his New Year outburst, Don Momigli took other initiatives. He summoned all fifteen parliamentary representatives for Florence, of both the senate and the chamber of deputies, for a meeting. Nine of them showed up. As a result, questions were asked in parliament. And one of the deputies, Valdo Spini, then an under-secretary at the interior ministry, and incidentally a Socialist and Waldensian, later convened a meeting of high-ranking officials of the concerned ministries and agencies, including guardia di finanza, prefectura, foreign ministry, immigration, police, health and labour to discuss an operational plan to deal with the problem.

At the end of April 1992, a new Florence–Chinese friendship association was inaugurated, providing for the first time an organization or body which could speak for the interests of the Chinese community. Since its founding it has initiated the first tentative dialogue with the Popular Committees in San Donnino. But there have been fights between the groups over the most trivial matters, indications according to the parish priest of the high level of tensions that remain.

Hope may lie with the children. They are much better integrated into Italian life. Their schoolteachers complain that they can hardly stay awake during their lessons, because they have been working most of the night. But they all pick up Italian rapidly. Outside one of the village shops some young Chinese girls and boys, barely six or seven years old, smiled and chatted volubly in Italian among themselves.

The record of integration of foreigners into the Italian community is poor. The Albanians who came in the sixteenth century remain a closed society. They have their own schools in parts of Southern Italy and Sicily where they settled. They have preserved their own language, so much so that scholars from Albania have come to listen to it in its purest form. Yet in reality, the separateness is cultural, not biological. Studies have shown that the original blood of the migrants has been much diluted by intermarriage. Although they maintain a cultural and linguistic distinctiveness, ethnically they have become more Italian than Albanian.

There are too few recent examples of immigrant communities establishing themselves in Italy to try to predict how well present and future immigrants will be absorbed or integrated into society. Such integration will depend on three facts: the will of Italians to integrate them and the will of the immigrants to be integrated; the capacity of the country to take in large numbers of people from often alien cultures; and, of course, the speed with which they are welcomed. But as yet few foreigners coming to Italy have done so to seek citizenship and permanent residency.

The most intractable group of immigrants in Italy is undoubtedly the Gypsies. The unwillingness of the *nomadi* or *zingari* to integrate into society is not peculiar to Italy. It is a problem faced throughout Europe. Immigration ministry officials decry them as the sole example of people unwilling to discuss community matters. For years the slips of Gypsy girls have been the scourge of life in the centres of Rome, Bologna, Florence and the main towns. Hunting in gangs they alight on the unwary and separate him or her from wallet, credit cards, papers with a deftness of the Artful Dodger. Watch them go down the buses (in Rome, the 64 route from the Vatican to the station is notorious). A Gypsy woman with babe in arms saunters down the bus swinging her bundle left and right. As passengers start at the jolt, they fail to feel the tiny mite following in her skirts lifting wallets from back pockets and shoulder bags. The figures point to the extent of the problem. Of 6,738 crimes committed by minors in Rome in 1991, according to the head of the juvenile court, 3,120 were carried out by Gypsies, or 46 per cent of the total.

The authorities all too frequently argue they can do nothing to root out this plague. They say that since the children accused of pickpocketing are minors, they have difficulty in making arrests; and if they are taken in, they will almost invariably be released. Then they hit on a more effective strategy. They questioned a number of the young girls and boys who confessed that they were sent out by the menfolk to work the streets. They were to beg or steal from passers-by, and had to declare a certain quota of takings, so to speak, each day, on pain of being given a good drubbing. After the confessions, the authorities had their pretext. They raided some of the Gypsy encampments, and charged several of the men with enslavement. Rome's Romanies were temporarily kept from the city gates. But within a matter of weeks they were back, as pestilential as ever, as the Roman police succumbed to their traditional inertia and indifference.

The Gypsy presence in Italy is varied. Sociologists reckon that by 1992 there were between 80,000 and 100,000 Gypsies in Italy in five main tribes. Most came after the Second World War from the former Italian areas of what was briefly Yugoslavia. Most settled in the South and centre of the country and along the Adriatic. Many have given up their nomadic ways, as well as their traditional occupations as blacksmiths and horse dealers. Some, advancing with the times, now deal in cars. The vast majority (80,000) have Italian citizenship according to the immigration ministry but still fall foul of Italian bureaucracy. As nomads, few spend enough time in any one place to meet the requirements of residency that would entitle them to benefits such as schooling, obtaining driving licences and health care.

The second main wave came between 1987 and 1990, from Bosnia and Kosovo, two mainly Muslim republics in what was then the Yugoslav federation. Desperately poor, these people turned to whatever means they could to fend for themselves.

By the late 1980s, the now rapid arrival of migrants from outside the European Community led to a number of strains. Immigrants were often victims of violent incidents. On 23 August 1989 a thirty-year-old Southern African tomato picker was brutally murdered. On 18 August 1991, two Senegalese were shot and killed from a passing white Fiat Uno at San Mauro Pascoli. A number of telephone calls of a racist nature were made to the police. Bangladeshi workers at a hostel outside Cisterna near Naples were attacked by gangs of bored, well-off Italians. Some of the attacks were undoubtedly racist in inspiration. Others had more commercial motives. In one case, a group of North African drugs pushers were trying to muscle in on a patch controlled by criminal gangs, and to undercut their prices. In the Monte Oppio area of Rome, near the Colosseum where slave gladiators were thrown to the lions, Tunisians were found beaten up in a park, having been set upon by rabid racists known as Naziskins, who had a clubhouse near by.

All around that area, anti-Semitic and racist graffiti have been painted on the walls of the school buildings. A disturbing sign of a rising racist sentiment in Italy? It is hard to gauge. Graffiti are little indication of the scale or extent of the feeling. After all, a couple of lads with cans of spray paint can cover the outside walls of every school in a district in an evening and promote a wholly misleading sense of their power and influence.

According to the interior ministry, the Naziskins first appeared as a phenomenon in 1988. They were called to Wunsiedel in what was then West Germany on the first anniversary of the death of Rudolf Hess. The Italian chief of police Vincenzo Parisi declared that the 'evolution of skinheads seems directed by extreme right-wing groups who use them'. The Digos anti-terrorist unit suspects the Movimento Politico of recruiting marginals for racist motives. They took the name from a right-wing group, Movimento Politico Nuovo Ordine, that was disbanded in 1974. The two groups, however, are socially different. The 1970s group brought together disaffected students during that whole fervid period of Italian political life. Nuovo Ordine was as much anarchist, against all political parties, as right wing. The new movement drew its support from much rougher ground: the marginalized, out-of-work, ignorant young men in the run-down suburbs of Rome and other Italian cities. They blamed foreigners for taking their jobs.

Italians were surprised and shocked at their own racism. But how significant were the Naziskins? Were they merely a passing fad, the rather lukewarm Mediterranean version of a harsher Northern European phenomenon, as the punks were before them? Or were they the early symptoms of a growing sentiment of racial intolerance?

Numerically, they were few when they emerged. Only 400 were mustered to march on Rome on 29 February 1992, the first time that neo-Fascists had stomped beneath the balcony where Il Duce had addressed the crowds. But with their shaved heads and bomber jackets, and virulently racist chants and banners, they evoked worrying memories of the past.

The Naziskins established their bars and clubs and favourite places to hang out in the drab peripheries of Rome in Quadraro, Prenestina, San Giovanni, Rione Monti, Via Mamiani, Talenti, Flaminio. The Movimento Politico had an office, if that is not too grand a term, on Via Domodossola, but initially it was ill-equipped. It was more a dingy basement, which also acted as a sales point for jackets and T-shirts and all the usual paramilitary paraphernalia and insignia such as swastikas.

Fiamma Nirenstein, a journalist whose nomination as head of the Italian cultural centre in Tel Aviv was one of the few appointments made by the then foreign minister Gianni De Michelis which did not arouse controversy, described the phenomenon of the archetypal racist in her book *Il Razzista Democratico* ('The Democratic Racist'). She felt that the neo-Nazis, with their hideous aspect and their espousal of the lunacies of historical revisionism, their denial of the existence of Auschwitz and Treblinka Nazi death camps, were really only rather pathetic individuals on the margins of society. The real danger was the unconscious racism of those who in all sincerity denied they were racist, but declared the need to preserve democracy and society from extraneous and alien elements.

*

A whole vocabulary has arisen to denote or connote racial characteristics. Italy's lack of experience in racial issues makes it much less coy than other countries to talk about colour. Cars can be blue (the standard Alfa Romeo or Lancia limousine to transport politicians, officials or captains of industry); green (environmentally friendly, if they run on lead-free petrol and are fitted with catalytic converters); or yellow (either taxis, or Japanese). Black and brown people are known as *extracomunitari* as though giving them a legalistic label in some way is less discriminatory. Italy's best-known clothes brand exploited colour for its marketing slogan of the United Colors of Benetton.

Colour, however, is not the main issue to Italians. That at least is the view of the victims of prejudice. A Senegalese I met in Florence, one of those fluent French-speaking university graduates who ended up selling trinkets along the Arno, told me that Italians discriminate against culture not colour. 'When I first came here I spoke English and passed as a black American. I had no trouble picking up girls. It is only when they learn I am African that they treat me differently.'

The coloured Dutch football stars with AC Milan, Ruud Gullit and Frank Rijkaard, have suffered very few racial taunts from visiting fans. Anti-Semitic taunts levelled against their compatriot Aron Winter, a player in the Italian league, were a rarity (and also an aberration: despite his name, he is not Jewish but manifestly coloured).

Cases have arisen of the Church or parents trying to block mixed marriages between North African immigrants and Italian girls. The Church has explained its opposition in cultural terms: marriages are more likely to founder if the cultural divide is too great. In such cases, under Islamic law, the father of any children will almost invariably obtain custody should the marriage break down. In a small village on the tranquil shores of Lake Iseo, near Brescia, a Tunisian and his girlfriend found their marriage blocked. They also could not get into council housing. He cried prejudice. Her parents, and the mayor, said they had first to check he had not been married before. And on the housing list, everyone had to queue.

One possible stumbling block towards true integration within a pluralist society is not race, but religion. Now, of course, it is evident, as we have seen, that Italy is fundamentally a secular society, albeit with a strong Catholic culture. There is no reason why such a society should not welcome people from different cultures and religions. Tensions could arise, however, if some of the immigrants erect obstacles to their integration. Islam, in its more militant forms – which it must be stressed has not manifested itself until this point – poses specific problems. For it is a revealed religion. The basis for Islamic law is what its followers hold is the word of God as contained in the Koran and the sayings and doings of the Prophet Muhammad. It accordingly presents an alternative set of ideas that by their nature cannot be integrated into the cultural whole. This is not just a question of such comparatively minor issues as ritual slaughter, an argument faced too by the Jewish community. But as has been seen in other European countries such as France and Britain, more militant Muslims are prepared to agitate and demand that society tolerate practices dear to them, even when they are in conflict with the avowedly secular customs of the countries they are residing in. In France the issue exploded over whether Muslim girls should be allowed to wear headdresses in schools that were, by law, non-sectarian and secular. This problem has not yet hit Italy. The question that, in time, Italian liberal democracy may have to face is: can it tolerate the erosion of its own values of tolerance? It is a variation on the old conundrum. To what extent should a tolerant society tolerate intolerance, or a secular society accept religious rigidity?

One group does have a long experience of coping with being outside the dominant Catholic culture of Italy throughout the centuries. The experience of the Jewish community in Italy illustrates a people's odyssey through acceptance, rejection, discrimination, reintegration, and persecution. Jews in medieval Italy were engaged in banking, but were always unpopular with the Franciscans whom they undercut in the same business. In the sixteenth century, the Jews of Rome were expelled by the papal authorities to the left bank of the Tiber and walled up in a ghetto along the model devised in Venice and replicated throughout Europe. After the unification of Italy, they broke down the walls of the ghetto and built their great synagogue. Its huge cupola was constructed if not to rival St Peter's, at least to challenge it, to announce after these generations of enforced humiliation and separate development that they were indeed a presence. But that separate development had its benefits. Jews had a far higher standard of literacy and education, and were well adapted to the requirements of the new, anti-clerical administration. Jews served in government with distinction. Integration went further. Five Jews were among the founding members of the Fascist movement in 1919. And one of Mussolini's favoured mistresses, Margherita Sarfatti, was from a well-to-do Milanese Jewish family. This may account in part for why in the 1930s and 1940s Italy was one of the few countries in Europe where all anti-Jewish measures were decidedly unpopular. According to the chronicler of the Eichmann trial, Hannah Arendt, it was only with reluctance, and under great pressure from Hitler, that Mussolini enacted anti-Jewish laws in 1938, so poignantly captured in the classic film of Giorgio Bassani's book, *Il Giardino dei Finzi-Contini*. Some then chose to leave.

One of the most distinguished families to do so was that of the eight Pontecorvo children, who have contributed so much in their different ways to the twentieth century. They were not a religiously observant family, and were fully assimilated into the social and cultural life of Italy. But after the enactment of Mussolini's racial laws, under which Jews could not obtain senior university posts, or marry non-Jews, most of the children were sent abroad. Four came to Britain. Of these, one became professor of genetics and fellow of the Royal Society, another a nurse, the third a spokesman for Olivetti, and the fourth, Bruno, a distinguished nuclear scientist who in 1951 defected to the Soviet Union.

It was not until the Italian surrender in 1943, when half of Italy fell directly under German control, that measures were implemented to carry out Hitler's grand design for the Final Solution. A plaque on the wall of the Rome synagogue records how that design was implemented. It pays tribute to the 8,000 Italian Jews who were massacred. According to Hannah Arendt, the reluctance of Italian officials to assist in the Nazi plan to murder Jews was 'the outcome of the almost automatic general humanity of an old and civilized people'.

Today, the Jewish community in Italy is one of the smallest in Europe – about 36,000. This figure is calculated by the number of those who pay their dues to the Community. It excludes many of the Jews who fled persecution in Libya, most of whom went to Israel. A few, however, came to Rome, where they have established their own synagogue in Piazza Bologna, and remain wary and aloof from the established Jewish community.

The Jewish community is afforded special protection in the Italian state in fact rather than in law because of past outrages committed not by anti-Semitic Italians but Arab groups or individuals. The attacks have been directed not only at specifically Israeli targets. The bombing of the El Al counter at Fiumicino airport in 1985 killed an American girl. It was an Italian cruise ship, the *Achille Lauro*, named after the Neapolitan shipping magnate, which was hijacked in the Mediterranean by Palestinian extremists in 1985. In 1989 a bomb was thrown at the Rome synagogue, causing some damage but no casualties. The main Rome synagogue today is ringed with armed police, and the Jewish school on the Tiber, the Liceo Gallileo, has anti-grenade meshing on its windows, bulletproof glass doors, and a permanent guard of uniformed police and young men in dark glasses.

It was not until the summer of 1990 that, to appease a concerned public, the government recognized the immigration problem as needing specific measures. A portfolio for immigration was created. The first minister was the Socialist Margherita Boniver, whose experience of living in the United States had encouraged her faith in the richness of diverse cultures in a single country. However, her office had little or no power. She had no separate department, and her ministry was merely an adjunct to the prime minister's office. Although her job description was to co-ordinate activity relating to immigrants between the different ministries (interior, foreign affairs, housing, health and so on), in effect decisions were taken by others. At the time the ministry was set up the country was prepared to accept and absorb some 25,000 Albanians who came in the first wave of immigration across the Adriatic in an armada of rafts and small boats, fleeing the last desperate days of the Hoxha regime. A year later the Italians had another influx of

Albanians. But these were not welcomed in the same way. The justification used was that the government in Albania had changed, these refugees were now no longer fleeing an oppressive political regime, but merely seeking a better standard of living in the west. They were allowed off their creaking steamer at the port of Bari, then led to the stadium where they were temporarily housed pending a decision. They were tricked into leaving the stadium and put on planes, which shuttled back and forth to Tirana. The decision to deport the Albanians was taken by the police and interior ministry who acted without consulting Signora Boniver.

A more substantial move was the enactment, at last, of legislation to regulate immigration, to bring Italy more into line with its European partners. Until then, Italy was the odd man out in the EC. It had no statutory immigration controls. Foreigners were allowed to enter freely both by law and in fact because of the porousness of Italy's borders. As a result, many used Italy as an entry point into Europe. Officials elsewhere in Europe looked aghast at Italy as the soft underbelly of the continent, an easy touch for immigrants coming from North Africa or Eastern Europe seeking a better life.

The law parliament passed was designed to curb future immigration. Known as the Martelli Law, after its sponsor the Socialist minister Claudio Martelli, it in effect closed an official eye towards those non-EC nationals already in Italy. These were granted an amnesty, provided they registered with the *questura*. At the same time, the law assured registered foreigners a certain level of social services in terms of housing, health care, and social insurance. By the same token, it placed restrictions on new immigrants.

The Martelli Law has inevitably been abused. In and around Rome is a community of 2,500 Bangladeshis, the largest in Europe outside the United Kingdom, who made a headlong dash into Italy from France, Germany and the Netherlands, where they were working illegally, to get to Italy before the amnesty and thereby qualify for work permits and residency.

The law was not without its critics. The most articulate was Giorgio La Malfa, whom I spoke to when he was still leader of the Republican Party. 'My argument at the time', La Malfa explained to me in his reedy voice, 'was that if you accept those already here, you create an inflow afterwards of those who will be convinced that sooner or later an amnesty will be extended to them. If you tell people that those who are in illegally can stay, there will be lots of people who will say that this was the case once, it will be the case a second time. So instead of stopping the inflow you are going to create an inflow of illegal immigrants.'

He argued that there were very clear quantitative limits to any immigration which a Western European country could take before entering into a situation of social strain. You cannot set a figure easily, he said. Italy does not have a labour market with room for millions of newcomers.

So what was he suggesting in terms of new arrivals? 'Basically none. For special jobs or needs, you can have a few thousand a year.' Some Northern health authorities had, for example, taken on non-EC nurses to make up a staff shortfall in city hospitals. This provoked little reaction.

La Malfa's next argument was that if people from neighbouring countries like Albania escaped, Italy could not be too hard on them. 'You cannot be hard on Albanians and then shut your eyes to illegal immigration from Tunisia. Then you have a situation in which you are both unjust and unfair and unreasonable. We should have had a very different attitude towards the Albanians.'

He blasted the lack of control of illegal immigration. Very few people have been expelled from the country for being found without papers. The authorities exerted an amount of firmness with respect to Albanians which they never showed to people coming from other countries. Their decisiveness in dealing with the Albanians merely showed up their lack of resolve in other cases. It was an attempt at bravado, at posturing.

'We don't have barriers. We can discourage people from doing things by not condoning them. Europe cannot become a fortress. That's for sure. If you want to stop the inflow, then you have to take care. The European Community should make itself spend money in Eastern Europe, in North Africa, to stem the inflow. You must invest money, transfer technology, which is costly, but in my view it's much more costly to have the social and economic strains of illegal immigration.'

Today the population of North Africa is basically the same as that in Southern Europe. By the year 2025, that is in one generation, the population will be a staggering 400 million against 200 million in Southern Europe. La Malfa's fear is that unless the possibility of development is created, unless a more rigorous effort is made to control population growth, even though it runs counter to the teaching of the Catholic Church, then the problem can only worsen.

'You can test the strains by seeing whether they occur or not. Italy is not a country where you have sentiments of hatred towards foreigners. There is no racial hatred. There is no tradition of anything of that sort. Now we see examples of racial intolerance that are becoming more frequent in the urban peripheries, in relatively poor areas. We now have examples of social strain. The signs are that you may be hitting the ceiling of tolerance.'

La Malfa was basically right. Italy had little history of racial or religious intolerance. But as we have seen, even with this record, a third of the Jewish population had been murdered during the Second World War. The rise in racist sentiment today on Italy is as much linked to the increase in petty crime and other urban ills for which foreigners provide a ready scapegoat. Anti-foreign sentiment also has less ideological content. Even those on the far right seldom talk of any biological differences between races. Rather they seek to preserve what they regard as their own cultural identity. They see the influx of outsiders as threatening their cultural and traditional roots. Social factors play a part. Those who come to Italy in search of work from the Third World almost inevitably find the kind of menial work that Italians no longer wish to do, even though many are highly educated.

It is too early to see how easily non-Italians will be absorbed within Italian society. Most Italian 'migrants' were Southerners who flooded north in search of jobs. The difficulties in integration of large numbers of Southern Italians into society in the North show just what challenges are posed. The concern has been to manage the immigration, in terms of numbers, concentration and speed of integration.

There has been a characteristically Italian reaction to the problem: call it a European issue, and seek EC funding. Hence the reaction of Nadio Delai, director-general of the social research organization Censis. 'In my mind we should set up a sort of European fund, a fund of money and a fund of culture to treat the problem. Because it's absolutely incredible all the criticism we had from the Germans over the treatment of the Albanians. We *have* managed to absorb migrants, up to 700,000 per year. From Southern Italy to Milan, Turin. And we had problems of racism, or of reaction. If you go to Turin, it's incredible. They have integrated everyone. Of course you can say, they are not black. In a certain sense I agree. If you have a long time it's different. Germany and France needed to have people to have manpower available.'

What Dr Delai did not say was that Germany was prepared to take far more immigrants than Italy, and at a faster rate. In 1992, when it was already coping with the integration of the Germans of the former East Germany, it opened its border to a mass influx of refugees fleeing fighting in what was Yugoslavia. At the same time, Italy sought to internationalize the problem, to obtain US financial assistance for housing the refugees, mainly Muslims from Bosnia, in North-eastern Italy. At that stage, Italy had received no more than a thousand refugees; Germany had accepted uncomplainingly twenty times that number.

The tolerance shown towards non-Italians will depend largely on factors outside their control. If Italy has not had a tradition of racial intolerance, that is not simply because of the absence of racial minorities of which to be intolerant. There are other reasons too. The dominant political cultures of the postwar years, Catholicism and Communism, have both preached some form of betterment of society. Each in its way is avowedly humane, with a strong belief in the equality of man. This has always made Italy such an agreeable and welcoming place for the foreigner whether visitor or resident.

An absence of economic difficulties was a key reason for the low level of racial tension. Elsewhere, in times of economic recession, of job shortages and inflation, of high prices and social strain, scapegoats may be found in outsiders, be they foreigners or merely from groups outside the main stream. Italy, though always appearing to lurch from one scandal to another, was actually thriving for much of this period.

As soon as Italians start losing their jobs in the austerity resulting from an economic downturn, they will pick on the easiest and most vulnerable targets for their frustration, and those least able to defend themselves: be they *clandestini* (illegal immigrants), or the *vu cumprà* street hawkers (a Neapolitan corruption of 'You wanna buy?'), doing the work that Italians now disdain doing.

Italians like La Malfa pride themselves on their racial tolerance, on their lack of prejudice. But as I have tried to show, Italians had no reason to harbour racial prejudice or show it because they had with the exception of small Jewish communities no long history of distinct racial groups living among them. Rapid immigration and growing economic strains could test quite how deep the much vaunted tolerance of the Italians really is, and how ready society is to welcome strangers in its midst.

In Britain in 1968, the Conservative politician Enoch Powell sparked a storm of protest when he evoked Virgil in voicing his concern at the pace of immigration and the effect this had on the indigenous population. 'We must be mad to be permitting the inflow of some 50,000 dependants a year. As I look ahead I am filled with foreboding. Like the Roman I seem to see "the River Tiber foaming with much blood".'*

Twenty-five years on, his fears had not been realized. I, unlike the Roman, do not foresee the Tiber foaming with much blood. But as immigration increases, and economic problems cause social strains, foreign communities are likely to suffer more discrimination and abuse than they have until now.

Bella, horrida bella,
  Et Thybrim multo spumantem sanguine cerno.

(I see wars, horrible wars and the Tiber foaming with much blood.) Virgil, *Aeneid* Book VI, line 86

TWELVE

Can the centre hold? Bossi v. *i boss*

Medieval historians might be better equipped than cartographers of contemporary history to position Pontida on a map of Europe. But not for long. For Pontida has already been established as a place of pilgrimage for followers of one of the most popular political movements of the end of the twentieth century. It was the focus of centrifugal forces which for a time were threatening to tear Italy apart and to break the North off from Rome little more than a century after the country was unified.

It was to Pontida, an hour or so's drive from Milan, that the one-time medical student and salesman Umberto Bossi enticed his faithful followers in the Lombard League. There he urged them to renew their commitment to their autonomist cause. Pontida evoked powerful associations of self-help against a shared enemy. The Lombard League took its name from the grouping of independent city states of Northern Italy that joined together at Pontida in 1167 to resist the common threat posed by Frederick Barbarossa and the Holy Roman Empire.

The modern-day successor to this League held its first major rally at Pontida in May 1990. By this stage, the League was calling itself the Lega Nord, the Northern League, a loose alliance of the Lombard League and other smaller regional leagues. The movement's leaders and members, who had won local and other elections, pledged their commitment to the federalist ideal. A year later, at Pontida again, the Lega 'proclaimed' a Republic of the North.

The evocation of these medieval antecedents was displayed everywhere. Lega supporters wore gold-plated lapel badges depicting the movement's symbol, a knight in armour with a sword held high in one hand and a shield in the other. The warrior was

Alberto Da Guissano, who led the forces of the Lombard (meaning long beard) League to victory against Frederick Barbarossa at Legnano in 1176. It was the Long Beards against the Red Beard – and the Long Beards won.

Yet there was nothing retrogressive in the modern League. It started as a tax revolt and became a more generalized protest against inefficiency and corruption in government. That it should have had its roots in the most industrious, hard-working, prosperous, modern and European-focused part of Italy was a demonstration of the depth of frustration and resentment against the excesses of the political parties. In recent times Northerners have generally left politics to Southerners. They concentrated on making money instead. But once the burdens of government policies, of high interest rates and taxes, and the difficulties of maintaining market share in competitive export markets became too great, tolerance of the status quo began to lessen. The League became a protest against everything that Rome stood for: the state of the economy, high taxes, the South, the Mafia, the government, corruption in local government, corruption in regional government, corruption in national government.

One of the League's early electoral successes was for the town council in Brescia, the second largest industrial centre in Italy. The city's wealth was based on mills forging steel and iron rod that reinforced the concrete buildings and bridges of Italy's economic development boom. Brescia was also a heartland of the Christian Democrats. There the Church enjoyed a formidable presence in the life of the community, with schools and publishing houses. There, too, the brash public-works minister Gianni Prandini had used the allocation of contracts in a blatant attempt to shore up the Christian Democrat vote. To no avail. For it was Brescia – albeit briefly – which became the first major city of Italy to fall to the men of the North.

An early book on the League dubbed its supporters the Brigate Rozze, the Raucous Brigades, a play on Brigate Rosse, the Red Brigades, which had attacked the heart of the state in the 1970s. But whereas the Red Brigades had been a small, ideologically motivated urban terrorist group, the League quickly evolved into the largest mass movement of Northern Italy. Its message was simple, the language of its delivery crude and brash. Emblazoned across the front of boxer shorts sold at League functions was one of Bossi's immortal sayings: *'La Lega ce l'ha duro'* ('The League has a hard-on'). Since the League was outside government, it had no access to the *tangenti* on public contracts that financed the other parties, and so had to resort to selling trinkets such as Northern League coinage to raise money. Its posters proclaimed the message directly: *Roma Ladrona, la Lega non perdona* (Thieving Rome, the League will not forgive you).

The League's leader hardly had the standard curriculum vitae of an aspiring politician, least of all a national figure. Bossi provoked the scorn of his colleagues in parliament for the coarseness of his language, and his apparent delight in his own complete absence of intellectual pretensions. He would refer to the prime minister Giulio Andreotti as 'the hunchback', and prided himself on not remembering when he last read a book.

Bossi was born in 1941, the son of a textile factory worker, on the outskirts of Varese, one of those small prosperous towns that dot the countryside around Milan. He did not go straight into higher education, but was a member of a rock band for a time and then worked as a salesman. Both occupations served him well. He still moves around on stage with the energy and presence of an experienced performer. And his patter has the crude persuasiveness of the barrow boy. Bossi decided late in life to return to his studies. As such he was a beneficiary of the great increase in educational opportunities offered to people of humble origin by Italy's economic boom. He did radio electronics by correspondence course before going on to medical school. It was while he was working as a laboratory technician in heart and lung transplant experiments on pigs that he became actively engaged in regionalist politics. The formative moment was his meeting in 1979 with Bruno Salvadori, leader of the Union Valdôtaine, which promoted a sort of autonomy and cultural awareness for the Valle d'Aosta, bordering France. But the movement was essentially flawed. Whereas the educated spoke both French and Italian, the ordinary people conversed in a local Occitaine patois. There was no real cultural or linguistic unity across the social divide.

The experience, however, gave Bossi many ideas for his own

movement. This came from nowhere. It was founded in 1982 as the Lega Autonomista Lombarda and a year later began contesting elections at the local and national level. After dropping 'Autonomist' from its name, in 1987 it won 2.5 per cent of the vote in national elections, and Bossi became senator in Rome. At this early stage the movement was still seen as a tiny band of quaint autonomists. It was not until December 1989 that it held its first congress. Then, for the first time, the League toned down some of its more strident demands and came up with some specific policies. Yet its programme never constituted much more than the simple message of less control from Rome and was dismissed by its critics as a latter-day revival of the postwar movement of the *uomo qualunque*. This term became a general expression of denigration for anyone who was against anything connected with the state but who had no real policy or ideology other than 'I'm all right Jack'. All the League's subsequent elaborations of policy, of free-market economics, its protests against organized crime, the tax revolt against Rome, stemmed from the single principle of wanting to loosen the control of a distant and administratively inefficient central government. It did not want the kind of centralized state that Mussolini created. That is why Bossi so resented being compared with the Fascists. There were similarities of style in their rabble-rousing rhetoric and autocratic control over their parties, but their policies could not differ more fundamentally.

The first time I met Bossi he was late for our appointment. His car had broken down on the way into Milan and he had been obliged to hire a replacement. He drove himself, in a small Citroën ZX – the current European Car of the Year. Foreign makes were still the minority in Italy. But why should he have had qualms? After all, he believed in a Europe without frontiers and envisaged a future for Lombardy in a Europe of the regions. Nothing could symbolize better the difference between Bossi and the pampered politicians in Rome. Not for him a bulletproof regulation-blue high-power Fiat or Lancia. Not for him a driver or bagman. There were no motorcycle outriders or armed escort fore and aft. Not even a personal assistant. Since that time he has acquired some of the trappings associated with the leader of a major party. He is usually driven in a large car – though not

Italian but a BMW. I saw him when he was the only member of parliament the League had. A fortnight later he was sitting at the head of a party that had swept in like a wind from the North to seize fifty-five seats in the chamber of deputies and twenty-five in the senate.

We pulled up at a red light. Two young men in the car in front recognized him. The driver got out. There was no cause for concern. He gave the thumbs up sign and a huge grin. Bossi was going to address an election meeting at Como, a kilometre from the Northern confines of the state. Como, silk capital of Italy, had more recently become an international centre for trade – or more often than not, the fraudulent commerce – of other more deadly substances from the East: nuclear materials from the old Soviet bloc.

As we cruised up the motorway, *il senatur*, as Bossi was known in mimicry of the Lombard way of saying senator, gabbled away about his vision of a federal Italy. Simply put, he wanted the North to govern the North, the Centre the Centre, and the South the South. Certain functions and responsibilities would remain with a federal government. He emphasized that the Northern League was not a separatist movement. He wanted a federal solution, not a separate state in the North. What had impressed and inspired his movement was the sight of Barcelona as the venue for the 1992 Olympic Games within a model of Catalan regional autonomy.

In Bossi's Italy, the North would include all those areas that were industrially most advanced and socially most integrated with those parts of Europe on the other side of the Alps. Milan, after all, was closer to Munich than to Messina, and Brescia had more business with Bavaria than with Bari. The Republic of the North, sometimes called the Republic of the Po Valley (Padania), would embrace Piedmont, Lombardy, Veneto, Liguria, Emilia-Romagna, Friuli and Tuscany. It would therefore include the industrial triangle of Turin, Milan and Genoa, as well as the great mass of productive small- to medium-sized industrial enterprises of the North and Northern Centre. If Italy did not introduce a federal system, then the Northern regions would simply band together and declare themselves a republic. Italy had a date with Europe. If the

South could not make it, too bad for it. 'We can go in one after the other.'

The distinction between federal solution and secession was to dog the League over its early years. It caused a rift between Bossi and Gianfranco Miglio, the professor of constitutional law and political science at Milan's Catholic University, who was the one person of standing in this rag-tag movement, and who was once regarded as its ideologue. The outcome of the dispute demonstrated that Bossi, and Bossi alone, spoke for the League. Professor Miglio, a senator for Como, had gone further than most, proposing in effect that Sicily and Sardinia should be politically cut off from the mainland and left to sink or swim in the Mediterranean. His anti-Sicilian rhetoric gave ammunition to those who have maintained that all the talk of a federal solution was in fact a euphemism for rabid anti-Southern prejudice. The outcry Professor Miglio's remarks provoked, and the fears expressed up and down the country about how the League was proposing the dismemberment of the unified state, forced Bossi into what was tantamount to an abandonment of any separatist policy, even one under the guise of the unilateral declaration of a Republic of the North.

The church bells were ringing as we pulled into Como. Along the road, rough painted signs marked 'Sen Bossi' pointed the way. Posters spread the message: 'Thieves of Rome, it's over.' The auditorium, in a technical school, all bleak concrete, was packed. Most were young, first-time voters, both boys and girls. Many were forced to spill into the corridors and a side room, where *il senatur*'s message was carried by loudspeaker.

The senator knew the tricks. He understood how to appeal to the crowd, to tell them what they wanted to hear. And they responded. When his cellular phone rang as he was being introduced, he got up to turn it off. They, the crowd, his people, were more important. They loved it. 'Bos-SI. Bos-SI,' they shouted. 'UM-BER-TO, UM-BER-TO,' they chanted as he ranted against the corruption of a government which squandered vast sums of tax money, money they had earned through hard work and paid because they were honest folk – which went to buy off *i boss*, the Mafia bosses, in the South and the corrupt political parties.

He rattled away, without notes, moving his hands up and down to make a point. In the South, he said, he had met young people who supported him. There were people there who wanted work, real work, not merely the 'posts' in the gift of local political bosses, or disability pensions. It was not a question of North versus South. It was a question of attitude. In the North, people tended to work and pay taxes. In the South, they waited for hand-outs from the government granted in exchange for votes. 'There are two ways of reducing the public deficit. Cutting costs or raising taxes. The current political classes, the four parties which make up the governing coalition, have no intention of cutting costs. Why? Because what we consider wasteful expenditure is electoral bribes, their way of buying votes. They talk of investment in the South. What do they mean by investment? In-vestment,' he leered, pushing his hand into his pocket, playing on the Italian word for jacket. The crowd erupted. And he responded, giving them an encore, repeating the jibe with even more grotesque pocketing of the imaginary bribe.

He turned to government waste. 'Consider pensions. In England, they know that the government invests pension contributions wisely, and they generate interest. Here they say the state pension scheme is out of cash. We are in a country where five million people have disability pensions. That's 10 per cent of the population. More even than in Iraq after the bombing. We have great need of institutional reform. There are fiscal laws passed in Rome which apply equally in the Alps and in Sicily, which ignore the differing social and economic realities.'

Bossi proposed the withholding of payment of some taxes as an act of civil disobedience. When he suggested that citizens should not buy any more government bonds, he was accused of being unpatriotic and seeking to undermine the national economy.

Roberto Ronchi, an early director of the League's political secretariat, explained what the League was fighting against. 'We are against billions of lire earned here being taken for the development of the South and ending up in the hands of the criminal organizations, the Camorra, the 'ndrangheta, and Cosa Nostra. The problem is not a system which works badly and has to be reformed, it is the system itself.'

The League was always more than a movement of artisans and small shopkeepers who resented paying high taxes. The support the League gained spanned all ages and social classes. There were manufacturers exasperated that it could take three days to complete the paperwork to ship goods from Bergamo to Bavaria when it would only take one if they rang the shipper in Bavaria direct. There were contractors fed up with having to pay bribes to secure work. They were not just North against South, but small against big. They resented paying taxes so that huge and wasteful state subsidies could be paid to the industrial giants to build non-productive enterprises in the South. They worked hard, but were deprived of what they saw as their just rewards. A small family-run construction company in Milan could only go so far without paying *tangenti* to secure contracts.

There were people like Angelo Maraini, who had come to the League late. For most of his working life he had run a restaurant in London, providing snacks for the stars and crews at Elstree film studios. Even before he decided to retire near the Italian lakes, he became actively engaged in League politics. On his return to Italy he had found much rotten in the country and blamed the poor administration on the people at the top. 'Look, in a restaurant there may be waitresses who don't serve you well. They sit in a corner chatting and painting their nails. It's not their fault. It is the head waiter who should supervise. There are no ifs and buts. They are not answerable to anybody. They have no one to refer to. It is a rot which sets in.'

The culprits were the politicians in the South who had corrupted the minds of the people. 'Thank God we in the North were invaded by the Austrians, and the Habsburgs left good traces in our blood.'

Like many, he rejected the suggestion that Southerners were culturally inferior, or workshy. 'Sicilians and Southerners work hard. It is not a cultural thing. It is a question of opportunities and the Mafia.'

Maraini's was the less crude view of the South and Southerners. The same could not be said of Bossi. Bossi had always rejected the charge that he himself was racist, against immigrants whether from North Africa or the South. He could point out his wife was half-Sicilian. Yet chauvinism and prejudice undeniably played their part in the Northern culture from which the League derived its support. In the North you would experience such prejudice in the slogans and hear it in the everyday comments: '*Terroni ladroni*' (Southerners are thieves) or 'Milan is European not African.'

League supporters will often illustrate what they see as the fundamental ways in which the North and the South differ by describing how the two handled very similar natural disasters. We have already seen what happened in the aftermath of the earthquake which struck Irpinia, outside Naples, in 1980. Four years before, on 6 May 1976, a huge earthquake struck an area of 5,725 square kilometres (2,210 square miles) in Friuli. Some 989 people were killed and 3,000 injured. The structural damage was enormous. But Friuli responded immediately. Lodging was found straight away for 40,000 people in hotels along the Adriatic coast. Emergency relief came almost at once, from neighbouring provinces and countries including Austria, Switzerland and Germany. Within a year and a half, most reconstruction was complete. The contrasting disaster management of the two earthquakes is often cited in League literature as proof of the cultural differences between the two parts of Italy.

The League was not alone in publicly expressing concern about the South. A high-ranking general, Luigi Federici – former army vice-chief of staff, and then commander of the 4th Army Corps (the Alpine) – issued a warning in the early 1990s against what he saw as the growing Southernization of the army. As the service was moving away from a conscript body drawn from all over the country towards a more professional, volunteer force, most of its recruits came from the South. Up to 98 per cent came from Puglia, Sicily and Campania, he declared. High unemployment and lack of opportunities had always propelled Southerners to-wards the security of government service. The general's warning was based less on prejudice than on wider security concerns. Many Southerners tended to have lower skill levels than Northerners, at a time when modern weapons systems needed ever more technic-ally able operators. And on a political level, the general questioned whether it was wise to have a largely Southern army protecting what in many cases might be Northern interests.

The general's intervention in what many might have regarded

as a delicate and sensitive political area did his career no harm. He was appointed commandant of the carabinieri shortly afterwards. The political arena had long been dominated by Southerners. Southerners made up about a third of the population, but nearly half the ministers in Andreotti's last government, and 44 per cent of the under-secretaries or junior ministers, were from the South.

Yet fears of geographical fissure were allayed over time. The metamorphosis of the Lombard League into the Northern League broadened its appeal. At the same time its stridency was tempered by its greater participation in government at local level, and by the imperatives of being one of the larger parties represented in parliament at a national level.

It is too early to say, as its critics hopefully predict, that the League will disappear as a political force. Yet the existing order is under challenge as never before. Will it be Bossi or *i boss* of the Sicilian Mafia who will gain the ascendancy in the new Italy? The rise of both organized crime and the League was a mirror to the weakness of the central state. Yet neither wanted the disintegration of that unified state. The Mafia had always preferred order to chaos and increasingly fed off the fat contracts which central government provided. And the League fully understood that a divided Italy would have even less say in world affairs and less influence on the economic councils of the globe than the modest role it had hitherto ascribed to itself.

The early 1990s were a turning point. It was the time when the single European market was to come into effect and fulfil the dreams of the European federalists. In Italy, it was the time when the bills which had been piling up – political, economic and fiscal – were presented for payment. The politicians, for so long unchallenged by the electorate, were finally cast aside. And suddenly the Italians also began to feel the chill winds of recession, which had been swirling around countries to the North, as they swept down through the Alps. Public-sector workers, who thought they had jobs for life, found they were being laid off. Several cases of attempted suicide were reported as despair gripped those who suddenly had to face the reality that the government was no longer going to feather-bed them.

And yet, and yet. It was true that Italian manufacturing industry had thrived in a business environment which was among the most protected in the Western world. But past experience suggested that Italian manufacturers would rise to the challenge of greater competition. Italians have a reputation as astute men of affairs, of people who not only desire to make money, but who have a great aptitude for doing so. The concept of *dolce far niente*, of doing sweet nothing, is a likeable but wholly baseless myth of this hard-working people. Italians are not driven by any Protestant work ethic, by the sense that they have a moral and religious duty to strive on this earth. Rather they work hard because they take pride in it and enjoy the fruits of those labours. They are the most dynamic, flexible, quick-thinking, irrepressible workforce in Europe. They will bounce back from the recession, even if Italy, later than other countries, has to come to terms with the economic realities of the reduced world demand for goods and the need to cut the manufacturing sector.

There will be tensions, which in Italy have a long tradition of erupting in violent form. Bomb attacks in Rome, Milan and Florence in the summer of 1993 were demonstrations, if any were needed, that there are still forces, whether aligned with the secret services, ultra right-wing groups, or the Mafia, which will take any measures necessary to block attempts at political reform that threaten their interests.

Yet the Italians have an uncanny ability to make the most of a given situation. Their disregard for the rules, whatever they may be, has been the undoing of their political system. But this same disregard remains the fount of the richness and vitality of Italian society. With demographic changes, the New Italians are older Italians, but Italy has the youthful vigour of a modern society. For the past forty or more years Italians have channelled their energies into economic development. If, in this new climate, with this more general desire for moral and political reform, they can manage to overhaul some of the institutions which have short-changed them for so long, then Italy will not only remain a wonderful place to visit. It will also provide a more equitable society for its own people.

If the elections of 1992 were the parting shot of the old regime, those of March 1994 were to consecrate Italy's induction into a new era. Or so it was said. Most of the political shoots that popped up in this Italian spring were green with inexperience. Over two-thirds of the intake to parliament had never before held an elected post. Fewer still had run ministries. However, some were grafted on to old stems that reached deep into the rich soil of Italian political culture. In this category must be placed the central figure of the piece, the man who swept all before him, the media mogul turned politician, Silvio Berlusconi.

No one can say now that they did not know who they were voting for. Throughout the eighties Berlusconi had been the hate figure of the liberal-left in Italy. Newspapers like *La Repubblica* had long attacked his growing control of the media. Here was a man whose very public friendship with the Socialist leadership – Bettino Craxi was godfather to one of his children – had ensured that the anti-trust legislation limiting ownership of the media would not be too restrictive. The political fudge that resulted in the so-called Mammi law of August 1991 consolidated Berlusconi's grip over three channels: Canale 5, Rete 4 and Italia 1, representing 90 per cent of commercial television in Italy and 45 per cent of the national audience. Such a monopoly has no equal in Europe. When, in order to comply with the new limits on media owner-ship, he was obliged to sell off some of his newspaper holdings, he put them in the name of his brother Paolo.

For all his appearance as the new face for a New Italy, Berlusconi's past associations confirmed that he had reached his current pinnacle atop the second largest media empire in Europe by playing according to the rules of the old game. His association with Craxi was not the only cause for disquiet. When the P2 membership list was disclosed, his name was on it – a fact he later dismissed as insignificant, undertaken merely as a favour to a friend who asked him to join. Such protestations convinced few. The veteran journalist Indro Montanelli, who had Berlusconi as a proprietor for many years, said he was always full of ideas and fantasies but was essentially untrustworthy. 'I never believed anything he said.' He publicly advised Berlusconi against his planned transition from business into politics. But, as Montanelli recounted, Berlusconi said, 'I want a heroic life.'

Another unrelenting critic of Berlusconi was Eugenio Scalfari, editor of *La Repubblica*, who fought a major battle with him over control of the Mondadori group of Italy's leading newspapers and news magazines. He dubbed Berlusconi the 'great seducer'. And what a seduction. In 1994 this former cruise-ship crooner with the permanent tan and dazzling smile charmed a quarter of the Italian electorate with his promises of miracle cures for the Italian economy. He spoke of creating a million new jobs, of cutting the public deficit and simplifying the tax system and of allowing Italians to hold their heads high again.

It was intoxicating stuff, fed to the public on a constant drip across his TV networks with the help of catchy, sugary jingles. It was not just illusions and showmanship that Berlusconi was ped-dling. For was he not the apotheosis of the Italian miracle, a self-made billionaire, the son of a modest bank official who had risen to become one of the richest men in Italy? His very success was his strongest card.

Excelling at marketing and sales, Berlusconi brought the skills and techniques of his business organization to the task of promoting his political concept. Forza Italia or 'Come on, Italy' was a slogan, more a rallying cry than a party label expressing an ideological orientation. The roar of '*Forza Italia*' had long resounded round the terraces at football stadiums, and Berlusconi's marketing team had no quibbles about invoking this call. It also expressed the more nationalist, can-do approach of a movement after decades during which Italians had looked to Brussels for a lead. The very structure of the party was based on the successful formula for supporters' clubs of Berlusconi's own team, AC Milan. Thousands of branches were set up, selling trinkets and T-shirts to promote the cause. Berlusconi told his party workers, as he told his salesmen, to market their goods as though they had the sun in their pockets.

Actually, Berlusconi was not the first to borrow the slogan. In his wartime diary *Naples '44* Norman Lewis recalls trying to track down subversive political movements during the Allied occupation.

> Some are regarded as more purposeful and sinister including the one to be investigated, called *Forza Italia!*, which is suspected of Neo-Fascist leanings. My contacts in Benevento dismiss it with scorn as just another maniac right-wing movement backed by the landlords and the rural Mafia, run in this case by a half-demented *latifundista* who proclaims himself a reincarnation of Garibaldi.

The purpose of Berlusconi's Forza Italia was not to coalesce into a true political party; rather it was to form the launching pad from which to propel the unbounded political ambitions of its founder. Candidates standing for Forza Italia in the 1994 elections were auditioned, rather than selected, to ensure they could come across well on television. Those who could not were given speech lessons and trained to use a microphone. The single requirement was that they should never have been politically active in the past. It was an extraordinary indictment of the old system. It was also a brilliant analysis of what the voting public wanted.

Many of Berlusconi's key lieutenants were seconded directly from his Fininvest holding company. Forza Italia was founded with Fininvest money. Fininvest trusties ran the election campaign. Several were to win seats in parliament and a couple were given cabinet portfolios.

Even days before the general elections few had any inkling that they would produce such a clear winner. Berlusconi's overwhelming victory said much about the people of the New Italy. For all their wish to rid themselves of the old, to turn a new leaf, people were happy to delude themselves that somehow Berlusconi's past associations with Craxi and P2 did not disqualify him from office any more than his total inexperience of either government or party politics.

Many factors explain Berlusconi's phenomenal success. A key element was the disarray of the only real opposition, the left. The left overconfidently predicted that its hour had finally come after half a century of exclusion from the highest offices of state. Yet in the weeks before the elections evidence emerged that it too was tainted by the corruption scandals. The right-of-centre parties continued to play on the latent fear of a Communist take-over, even though the Berlin Wall had long since fallen. And in the event the majority demonstrated once again that they could no more bring themselves to vote for the ex-Communists in their reformist Social Democrat guise than they could vote for the same people when they stood as Communists.

In effect, voters had few choices. A political vacuum had been left by the disgrace of the old order, and Berlusconi seized the opportunity to fill it. Voters had precious few other outlets for the expression of their political will.

The voices of liberalism and the left were as dismayed at Forza Italia's victory as at their own failure to capitalize on the political turmoil. They were especially appalled that the younger, first- and second-time voters had renounced idealism for the promise of protection of the consumer society and the glitzy showmanship of the 'great seducer'. They should not perhaps have been surprised, given that these younger voters had all grown up during the period of Italy's great economic boom.

The elections left the reformers, those who had helped create the circumstances for the change, wondering how their revolution had been hijacked. One of the casualties was Mario Segni, a victim of the fickleness of voters and of the very electoral change, first-past-the-post voting, which he had brought about. Other would-be reformers, including a number of anti-Mafia candidates in Sicily, were also defeated by candidates for either Forza Italia or the Alleanza Nazionale, confirming the power there of party organizations over mere protest.

The results showed that Italy voted along regional lines. The red belt in the centre voted, as always, for the Communists and their heirs, both moderate and hardline. The north voted largely for the Northern League or Forza Italia, and the south for the Alleanza Nazionale or Forza Italia.

For all the changes in the voting system, the result, as before, was that no party won an outright majority. Forza Italia won the largest number of seats but not enough to form a government except by constructing a coalition with other parties. It was Berlusconi's partnership with one of these that provoked serious concern outside Italy. For the first time since the fall of Il Duce in 1943 a party with Fascist associations was to be part of the government of Italy. These were members of the Alleanza Nazionale, the National Alliance, which had emerged out of the old MSI in December 1993. Although not all the Alleanza Nazionale members had belonged to the MSI, over two-thirds had.

But what was the Alleanza Nazionale? Neo-Fascist? Post-Fascist? Crypto-Fascist? The party's smooth, moderate-sounding secretary general, Gianfranco Fini, insisted that his party was very different from its antecedents. It believed in democracy and played by the rules of the country. In the past, Fascism was a response to the circumstances of the time. Those circumstances have now changed, Fini argued. The Alleanza Nazionale was post-Fascist, he insisted.

On many issues, the MSI were less hardline than, say, right-wing Conservatives in Britain or Republicans in the United States. Some of its supporters and members, however, were of the old Blackshirt tradition. Many were inspired mainly by a folkloric nostalgia for what was falsely remembered as a period of efficiency and punctuality and order in Italy. Some members openly favoured a renegotiation of the 1975 Treaty of Osimo with the former Yugoslavia, and hankered after a return to Italian sovereignty of the old Italian enclaves of Istria, Fiume and Dalmatia on the Adriatic coast. Fini spelt out his policies clearly. He was for tight control on public spending, an efficient bureaucracy, stricter controls on immigration and a more centralized state.

In style and substance he was the polar opposite of the third component in this unlikely government coalition, Umberto Bossi, with his populist rhetoric and commitment to devolution. Bossi exploited every opportunity to disrupt the coalition of which he was part, and Berlusconi appeared to have difficulty in holding his partner in check. Yet their supporters had much in common. Both groups were hardworking Italians looking for honest government and efficient administration. Where the Alleanza Nazionale differed was in its championship of the south, thus sweeping up support from territory that was the former preserve of the old Christian Democrats.

These coalition partners were to prove more than a handful for Berlusconi. Here, after all, was a man used to the more rigid management of corporate business, where he ruled by *diktat*. This was very different from heading an uneasy coalition of apparently irreconcilable associates. He tried to run the country as he would his company, issuing orders in the expectation they would be implemented. His previous life had hardly prepared him for the cultural difference of ruling by consensus and compromise. Despite his massive personal vote, he was still only President of the Council of Ministers, not the kind of executive president he – like his friend Craxi – had envisaged for Italy.

Whether from political naïvety or arrogance Berlusconi never divested himself of his true role in his Fininvest empire, thereby raising questions about a conflict of interest. This became apparent in assaults on two national institutions. He tried to appoint his own men as directors of the Bank of Italy, hitherto ring-fenced from interference by the government. And he swept aside the board of governors of the state television network RAI, raising suspicion he wanted control of both private and public broadcasting.

For all his ambition to be Prime Minister, Berlusconi did not appear to relish his new role. The burdens of office hung heavily on a man who had always appeared to enjoy life. He complained that his time was no longer his own, and he felt obliged to attend interminable meetings. He lashed out at the press that dared criticize him. Over-sensitive to any adverse comment, he retaliated by identifying his policies with the national interest. Any attack on him was an attack on the nation, he said.

His single most ill-judged act was the decision to pass a decree restricting the powers of investigating magistrates to use preventive detention against those suspected of corruption. There was a strong legal argument for the move, which enjoyed support from former radicals and other traditional defenders of civil liberties. They felt, with reason, that the magistrates enjoyed powers of arrest and detention that were too arbitrary. They saw that to put a suspect in prison without charge for months on end was a gross breach of natural justice. It was a means to extract confessions under duress and a tool more appropriate to a police state than a modern functioning democracy.

Antonio Di Pietro and the other magistrates of the Milan pool conducting the Clean Hands investigations protested vocally against this interference in their independence by the executive. Without these powers, none of the more than 600 formally charged with serious crimes (out of thousands investigated) would have entered prison. Releasing the 2,000 people currently in preventive detention would permit many to go out and tamper with the evidence by nobbling witnesses. Their threat to resign provoked a U-turn by the government.

In political terms, the attempt to curb magistrates' powers was a disaster for Berlusconi. For all the opinion polls of his market research teams, he completely misjudged the popular revulsion at the sight of the most voracious of corruption suspects being released from jail to enjoy the fruits of their theft. Furthermore he over-estimated his own popularity. And the cynical Italians could only believe that the decree was intended to help Berlusconi's own, whether members of his family, his company or his former political associates. This sense of ulterior motive was enhanced by the disclosures that executives of Fininvest had confessed to paying bribes to the guardia di finanza in a tax fraud.

The Berlusconi prime ministership at best continued the process of transition. For all the new faces, in the way it lurched from one coalition crisis to another it appeared remarkably like the other fifty-two post-war governments that preceded it. And like them, it only lasted a few months, torn asunder by the internal contradictions of the coalition before the year was out.

It was a period which promised so much to those who bought the Berlusconi dream, and were to be so cruelly disillusioned. It was in addition deeply disturbing to his critics. For whereas the previous political cronies had known the rules of the game, and abused and exploited them to their own ends, Berlusconi ripped up the rule book, or tried to. He achieved little other than to confirm Italians in their cynical disdain of the political classes. Such is his legacy that Italy still faces the problems it always has: the growing dangers of organized crime, the rising public debt, the huge hole in the national pension fund. Some considerable distance has been covered towards the reform of political life, but Italy is still waiting for its Second Republic.

abusivo unlicensed

al fresco in the cool, or (slang) in prison

all'aperto in the open

amante lover

anagrafe register of births, marriages and deaths

anni di piombo years of lead

aviso di garanzia judicial notification of being under investigation

avvocato lawyer *Il avvocato* Fiat boss, Gianni Agnelli

basta enough

bella figura a good impression (opposite of *brutta figura*)

belpaese beautiful country, a.k.a Italy

belva the wild beast, a.k.a Totò Riina

boss (singular and plural) not corporate leaders but heads of Mafia Inc.

Camorra the Mafia of Naples and the surrounding Campania area

campanilismo parochialism

campo field (pl. *campi*)

capo head, chief *capo dei capi* the head of Cosa Nostra

carabiniere paramilitary police (pl. *carabinieri*)

carta bollata paper with an embossed government duty stamp (pl. *carte bollate*)

ciellini followers of the Christian revival movement Comunione e Liberazione

clandestini illegal immigrants

commissione ruling body of Cosa Nostra

compagna partner

comune town council (pl. *comuni*)

concorso competitive exam

concussione extortion

condominio condominium, block of apartments

consigliere adviser

contadino peasant, countryman   *Il contadino* Raul Gardini

corrente faction

corruzione corruption

Cosa Nostra the Sicilian Mafia (literally, our thing)

cosca clan (literally, the leaf of an artichoke) (pl. *cosche*)

cronaca nera crime news

cupola ruling body of Cosa Nostra

dietrologia the Italian version of Let's all play conspiracy theories

dolce far niente sweet idleness

famiglia family

figlio di papa daddy's boy

Fuan neo-Fascist students' movement in the 1940s

furbo sly, cunning, devious, crafty (pl. *furbi*)

galantuomini gentlemen

galoppino fixer (pl. *galoppini*)

gattopardista subscriber to the fatalistic views expressed in the novel
   The Leopard by Giuseppe di Lampedusa.

gattopardo leopard

guardia di finanza fiscal police

incaprettamento tied up like a goat

individualismo selfishness

ingegnere engineer   *Il ingegnere* Olivetti boss Carlo De Benedetti

intrecci plots

killer assassin

latifondo estate (pl. *latifondi*)

leva military service, draft

liceo grammar (high) school

lottizzazione division of spoils according to party affiliation

lupara bianca murder in which the body is never found (literally,
   the white shotgun)

mafioso Mafia member (pl. *mafiosi*)

mamma-nonna post-menopausal mother (literally, mummy-
   granny)

'ndrangheta the Calabrian Mafia

omertà conspiracy of silence

onorevole the honourable Courtesy title given to members of parliament, not to be confused with *uomini d'onore*, the men of honour, or *mafiosi*

pacchetto package deal on Alto Adige

palazzo big building, therefore (in plural) the headquarters of the political parties (pl. *palazzi*)

partitocrazia rule by the parties

pentito supergrass (pl. *pentiti*)

perbene decent

permesso di soggiorno temporary residence permit

picconate blows of a pickaxe

piovra literally, the octopus Popular name for the Mafia; also name of TV series on the bosses

pizzo protection money

portaborse bagman

pregiudicato convict (pl. *pregiudicati*)

questura police station

raccomandazione recommendation

salotto salon

sbirro police informer

separati in casa separated, but living under the same roof

soggiorno obbligato form of internal exile

soldati footsoldiers of the Mafia

sottogoverno parallel government

stidda Sicilian dialect for star (pl. *stidde*) Came to mean freelance gangs working outside the hierarchy of Cosa Nostra

tangente a pay-off (pl. *tangenti*)

tangentopoli bribesville

terrazza terrace the Terrazza Law: the rule of life in a café society whereby because the sun shines, and people can enjoy being outside, all troubles will eventually evaporate

VIP – visto in prigione – seen in prison

vu cumprà street hawkers (from the Neapolitan dialect for 'You wanna buy?')

zingari Gypsies

zio uncle Mafia-speak for a local leader

SELECT BIBLIOGRAPHY

The author consulted annual and other reports of the state statistical office ISTAT and of the social trends research institute CENSIS

Arendt, Hannah, *Eichmann in Jerusalem*, Harmondsworth: Penguin Books, 1964

Arlacchi, Pino, *Mafia Business*, Oxford: Oxford University Press, 1983, 1986, 1988

—, *Gli Uomini del Disonore*, Milan: Mondadori, 1992

Barzini, Luigi, *The Italians*, London: Hamish Hamilton, 1964

—, *The Europeans*, Harmondsworth: Penguin Books, 1984

Biagi, Enzo, *L'Italia dei Peccatori*, Milan: Rizzoli, 1991

—, *Incontri e Addii*, Milan: Rizzoli, 1992

Bocca, Giorgio, *Il Provinciale*, Milan: Mondadori, 1991

—, *L'Inferno. Profondo sud, male oscuro*, Milan: Mondadori, 1992

—, *La disUnità d'Italia*, Milan: Garzanti, 1992

Caffo, Ernesto, *Telefono Azzuro*, Milan: Feltrinelli, 1991

Cazzola, Franco, *Della Corruzione*, Bologna: Il Mulino, 1988

—, *L'Italia del Pizzo*, Turin: Einaudi, 1992

Cornwell, John, *A Thief in the Night: the Death of Pope John Paul I*, London: Viking, 1989

Cornwell, Rupert, *God's Banker: The Life and Death of Roberto Calvi*, London: Victor Gollancz, 1983

Dibdin, Michael, *Ratking*, London: Faber and Faber, 1988

—, *Vendetta*, London: Faber and Faber, 1990

—, *Cabal*, London: Faber and Faber, 1992

Economist, The, *The Economist Guide to Italy*, London: The Economist, 1990

Enzensberger, Hans Magnus, *Europe, Europe*, New York: Random House, 1989 and London: Pan Books, 1990

Falcone, Giovanni, in collaboration with Marcelle Padovani, *Cose di Cosa Nostra*, Milan: Rizzoli, 1991 (in English as *Men of Honour*, London: Fourth Estate, 1992)

Fox, Robert, *The Inner Sea: the Mediterranean and its People*, London: Sinclair-Stevenson, 1991

Friedman, Alan, *Agnelli and the Network of Italian Power*, London: Harrap, 1988

Ginsborg, Paul, *A History of Contemporary Italy: Society and Politics 1944–1988*, Harmondsworth: Penguin Books, 1990

Gobbi, Romolo, *Il Mito della Resistenza*, Milan: Rizzoli, 1992

Goethe, J.W., *Italian Journey*, Harmondsworth: Penguin Books, 1982

Haycraft, John, *Italian Labyrinth*, London: Secker and Warburg, 1985

Hebblethwaite, Peter, *In the Vatican*, London: Sidgwick and Jackson, 1986

Hibbert, Christopher, *Garibaldi and his Enemies*, London: Longman, 1965

Hine, David, *Governing Italy: the Politics of Bargained Pluralism*, Oxford: Oxford University Press, 1993

Jamieson, Alison, *The Heart Attacked: Terrorism and Conflict in the Italian State*, London and New York: Marion Boyars, 1989

—, *The Modern Mafia: its Role and Record*, London: The Centre for Security and Conflict Studies, 1989

Johnson, Paul, *A History of the Jews*, London: Weidenfeld and Nicolson, 1987

Keates, Jonathan, *Italian Journeys*, London: Heinemann, 1991

Kogan, Norman, *A Political History of Italy: the Postwar Years*, New York: Praeger, 1983

Lanaro, Silvio, *Storia dell'Italia Repubblicana*, Milan: Saggi Marsilio, 1992

LaPalombara, Joseph, *Democracy, Italian Style*, New Haven and London: Yale University Press, 1987

Lewis, Norman, *The Honoured Society*, London: Collins, 1964

—, *Naples '44*, London: Collins, 1978

Mack Smith, Denis, *Italy and its Monarchy*, New Haven and London: Yale University Press, 1989

—, *Cavour*, London: Methuen, 1985

—, *Mussolini*, London: Paladin, 1983

Mafai, Miriam, *Il Lungo Freddo*, Milan: Mondadori, 1992

Maraini, Dacia, *Bagheria*, Milan: Rizzoli, 1993

Mazzantini, Carlo, *A Cercar la Bella Morte*, Milan: Mondadori, 1986 (translated as *In Search of a Glorious Death*, Manchester: Carcanet, 1992)

Menzies, Yve, *Living in Italy*, London: Robert Hale, 1987

Miglio, Gianfranco, *Come Cambiare*, Milan: Mondadori, 1992

Moss, David, *The Politics of Left-Wing Violence in Italy, 1969–85*, London: Macmillan, 1989

Newby, Eric, *Love and War in the Apennines*, London: Hodder and Stoughton, 1971

—, *On the Shores of the Mediterranean*, London: Harvill Press, 1984

Nichols, Peter, *Italia, Italia*, London: Fontana/Collins, 1973

Nirenstein, Fiamma, *Il Razzista Democratico*, Milan: Mondadori, 1990

Norwich, John Julius, *A History of Venice*, Harmondsworth: Penguin Books, 1982

Parks, Tim, *Italian Neighbours*, London: Heinemann, 1992

Putnam, Robert D., *Making Democracy Work: Civic Traditions in Modern Italy*, with Robert Leonardi and Raffaella Y. Nanetti, Princeton N.J.: Princeton University Press, 1993

Rocchini, Piero, *Le Nevrosi del Potere*, Pontremoli: Editoriale Città del Libro, 1992

Sassoon, Donald, *Contemporary Italy*, London: Longman, 1986

Scoppola, Pietro, *La Repubblica dei Partiti*, Bologna: Mulino, 1991

Severgnini, Beppe, *Inglesi*, London: Coronet, 1991

—, *Italiani con Valigia*, Milan: Rizzoli, 1993

Spotts, Frederic and Theodor Wieser, *Italy: a Difficult Democracy*, Cambridge: Cambridge University Press, 1986

Tomasi di Lampedusa, Giuseppe, *The Leopard*, London: Collins/Harvill, 1958

Ward, William, *Getting it Right in Italy*, London: Bloomsbury, 1990

Willan, Philip, *Puppet Masters: The Political Use of Terrorism in Italy*, London: Constable, 1991

Willey, David, *God's Politician*, London: Faber and Faber, 1992

—, *Italians*, London: BBC Books, 1984